STUDENT WORKBOOK 

Biblical Studies

The Old Testament Witness *to* Christ & His Kingdom

The Promise Given

The Promise Clarified

The Promise Personalized

The Promise Universalized

Capstone Module 9: The Old Testament Witness to Christ and His Kingdom Student Workbook

ISBN: 978-1-62932-009-0

First edition 2005, Second edition 2011, Third edition 2013, Fourth edition 2015.

The Urban Ministry Institute is a ministry of World Impact, Inc.

Contents

About the Instructor

Rev. Dr. Don L. Davis is the Executive Director of The Urban Ministry Institute and a Senior Vice President of World Impact. He attended Wheaton College and Wheaton Graduate School, and graduated summa cum laude in both his B.A. (1988) and M.A. (1989) degrees, in Biblical Studies and Systematic Theology, respectively. He earned his Ph.D. in Religion (Theology and Ethics) from the University of Iowa School of Religion.

As the Institute's Executive Director and World Impact's Senior Vice President, he oversees the training of urban missionaries, church planters, and city pastors, and facilitates training opportunities for urban Christian workers in evangelism, church growth, and pioneer missions. He also leads the Institute's extensive distance learning programs and facilitates leadership development efforts for organizations and denominations like Prison Fellowship, the Evangelical Free Church of America, and the Church of God in Christ.

A recipient of numerous teaching and academic awards, Dr. Davis has served as professor and faculty at a number of fine academic institutions, having lectured and taught courses in religion, theology, philosophy, and biblical studies at schools such as Wheaton College, St. Ambrose University, the Houston Graduate School of Theology, the University of Iowa School of Religion, the Robert E. Webber Institute of Worship Studies. He has authored a number of books, curricula, and study materials to equip urban leaders, including *The Capstone Curriculum*, TUMI's premiere sixteen-module distance education seminary instruction, *Sacred Roots: A Primer on Retrieving the Great Tradition*, which focuses on how urban churches can be renewed through a rediscovery of the historic orthodox faith, and *Black and Human: Rediscovering King as a Resource for Black Theology and Ethics*. Dr. Davis has participated in academic lectureships such as the Staley Lecture series, renewal conferences like the Promise Keepers rallies, and theological consortiums like the University of Virginia Lived Theology Project Series. He received the Distinguished Alumni Fellow Award from the University of Iowa College of Liberal Arts and Sciences in 2009. Dr. Davis is also a member of the Society of Biblical Literature, and the American Academy of Religion.

Introduction to the Module

Greetings, in the strong name of Jesus Christ!

The Spirit-breathed Scripture is anchored on the witness of Jesus of Nazareth. He and he alone provides unity, continuity, and coherence to both the Old and New Testaments, and no one can claim a holistic or accurate view of the Bible without him being central in all phases of exegesis. He is the Bible's theme (John 5.39-40). In this module we trace some of the significant markers of the OT's witness to Messiah, and see how those markers provide us with a strong handle on the meaning of the entirety of Scripture.

In our first lesson, ***The Promise Given***, we will examine the relationship of the Old Testament to the New Testament through the idea of progressive revelation. We will look at the complimentary connections which exist in the OT and NT as they relate to the person of Christ and his Kingdom, and consider the unique motif of *promise and fulfillment*, and how this integrates and makes one the teaching of Scripture on the person of Jesus Christ. This unity of truth is seen in God's marvelous promise to send a redeemer to humanity through whom God's enemy would be destroyed, and humankind would be redeemed. In the *protoevangelium* (i.e., the first telling of the Gospel in Genesis 3.15), through the covenant promise of Abraham and its extensions we see how the Messianic hope is the unifying principle of the OT and the joyous fulfillment of the New, all finding their climax in the person of Jesus Christ. He is both the seed of the woman and the seed of Abraham.

In lesson two, ***The Promise Clarified***, we explore the biblical typology that reveals how the experience of Israel, the descendants of Abraham and the people of God, represent an analogy where we can understand the larger relationship of God with all of the redeemed through Jesus Christ. We will look at the roles of types and analogies in our study of Scripture, and explore four distinct moments within Israel's history which can help us understand the OT essentially as a witness to Christ and his kingdom reign (i.e., the Exodus, the conquest of Canaan, the entering into the Promised Land, and the restoration of Israel from the Babylonian Captivity). In this lesson we will also see further how the OT provides witness to Christ in the OT sacrificial system. Jesus of Nazareth is the substance and fulfillment of the Tabernacle, the Levitical Priesthood, the Temple sacrifices, and the feasts and festivals of Israel. In a real way, all of these personages, events, and institutions prefigure the person and work of Jesus Christ as the fulfillment of God's promise to Abraham.

Lesson three focuses on ***The Promise Personalized***, whose aim is to see how many of the character types in the OT point to and illustrate the ministry of Jesus Christ in the NT. We will explore the types in the OT which point to Jesus' roles as a prophet, priest, and king, considering Moses as a type of Christ in his prophetic role, Melchizedek as a type of Christ in his priestly order, and David as a type of Christ in his role as King of God's people. We will also look at several cases of character types which deserve special mention because of their significance in understanding Christ's role as head of humanity, redeemer of his kinsmen, and warrior in God's conquest. These characters represent the person of Adam, Joseph, and Joshua. In these figures the promise of God for redemption and restoration are made personal and visible for all to see.

Finally, we will close our module with lesson four, ***The Promise Universalized***. Here we will consider the nature and scope of OT Messianic prophecy as it relates to providing us with a clear OT witness to Christ and his Kingdom. We will provide the rationale of OT Messianic prophecy, and quickly outline the OT Messianic predictions which are repeated in the NT, specifically predictions fulfilled in Jesus Christ concerning his birth, his person and life, his death, his resurrection, and coming glory. We will also consider the significant issue of how God has extended the promise and blessings of Abraham, a promise extended in the apostles' teaching, to include all peoples. We will also look carefully at the OT predictions about the Messiah in Acts and the Epistles, and a picture will emerge for us–that God Almighty, the true and living God, has not only fulfilled his promise for salvation to Abraham, but he has also included Gentiles in that salvation.

No greater work can be done on earth than becoming a workman or work woman of the Lord in regard to his sacred text: "Do your best to present yourself to God as one approved, a worker who has no need to be ashamed, rightly handling the word of truth" (2 Tim. 2.15). The accurate handling of the text demands a Christo-centric orientation that discovers and cherishes the OT witness to Jesus Christ.

My sincere desire is that the Holy Spirit will reveal to you the glory and majesty of the picture of Jesus in the OT text, and that this picture will transform us, even as Paul suggests: "And we all, with unveiled face, beholding the glory of the Lord, are being transformed into the same image from one degree of glory to another. For this comes from the Lord who is the Spirit" (2 Cor. 3.18).

May the Hebrew Scriptures unveil his glory to us, and transform us as we become diligent students of God's holy Word!

- *Rev. Dr. Don L. Davis*

Course Requirements

Required Books and Materials

- Bible (for the purposes of this course, your Bible should be a translation [ex. NIV, NASB, RSV, KJV, NKJV, etc.], and not a paraphrase [ex. The Living Bible, The Message]).
- Each Capstone module has assigned textbooks which are read and discussed throughout the course. We encourage you to read, reflect upon, and respond to these with your professors, mentors, and fellow learners. Because of the fluid availability of the texts (e.g., books going out of print), we maintain our *official* Capstone Required Textbook list on our website. Please visit *www.tumi.org/books* to obtain the current listing of this module's texts.
- Paper and pen for taking notes and completing in-class assignments.

Suggested Readings

- DeYoung, James, and Sarah Hurty. *Beyond the Obvious*. Gresham, OR: Vision House Publishing, 1995.
- Fairbairn, Patrick. *The Typology of Scripture*. 2 vols. Reprint. Grand Rapids: Baker Books, 1975.
- Kaiser, Walter C., Jr. *The Messiah in the Old Testament*. Grand Rapids: Zondervan, 1995
- Poythress, Vern S. *The Shadow of Christ in the Law of Moses*. Phillipsburg, NJ: P & R Publishing, 1991.

Course Requirements

Summary of Grade Categories and Weights

Category	Percent	Points
Attendance & Class Participation	30%	90 pts
Quizzes	10%	30 pts
Memory Verses	15%	45 pts
Exegetical Project	15%	45 pts
Ministry Project	10%	30 pts
Readings and Homework Assignments	10%	30 pts
Final Exam	10%	30 pts
Total:	100%	300 pts

Grade Requirements

Attendance and Class Participation

Attendance at each class session is a course requirement. Absences will affect your grade. If an absence cannot be avoided, please let the Mentor know in advance. If you miss a class it is your responsibility to find out the assignments you missed, and to talk with the Mentor about turning in late work. Much of the learning associated with this course takes place through discussion. Therefore, your active involvement will be sought and expected in every class session.

Quizzes

Every class will begin with a short quiz over the basic ideas from the last lesson. The best way to prepare for the quiz is to review the Student Workbook material and class notes taken during the last lesson.

Memory Verses

The memorized Word is a central priority for your life and ministry as a believer and leader in the Church of Jesus Christ. There are relatively few verses, but they are significant in their content. Each class session you will be expected to recite (orally or in writing) the assigned verses to your Mentor.

Exegetical Project

The Scriptures are God's potent instrument to equip the man or woman of God for every work of ministry he calls them to (2 Tim. 3.16-17). In order to complete the requirements for this course you must select a passage and do an inductive Bible study (i.e., an exegetical study) upon it. The study will have to be five pages in length (double-spaced, typed or neatly hand written) and deal with one of the four aspects of the Old Testament witness to Jesus Christ which are highlighted in this course. Our desire and hope is that you will be deeply convinced of Scripture's ability to change and practically affect your life and the lives of those to whom you minister. As you go through the course, be open to finding an extended passage (roughly 4-9 verses) on a subject you would like to study more intensely. The details of the project are covered on pages 10-11, and will be discussed in the introductory session of this course.

Ministry Project

Our expectation is that all students will apply their learning practically in their lives and in their ministry responsibilities. The student will be responsible for developing a ministry project that combines principles learned with practical ministry. The details of this project are covered on page 12, and will be discussed in the introductory session of the course.

Class and Homework Assignments

Classwork and homework of various types may be given during class by your Mentor or be written in your Student Workbook. If you have any question about what is required by these or when they are due, please ask your Mentor.

Readings

It is important that the student read the assigned readings from the text and from the Scriptures in order to be prepared for class discussion. Please turn in the "Reading Completion Sheet" from your Student Workbook on a weekly basis. There will be an option to receive extra credit for extended readings.

Take-Home Final Exam

At the end of the course, your Mentor will give you a final exam (closed book) to be completed at home. You will be asked a question that helps you reflect on what you have learned in the course and how it affects the way you think about or practice ministry. Your Mentor will give you due dates and other information when the Final Exam is handed out.

Grading

The following grades will be given in this class at the end of the session, and placed on each student's record:

A - Superior work	D - Passing work
B - Excellent work	F - Unsatisfactory work
C - Satisfactory work	I - Incomplete

Letter grades with appropriate pluses and minuses will be given for each final grade, and grade points for your grade will be factored into your overall grade point average. Unexcused late work or failure to turn in assignments will affect your grade, so please plan ahead, and communicate conflicts with your instructor.

Exegetical Project

Purpose

As a part of your participation in the Capstone *Old Testament Witness to Christ and His Kingdom* module of study, you will be required to do an exegesis (inductive study) on one of the following passages:

- ❒ Isaiah 53.1-12
- ❒ Isaiah 9.6-7
- ❒ Genesis 12.1-3
- ❒ Psalm 110.1-3
- ❒ 2 Samuel 7.4-17
- ❒ Psalm 118.22-23

The purpose of this exegetical project is to give you an opportunity to do a detailed study of an Old Testament passage which speaks of the promised Messiah and his ministry. All of the texts above highlight a specific dimension of the Messianic hope, and his particular work. The hope of the Messiah is the heart of the Old Testament message (cf. John 5.37-40; Luke 24.44-49), and doing a detailed study can help you better comprehend the significance of this major biblical theme. To master the OT's witness to the person of Christ is essential to every dimension of evangelism and pastoral care, helping others gain a full appreciation of the work of God. Your ability to make plain to others how Jesus of Nazareth fulfills the OT meaning of Scripture and then relate that meaning to the real life concerns of people is the heart of biblical ministry. In this study you are seeking to make clear the meaning of the passage, and also show how the passage's truth can impact your own personal walk of discipleship and your ministry in the Church and world.

Outline and Composition

This is a Bible study project, and, in order to do *exegesis*, you must be committed to understand the meaning of the passage in its own setting. Once you know what it meant, you can then draw out principles that apply to all of us, and then relate those principles to life. A simple three step process can guide you in your personal study of the Bible passage:

1. What was *God saying to the people in the text's original situation*?
2. What principle(s) does *the text teach that is true for all people everywhere*, including today?
3. What is *the Holy Spirit asking me to do with this principle here, today*, in my life and ministry?

Once you have answered these questions in your personal study, you are then ready to write out your insights for your *paper assignment*.

Here is a *sample outline* for your paper:

1. List out what you believe is *the main theme or idea* of the text you selected.

2. *Summarize the meaning* of the passage (you may do this in two or three paragraphs, or, if you prefer, by writing a short verse-by-verse commentary on the passage).

3. *Outline one to three key principles or insights* this text provides on the Old Testament's witness to Christ as the Messiah.

4. Tell how one, some, or all of the principles may relate to *one or more* of the following:

    a. Your personal spirituality and walk with Christ

    b. Your life and ministry in your local church

    c. Situations or challenges in your community and general society

As an aid or guide, please feel free to read the course texts and/or commentaries, and integrate insights from them into your work. Make sure that you give credit to whom credit is due if you borrow or build upon someone else's insights. Use in-the-text references, footnotes, or endnotes. Any way you choose to cite your references will be acceptable, as long as you 1) use only one way consistently throughout your paper, and 2) indicate where you are using someone else's ideas, and are giving them credit for it. (For more information, see *Documenting Your Work: A Guide to Help You Give Credit Where Credit Is Due* in the Appendix.)

Make certain that your exegetical project, when turned in meets the following standards:

- It is legibly written or typed.
- It is a study of one of the passages above.
- It is turned in on time (not late).
- It is 5 pages in length.
- It follows the outline given above, clearly laid out for the reader to follow.
- It shows how the passage relates to life and ministry today.

Do not let these instructions intimidate you; this is a Bible study project! All you need to show in this paper is that you *studied* the passage, *summarized* its meaning, *drew out* a few key principles from it, and *related* them to your own life and ministry.

Grading

The exegetical project is worth 45 points, and represents 15% of your overall grade, so make certain that you make your project an excellent and informative study of the Word.

Ministry Project

Purpose

The Word of God is living and active, and penetrates to the very heart of our lives and innermost thoughts (Heb. 4.12). James the Apostle emphasizes the need to be doers of the Word of God, not hearers only, deceiving ourselves. We are exhorted to apply the Word, to obey it. Neglecting this discipline, he suggests, is analogous to a person viewing our natural face in a mirror and then forgetting who we are, and are meant to be. In every case, the doer of the Word of God will be blessed in what he or she does (James 1.22-25).

Our sincere desire is that you will apply your learning practically, correlating your learning with real experiences and needs in your personal life, and in your ministry in and through your church. Therefore, a key part of completing this module will be for you to design a ministry project to help you share some of the insights you have learned from this course with others.

Planning and Summary

There are many ways that you can fulfill this requirement of your study. You may choose to conduct a brief study of your insights with an individual, or a Sunday School class, youth or adult group or Bible study, or even at some ministry opportunity. What you must do is discuss some of the insights you have learned from class with your audience. (Of course, you may choose to share insights from your Exegetical Project in this module with them.)

Feel free to be flexible in your project. Make it creative and open-ended. At the beginning of the course, you should decide on a context in which you will share your insights, and share that with your instructor. Plan ahead and avoid the last minute rush in selecting and carrying out your project.

After you have carried out your plan, write and turn in to your Mentor a one-page summary or evaluation of your time of sharing. A sample outline of your Ministry Project summary is as follows:

1. Your name
2. The place where you shared, and the audience with whom you shared
3. A brief summary of how your time went, how you felt, and how they responded
4. What you learned from the time

Grading

The Ministry Project is worth 30 points and represents 10% of your overall grade, so make certain to share your insights with confidence and make your summary clear.

The Promise Given

Lesson Objectives

Welcome in the strong name of Jesus Christ! After your reading, study, discussion, and application of the materials in this lesson, you will be able to:

- Define the relationship of the Old Testament to the New Testament through the idea of *progressive revelation,* which affirms that God has revealed himself progressively and definitively throughout the history of his people, and finally through Jesus Christ.
- Lay out the various aspects of progressive revelation, including God's continuous revelation of himself to us through creation, through specific manifestations and occasions, and in these last days through his Son.
- Show how the OT explains and reveals the NT through the person of Christ, and how both testaments focus upon God's final and full revelation of himself in Jesus Christ and his kingdom reign.
- Reproduce Augustine's epigram (saying) on the relationship between the two testaments: "In the OT the NT lies hidden; in the NT the OT stands revealed."
- Highlight the complimentary concepts which connect and explain the relationship of the Old and New Testaments, including the OT providing the introduction to the NT's conclusion about Christ, the OT as anticipation of Christ and the NT as its climax, the OT as the shadow (prefiguring) of the person and work of Christ and the NT as the embodiment of those figures, the OT as the ineffective former revelation of God's salvation and the NT revelation in Christ as the consummated latter, and the OT as the particularized form of God's salvation universalized to all nations in the NT.
- Lay out the definition and elements of the *promise and fulfillment* motif in OT revelation, which affirms the promise of God for his own chosen one to redeem humankind and to destroy the devil's work, a promise fulfilled in the person of Jesus of Nazareth.

- Identify the central texts in Scripture which affirm how the OT's work is to provide a compelling and definitive witness to the person of Messiah fulfilled in the person of Jesus Christ (cf. Luke 22.25-27, 44-48; Matt. 5.17-18; John 1.45; 5.39-40; Heb. 10.5-10 with Ps. 40.6-8).

- Describe the implications of the *promise-fulfillment* motif for OT study, especially the way in which it suggests that a clear picture of Messiah can be seen in the history of the patriarchs, the nation of Israel, the Messianic prophecies, and the moral standards of the Law.

- List the ways in which the *promise and fulfillment* motif affirms the unity of the Old and New Testaments, in terms of God's intention to reveal himself, to redeem his people, and to do this through the promise made to Abraham and his descendants fulfilled in the person of Jesus of Nazareth.

- Define and explain the concept of the *protoevangelium*, the first telling of the Gospel in Genesis 3.15, laying out the specifics of the promise including hostility between the serpent and the woman and their respective "seeds," the bruising of the heel of the woman's seed, and the crushing of the serpents head by the seed.

- Recite the theological implications of the *protoevangelium*, namely that God would provide humanity with a Savior through the woman's lineage who would destroy the serpent, albeit having his heel bruised; Jesus of Nazareth is this divine seed commissioned to destroy the devil's work.

- Trace the covenant promise of Yahweh with Abraham as the continuation of this divine promise, including the fact that Abraham and his "seed" would be the means whereby redemption and restoration would come to God's people as well as to the nations of the earth in him; Jesus of Nazareth is declared to be the seed of Abraham in the NT apostolic witness.

The Original Promise Keeper

Devotion

Gen. 3.15 - I will put enmity between you and the woman, and between your offspring and her offspring; he shall bruise your head, and you shall bruise his heel.

Do you keep your promises, or do you renege on what you say you will do? A popular men's group have given themselves the name of "Promise Keepers," laying out seven areas in which they pledge to the Lord and to each other their fidelity to him and the Kingdom. The idea of promise is a significant concept in our society, from our common romance notions of engagement, "I'm promised to Sherri," to the promissory notes associated with business and law. Truly, the idea of the promise is a significant and important notion in all of our modern day relationships: promises are made between nations, world leaders, militaries, business partners, family members, and contractors. Without the notion of making and keeping promises, our entire societal machinery would grind to a halt.

One of the simplest and most direct ways of comprehending the biblical story is the motif of promise and fulfillment. In one sense the entirety of the Bible can be seen as a movement of the sovereign God, the God of Israel, Yahweh, the God and Father of our Lord Jesus Christ who makes a promise to the rebellious first human pair and the serpent who deceived Eve. In this text God makes a promise, a promise that will affect the serpent and the seed of the woman. In theological circles this promise is called the "*protoevangelium*," the very first mention or telling of the Gospel message of salvation of humankind that occurs in Bible. Here God lays out the entire plan of salvation in a short passage that summarizes one of the most important ideas in Scripture.

1

The setting of this episode related to the text is that tragic moment when the first human pair, Adam and Eve, are caught in their shameful admission of eating the fruit of the knowledge of the Tree of Good and Evil against the direct commandment of the Lord. The serpent, who deceived Eve into her disobedient act, Eve, and Adam are all before the Lord who is calling down his judgment upon them. In speaking to the serpent, God makes a declaration about the future that literally makes this text the beginning of the end of the entire written revelation of Scripture.

God here unequivocally states that his sovereign purpose for the serpent will be perpetual and unending hostility between the serpent and the seed of the woman, between its offspring and that of the woman. This "seed" would have his heel bruised by the serpent, but the serpent would have his entire head crushed in by the seed of the woman. This graphic image of the serpent and seed lies at the heart of the salvific vision of the Bible. God says that as a result of the voluntary human rebellion, he has established relationships in the universe which will perpetually be in place, unbroken hostility and enmity between the serpent and the seed of the woman, between its offspring and that of the woman.

From the earliest readings of this text, Jewish scholars saw it as the first mention of the divine promise of the Messiah, this seed, this person who would come of the woman and yet would bring a brutal and final end to the serpent and its accursed lying, deception, and ill-will toward the human race. We know that this promise is renewed with Abraham whose seed would be blessed and would be a blessing to all the nations (Gen. 12-13). This promise of a seed, an heir, a blessed warrior who would make an end of the works of the devil, was renewed with Abraham's sons, Isaac and Jacob, and then passed on to Jacob's son Judah (Gen. 49). The promise weaves through the OT, through the house of Judah, until it is made explicit that the seed would be an heir of the house of David (cf. 2 Sam. 7), and the prophets add even more color, knowledge, and revelation about the character and work of this seed (e.g., Isa. 9.6-7; 53.1-12).

Finally, the seed is revealed in the NT to be the person of Jesus of Nazareth, who himself is the fulfillment of the ancient promise of the Lord to bring to the earth one who would redeem his people, restore creation, and reign forever as the Lord and King of God's universe. The apostles make it explicit that Jesus of Nazareth is in fact the long sought for seed of Abraham (e.g., Paul in Galatians 4.4, "But when the fullness of time had come, God sent forth his Son, born of woman, born under the law"). Likewise, John makes it plain what the purpose of Jesus of Nazareth was in coming in to the world: 1 John 3.8 "Whoever makes a practice of sinning is of the devil, for the devil has been sinning from the beginning. The reason the Son of God appeared was to destroy the works of the devil."

Truly, Jesus of Nazareth is the fulfillment of the ancient promise of Yahweh to send through the line of humankind, the seed of the woman, a person who would both redeem humankind from its guilt, as well as finally destroy the works of the devil. This image of the serpent whose head is crushed by the victorious warrior of the Lord is dominant in the imagery and rhetoric of the apostles. Notice these themes in the following representative texts of the NT:

Rom. 16.20 - The God of peace will soon crush Satan under your feet. The grace of our Lord Jesus Christ be with you.

Eph. 4.8 - Therefore it says, "When he ascended on high he led a host of captives, and he gave gifts to men."

Col. 2.15 - He disarmed the rulers and authorities and put them to open shame, by triumphing over them in him.

Heb. 2.14-15 - Since therefore the children share in flesh and blood, he himself likewise partook of the same things, that through death he might destroy the one who has the power of death, that is, the devil, [15] and deliver all those who through fear of death were subject to lifelong slavery.

1 John 3.8 - Whoever makes a practice of sinning is of the devil, for the devil has been sinning from the beginning. The reason the Son of God appeared was to destroy the works of the devil.

1 John 5.5 - Who is it that overcomes the world except the one who believes that Jesus is the Son of God?

These and other texts lay out for us the power of the promise of the Lord to "crush the head of the serpent" in his own self-chosen, anointed "seed of the woman." God has determined to connect the entirety of human history to the fulfillment of a single promise that he made in regard to the restoration and redemption of his creation through Jesus of Nazareth.

We now know that this promise has in part already been fulfilled in the coming and work of Jesus of Nazareth, and soon he will consummate his work that he began on the cross at his Second Coming. Is it not amazing that all of the history of the entire world and universe can be boiled down to a single promise and our sovereign and faithful God's absolute determination to fulfill his Word? This is the ground of our faith, the heart of our worship, and the basis of our reading of the Scriptures. This divine promise coursed through the sacred history of the people of Israel until it was fulfilled in the person of Jesus of Nazareth. He is the center and end of all salvific work that God conducts in this world.

Isn't it amazing that our God, this great God, is a God of promise who fulfilled it in the person of Jesus Christ? Isn't it wonderful to know that the one who promised us will never change his mind, but will fulfill his sacred promise, to the glory of his name, and the salvation of his own? Let us declare our faith in the simple affirmation of the promise of the apostle, and live as if we believe it with all of our hearts and minds:

1 Thess. 5.23-24 - Now may the God of peace himself sanctify you completely, and may your whole spirit and soul and body be kept blameless at the coming of our Lord Jesus Christ. [24] He who calls you is faithful; he will surely do it.

The God who laid out his sovereign purpose for the world in the Garden, the God and Father of our Lord Jesus Christ, indeed, he is the *original Promise Keeper!*

Nicene Creed and Prayer

After reciting and/or singing the Nicene Creed (located in the Appendix), pray the following prayer:

> *O everlasting God and Father of our Lord Jesus Christ, grant us thy grace that we may study the Holy Scriptures diligently, and, with our whole heart, seek and find Christ therein, and through him obtain everlasting life; through the same Jesus Christ our Lord. Amen.*
>
> ~John W. Doberstein, ed. **A Lutheran Prayer Book.** Philadelphia: Fortress Press, 1960. p. 102.

1

Quiz

No quiz this lesson

Scripture Memorization Review

No Scripture memorization this lesson

Assignments Due

No assignments due this lesson

CONTACT

Are We Using the Right Book in the Wrong Way?

1

One of the ongoing issues and problems associated with the mastery of the OT is its misuse by so many interpreters, both conservative and liberal. The OT is such a diverse library of literature that many OT scholars no longer seek to provide us with a coherent, unified OT theology. In place of a single unity, it is seen as a heavily edited (redacted) text that covers many centuries, dozens of authors, and one which provides no consistent or unified message for the interpreter. Even for many evangelical Christians, the Bible remains a closed book. Used primarily for devotional readings in the Psalms and Proverbs, large portions of the OT remain unpreached and unread by many evangelicals. What is the reason that these dear saints who love the Bible give for their systematic neglect of the OT? It is simply too hard to understand and use. For them it is seldom referred to because it is unintelligible, filled with difficult passages, and too heavily concentrated in portions of ceremonial law and/or symbolism and imagery. Frankly, for the new or growing Christian it is easier to focus on the NT and read the Epistles, and, if one is so bold, go to the Gospels and read the words of the Lord. But, in terms of understanding and desirability, many Christians testify that the OT is not an integral part of their spiritual journeys. What do you make of this situation, and how does the neglect of the OT play itself out in your experience?

Is the God of the OT the Same God as the God of the New?

2 In a day of tolerance, political correctness, and overall squeamish feelings about anything that smacks of judgment or punishment, the OT is a much maligned book. Admittedly, it is filled with many stories which cover all the dark shadows of human existence, and include graphic portrayals of murder, rape, violence, war, and tragedy. Examples of tough judgment are given in many of the stories, and those of certain beliefs and lifestyles are not only morally condemned, but in graphic detail we see them judged by the community and the Lord. The statements of God against a number of modern lifestyle choices makes the OT especially the lightning rod for much debate and discussion. Some liberal Christians have gone so far as to denounce the OT as the product of a primitive culture whose theological and moral ideas were more a reflection of their era and environment than what we as "reasoned and tolerant Christians" would find acceptable. What should we make of these modern attempts to drive a wedge between the God of the OT and the God of the NT, as revealed in the person of Jesus of Nazareth? What is the continuity between the two? Should we admit, even a little, that there might be a difference between the God of the OT and the God of the NT? Explain.

1

Jesus and Meaning of the OT

3 When Jesus of Nazareth referred to the Bible or Scripture, his referent was our OT. Today, it is referred to in non-Christian circles as the "Hebrew Bible," and the discussions are heated about the *meaning* of the OT. For most Christians, the highest and best authority on the meaning of the OT is the person of Jesus, who unequivocally in at least five different passages in the NT said that he himself was the theme of the Hebrew Bible (cf. Luke 24.25-27; 44-48; Matt. 5.17-18; John 5.39-40; 1.41ff.; Heb. 10.5-10 with Ps. 40.6-8). These texts give the sense that Jesus believed that the OT, the Hebrew Bible, was essentially a text that pointed to his person in terms of figure and prophecy, and that a correct reading of the OT had to, in some fundamental sense, find its meaning in his own person. This claim, by the way, lies at the heart of the constant controversy between Jesus and the teachers of the Bible of his own day; such a claim, that the entirety of the Scriptures found their

theological and spiritual end in relationship to him as the Messiah of God was unacceptable to them, even blasphemous. This Christo-centric use of the Bible is equally controversial today, especially in the world of biblical criticism, which sees such a laser-guided approach to such a diverse set of literature problematic. What is your thought? Based on what you know today, how would you understand the nature of the OT in its relationship to Jesus Christ? How far can you take this kind of hermeneutic before you skew or misread the basic message of the OT?

CONTENT

1

The Promise Given

Segment 1: Promise and Fulfillment in the Old and New Testaments

Rev. Dr. Don L. Davis

Summary of Segment 1

The relationship of the Old Testament to the New Testament can be effectively understood through the idea of *progressive revelation,* which affirms that God has revealed himself progressively and definitively throughout the history of his people, and finally through Jesus Christ. God in diverse manners and at different times made himself known to the nation of Israel in limited ways, but in these last days he has spoken to us through his Son. Jesus of Nazareth is God's final and full revelation of himself, now testified of in Scripture. As Augustine suggests: "In the OT the NT lies hidden; in the NT the OT stands revealed." The testaments have a complimentary relationship, the OT providing the introduction to the NT's conclusion about Christ, the OT as anticipation to the NT's climax about God's salvation story in Christ. Furthermore, the OT prefigures Christ's person and work fully embodied in the NT. While the OT is the ineffective former revelation of God's salvation, the NT can be seen as the consummated latter, and the universalized call of which the OT is particularized to the nation of Israel. The connection of the testaments can be seen in the *promise and fulfillment* motif, especially in the way the NT affirms how the OT's work is to provide a compelling and definitive witness to the person of Messiah fulfilled in the person of Jesus Christ in the history of the patriarchs, the nation of Israel, the Messianic prophecies, and the moral standards of the Law.

Our objective for this segment, *Promise and Fulfillment in the Old and New Testaments*, is to enable you to see that:

- The relationship of the Old Testament to the New Testament can be effectively understood through the idea of *progressive revelation*, which affirms that God has revealed himself progressively and definitively throughout the history of his people, and finally through Jesus Christ.

- The concept of *progressive revelation* includes God's continuous revelation of himself to us through creation, through specific manifestations and occasions, and in these last days through his Son. The OT explains and reveals the NT through the person of Christ, and both testaments focus upon God's final and full revelation of himself in Jesus Christ and his kingdom reign.

- Augustine's epigram (saying) nicely summarizes the relationship between the two testaments: "In the OT the NT lies hidden; in the NT the OT stands revealed." This complimentary relationship is seen in how the OT provides an introduction to the NT's conclusion about Christ, the OT's anticipation of the person and work of Messiah, and the NT's identification of Jesus of Nazareth as the climax of that anticipation. Also, the OT serves as the shadow (prefiguring) of the person and work of Christ and the NT as its embodiment, and the OT is seen as the ineffective former revelation of God's salvation consummated later in the NT revelation of Jesus. Finally, what was particularized to Israel in the OT was universalized to all nations in the NT.

- The motif of *promise and fulfillment* in OT revelation affirms the promise of God for his own chosen one to redeem humankind and to destroy the devil's work, a promise fulfilled in the person of Jesus of Nazareth.

- The NT provides several central texts which affirm how the OT's work is to provide a compelling and definitive witness to the person of Messiah fulfilled in the person of Jesus Christ (cf. Luke 22.25-27, 44-48; Matt. 5.17-18; John 1.45; 5.39-40; Heb. 10.5-10 with Ps. 40.6-8). This witness can be seen in the history of the patriarchs, the nation of Israel, the Messianic prophecies, and the moral standards of the Law.

I. Progressive Revelation: Affirming the Connection Between the Old and New Testaments

Video Segment 1 Outline

A. Definition of progressive revelation: God has revealed himself progressively through history and finally through Jesus Christ.

Heb. 1.1-2 - Long ago, at many times and in many ways, God spoke to our fathers by the prophets, [2] but in these last days he has spoken to us by his Son, whom he appointed the heir of all things, through whom also he created the world.

Augustine's epigram (little saying) about the relationship between the two testaments:

"In the Old Testament the New Testament lies hidden; in the New Testament the Old Testament stands revealed."

1

B. Aspects of progressive revelation

1. Through human history, God has provided a continuity (connected reality) of revelation to humankind.

2. God communicated on numerous occasions in the past using many different ways to speak to diverse individuals and groups.

3. God's earlier words, although entirely true, were partial and required completion.

    a. God's latter revelations explain the meaning of the earlier.

    b. God's earlier revelations give shape and meaning to the latter.

4. In these last days, God has spoken to us through his Son.

    a. Matt. 3.17

b. Matt. 17.5

c. John 1.14

d. John 1.17-18

e. Jesus as the center of biblical revelation bridges the testaments, himself being the Shadow of the Old Testament and the Substance of the New.

f. He fulfills the sayings of the OT, including the prophecies of the Law and the Prophets, Luke 24.25-27.

g. He reveals the very person of God in his own person (i.e., he is the express image of his glory, the "Word made flesh," cf. John 1.14-18).

5. The Old Testament explains and reveals the meaning of the New Testament.

C. Implication of progressive revelation for Christ-centered approach to Scripture interpretation

1. The testaments are intimately connected to each other.

2. The testaments both focus on God's revelation regarding Jesus Christ and his kingdom reign.

II. Complimentary Concepts that Connect the Old and New Testaments

Augustine's epigram (little saying) about the relationship between the two testaments:

"In the Old Testament the New Testament lies hidden; in the New Testament the Old Testament stands revealed."

A. *Introduction and conclusion:* the Old Testament provides us an introduction to the truths about Christ and his Kingdom, and the New Testament brings these to a conclusion (e.g., the teachings of Isaiah of the Servant in chapters 42-55 introduces a figure who in fact is shown to be Jesus Christ at his first advent [cf. 1 Pet. 1.22-25]).

1

B. *Anticipation and climax*: what is anticipated regarding Christ and his Kingdom in the Old Testament is brought to its final climax in the New Testament (the salvation of the remnant of Israel in Zech. 12.10-13.1 anticipates the climax of Jesus' return in Revelation 19).

C. *Shadow and substance*: what is embodied and prefigured in the Old Testament regarding Christ and his Kingdom is revealed and given substance in the New (the physical tabernacle of Hebrews 8.5 is the shadow of the true tabernacle mentioned regarding Jesus as priest in heaven).

D. *Ineffective former and consummated latter*: what is demonstrated and found to be ineffective in the Old Testament is finalized and consummated in the New (e.g., the entire book of Hebrews speaks of the insufficiency of the old sacrificial system to actually take sins away; Jesus' death is the effective reality behind the OT example, e.g., Heb. 10.1-10).

E. *Particular and universal*: what is particularized in the experience of the people of Israel in the Old Testament is extended and expanded to all who believe in the New.

III. Promise and Fulfillment: the Christo-centric Nature of the Old Testament Revelation

Christ Is the Theme of Each of the Eight Sections of the Bible

(Cf. Geisler, *A Popular Survey of the Old Testament*, pp. 21-24).

1. *The Law (Genesis - Deuteronomy): Laying the Foundation for Messiah*
2. *History (Joshua - Esther): The Preparation for Messiah*
3. *Poetry (Job - Song of Solomon): The Aspiration for Messiah*
4. *Prophecy (Isaiah - Malachi): The Expectation of Messiah*
5. *Gospels (Matthew - John): The Manifestation of Messiah*
6. *History (Acts): The Propagation of Messiah*
7. *Epistles (Romans - Jude): The Interpretation and Application of Messiah*
8. *Prophecy (Revelation): The Consummation of All Things in Messiah*

1

A. *Definition of the promise-fulfillment motif*: the promise of God for someone to redeem humankind from its sin and destroy the devil's work is fulfilled in the person of Jesus Christ.

B. Jesus' gives convincing testimony within Scripture that the Old Testament's purpose is to give witness concerning his person and work.

1. The road to Emmaus

a. Luke 24.25-27, 32

b. Here is a picture of Christ interpreting all the Scriptures (i.e., OT) as to how they explain and point toward his own identity.

2. The post-resurrection appearance to his own

a. Luke 24.44-48

b. Christ opened their minds to understand the Scriptures (i.e., the OT) concerning himself.

3. The Sermon on the Mount

a. Matt. 5.17-18

b. Christ's explicit teaching that he had come not to abolish the Scriptures but to fulfill them completely.

4. Dialogue with the Pharisees

a. John 5.39-40

b. Jesus explaining to the experts in Scripture that reading them without having his identity in mind is poor, ineffectual exegesis.

5. Prophetic quotation in Heb. 10.5-10 cf. Ps. 40.6-8

a. Ps. 40.6-8

b. Heb. 10.5-10

c. A prophetic psalm is attributed to Jesus Christ as he relates a text to his own offering of his body as a sacrifice for sin.

C. Implications of the promise-fulfillment motif

Luke 24.44-48 - Then he said to them, "These are my words that I spoke to you while I was still with you, that everything written about me in the Law of Moses and the Prophets and the Psalms must be fulfilled." [45] Then he opened their minds to understand the Scriptures, [46] and said to them, "Thus it is written, that the Christ should suffer and on the third day rise from the dead, [47] and that repentance and forgiveness of sins should be proclaimed in his name to all nations, beginning from Jerusalem. [48] You are witnesses of these things."

1. In the history of the Patriarchs, the nation of Israel, and its historical and spiritual development, the Old Testament provides us with a clear picture of Christ.

2. The central promise of God in the OT (i.e., that God would send a Seed/Servant who would remedy the downfall of his creation and all humankind) is fulfilled in the manifestation of Jesus Christ recorded in the NT.

3. The actual subject matter of the Scriptures is singular and dynamic: the revelation of Jesus Christ.

4. The OT can be profitably studied as the outline of God's promise for salvation and kingdom restoration of which the New Testament is its fulfillment.

Conclusion

» The notion of *progressive revelation* unites our understanding of the Old and New Testaments in the person of Jesus Christ and his kingdom reign.

» Both the Old and New Testaments compliment each other, and through the biblical motif of *promise and fulfillment* we can comprehend the meaning and application of our Old Testament.

Segue 1

Student Questions and Response

1

Please take as much time as you have available to answer these and other questions that the video brought out. In this segment we explored the relationship of the Old Testament to the New Testament in the ideas of *progressive revelation*, as well as the *promise-fulfillment* motif. The idea of progressive revelation affirms that God has revealed himself progressively and definitively throughout the history of his people, and finally through Jesus Christ. Likewise, the motif of promise-fulfillment suggests that the promise God made to redeem and restore his creation and people, made in the OT, is fulfilled in the person of Jesus of Nazareth in the NT. Explore these and the other ideas covered in this segment by reviewing the material through the questions below. Include Scripture in your answers, where appropriate.

1. What is the meaning of progressive revelation, and what does this idea affirm regarding God and his determination to make himself known in the world? Be specific.

2. How does the concept of *progressive revelation* help us understand how God has revealed himself to humankind before Christ? Now that Christ has come, what further revelation can we expect from God about himself and his purposes for his universe?

3. What saying of Augustine nicely summarizes the relationship between the two testaments? Explain its meaning.

4. What are some of the ways in which the OT and the NT are complimentary to each other, that is, explain and reveal one another? Be specific, and highlight what each concept means?

5. What does it mean to say that the OT serves as *the shadow* (prefiguring) of the person and work of Christ *embodied* in the NT? Give examples.

6. How can it be said that the OT is the *ineffective former revelation* of God's salvation, of which the NT is the *consummated latter* of that same salvation in Jesus?

7. In what sense does the NT make available for all people what was particularized to Israel in the OT? Explain.

8. How does the motif of *promise and fulfillment* affirm how the entire Bible can be understood as God making his promise for salvation which is fulfilled in the person of Jesus of Nazareth? Explain.

9. What are the central texts which affirm how the OT's theme and subject is the person of Messiah fulfilled in the person of Jesus Christ? How is this theme developed and laid out in the OT?

1

The Promise Given

Segment 2: The Ancient Hope of a Saving Seed

Rev. Dr. Don L. Davis

Summary of Segment 2

The major motif that links all biblical revelation in Scripture is the *promise and fulfillment* motif. This theme affirms the unity of Scripture; God intends to reveal himself and redeem his people through the seed, the one promised to Abraham and his descendants. This seed is fulfilled in the person of Jesus of Nazareth. The seminal text in Scripture outlining the promise is the *protoevangelium*, the first telling of the Gospel in Genesis 3.15. Here God promises the certainty of hostility between the serpent and the woman and their respective "seeds," the bruising of the heel of the woman's seed, and the crushing of the serpents head by the seed. In the NT, Jesus of Nazareth is revealed to be this divine seed commissioned to destroy the devil's work and to redeem humankind to God. Yahweh's covenant promise with Abraham serves as progressive continuation of God's divine promise for a Savior. In his covenant with Abraham, God promised to supply him a "seed" who would bring redemption and restoration to Abraham's descendants and all the nations of the earth. In the NT, Jesus of Nazareth is declared to be the seed of Abraham, the restorer and redeemer of creation and the world.

Our objective for this segment, *The Ancient Hope of a Saving Seed*, is to enable you to see that:

- The major motif that links all biblical revelation in Scripture is the promise and fulfillment motif. This theme affirms the unity of the Old and New Testaments, in terms of God's intention to reveal himself, to redeem his people, to do this through the promise made to Abraham and his descendants fulfilled in the person of Jesus of Nazareth.
- The seminal text of the promise is explained in the *protoevangelium*, the first telling of the Gospel in Genesis 3.15. Here in this text God lays out the specifics of his salvation promise, including the certainty of hostility between the serpent and the woman and their respective "seeds," the bruising of the heel of the woman's seed, and the crushing of the serpents head by the seed.
- The theological implications of the *protoevangelium* are plain and profound. Namely, these include the fact that God would provide humanity with a Savior through the woman's lineage who would destroy the serpent, albeit his heel would be bruised by the serpent. In the NT, Jesus of Nazareth is revealed to be this divine seed commissioned to destroy the devil's work and to redeem humankind to God.
- Yahweh's covenant promise with Abraham serves as progressive continuation of God's divine promise for a Savior. In the covenant with Abraham, this promise is specified to be the seed of Abraham who would bring redemption and restoration not only to God's people (Abraham's descendants), but blessing to the nations of the earth as well. In the NT, Jesus of Nazareth is declared to be the seed of Abraham, the one through whom Abraham, his descendants, and the all the families of the earth would be blessed.

1

I. Promise and Fulfillment: the Importance of the *Unity of God's Divine Revelation*

Video Segment 2 Outline

2 Cor. 3.14-16 - But their minds were hardened. For to this day, when they read the old covenant, that same veil remains unlifted, because only through Christ is it taken away. [15] Yes, to this day whenever Moses is read a veil lies over their hearts. [16] But when one turns to the Lord, the veil is removed.

Jesus of Nazareth Is the Fulfillment of the OT Precepts, Types, and Forecasts

Christ at once sums up in himself the perfection of the Old Testament precepts, the substance of the Old Testament shadows and types, and the fulfillment of Old Testament forecasts. Those truths about him which bud forth in the Old Testament come into full bloom in the New Testament; the flashlight of prophetic truth turns into the floodlight of divine revelation. The Old Testament foreshadows find their fulfillment in the New Testament in several ways:

(1) The moral precepts of the Old Testament become fulfilled or perfected in the life and teachings of Christ. (2) The ceremonial and typical truths were only shadows of the true substance to be found in Christ. (3) The Messianic prophecies foretold in the Old Testament were finally fulfilled in the history of the New Testament. In each of these relationships it can be seen that the Testaments are inseparably connected. The New is not only supplementary to the Old but it is the necessary complement to it. As the book of Hebrews puts it, "God had foreseen something better for us, that apart from us they [Old Testament believers] should not be made perfect" (Heb. 11.40). For what was contained in the Old Testament is fully explained only in the New Testament.

~ Norman Geisler. **To Understand the Bible Look for Jesus.** Eugene, OR: Wipf and Stock Publishers, 2002. p. 68.

1

A. Through the promise, the one true God reveals his intention for his universe to his own people (it is personal revelation).

1. He discloses *himself* in the revelation; the promise concentrates first and foremost on the nature of who God is.

2. He provides us with the ability to know what he is revealing.

B. Through the promise, the one true God discloses his purpose to redeem and restore his creation.

C. Through the promise, the one true God shows us his sovereign choice: he will bring the redeemer from the kindred of Abraham and his descendants.

1. It is given to a particular people (i.e., Abraham and his descendants).

2. It is given for the sake of all humankind (i.e, through *Abraham* all the families of the earth would be blessed).

3. It will touch all creation in its impact (i.e., all of heaven and earth are involved in the implications of this salvation).

D. Through the promise, the one true God shows us that Jesus of Nazareth is the fulfillment of his promise to Abraham.

1. Gal. 3.27-29

2. Col. 3.11

E. Implications of the promise of God for studying the OT

1. The promise unifies our understanding of God's divine revelation.

a. The God of Abraham is the God and Father of our Lord Jesus Christ.

b. The testaments deal with the same essential story: the unfolding fulfillment of God's promise to Abraham in the person of Jesus Christ.

2. The Bible may have numerous subjects and segments, but it only has a single unifying theme: the revelation (unveiling) of Jesus Christ. When read with Christ in mind, the veil of misunderstanding the OT is taken away.

   a. Matt. 16.17

   b. Luke 24.25-27

   c. Luke 24.44-46

   d. John 8.12

   e. John 12.46

   f. Acts 26.18

3. We ought to be able to set forth biblical history of salvation in such a way as to see Jesus present in the Old Testament, and completing the meaning of the Old in the New Testament, 2 Cor. 4.6.

II. The *Protoevangelium*: the Promised Seed of the Woman

Gen. 3.15 - I will put enmity between you and the woman, and between your offspring and her offspring; he shall bruise your head, and you shall bruise his heel.

A. The backdrop: the temptation and fall of humankind

B. The fall: voluntary rebellion of Adam and Eve

C. The result of the rebellion

1. Condemnation before God

2. Alienation between each other

3. Banishment from the Garden

4. Death (both physical and spiritual)

D. The promise: what are the specifics of God's promise?

1. The hostility between the serpent and the woman, and between their respective "seeds" (i.e., lineages, descendants)

2. The seed of the woman would crush the serpent's head.

3. The serpent would wound the heel of the woman's seed.

E. The implications

1. God would provide through humanity's lineage a Savior who would crush the head of the devil.

2. This crushing would result in the wounding of the heel of the seed.

3. This righteous seed is renewed in Seth and protected through Noah and his kin.

4. From the beginning of the Bible's story, we see the story of a righteous seed unfolding through history as one who would destroy the devil.

5. Jesus of Nazareth is this destroyer of the devil.

a. 1 John 3.8

b. Col. 2.15

c. Heb. 2.14

d. Rom. 16.20

III. The Covenant of God with Abraham

A. Biblical affirmations of God's covenant with Abraham

1. Gen. 12.1-3
2. Gen. 15.1-6
3. Gen. 17.1-8
4. Gen. 22.15-18

B. What precisely is promised in God's covenant with Abraham?

1. Greatness of his name and multiplied blessings upon him
2. God's protection on his clan (blessing those who bless him, and cursing those who curse him)
3. The multiplication of Abraham's offspring
4. The inheritance of the Promised Land as an eternal possession
5. The blessings of all the nations through Abraham's lineage

C. The implications

1. Redemption and restoration from the Lord are linked directly to Abraham and his clan.

2. The Promised Savior who is to be the blessing to the nations is Abraham's seed.

3. Renewed in Abraham's children

    a. Renewed in Isaac, Gen. 26.23-25

    b. Affirmed in God's selection of Jacob, Gen. 25.22-23

    c. Extended to the tribe of Judah through Jacob's prophecy, Gen. 49.9-10

D. Jesus of Nazareth is declared to be this seed of Abraham.

1. Through the lineage of Abraham (cf. Matt. 1.1)

2. As the seed of Abraham whom God elected, Gal. 3.16

3. As a descendant of David, from the tribe of Judah, Luke 1.69-70

4. In Jesus Christ, the promise first given in the Garden and renewed in Abraham is fulfilled: in his person God is now making available to all peoples redemption, blessing, forgiveness, and amazingly, eternal life through faith in him.

Conclusion

» In both the *protoevangelium* and the Abrahamic covenant God promised a seed to redeem humanity and restore what our first parents lost through disobedience and defeat the serpent, our mortal enemy, the devil.

» This promise of a seed was first spoken in the *protoevangelium* (i.e., the first telling of the Gospel in Genesis 3.15), and then in the covenant promise of Abraham.

» Jesus Christ himself is the singular fulfillment of these OT promises; he is both the seed of the woman who destroys the devil, as well as the seed of Abraham through whom all the families of the earth are blessed.

Segue 2

Student Questions and Response

The following questions were designed to help you review the material in the second video segment. In this last segment we briefly considered the major motif that links all biblical revelation in Scripture, is the *promise and fulfillment* motif. This promise of a seed was first spoken in the *protoevangelium* (i.e., the first telling of the Gospel in Genesis 3.15), and then in the covenant promise of Abraham. Jesus Christ himself is the singular fulfillment of these OT promises, being the seed of the woman who destroys the devil and the seed of Abraham blessing the families of the earth. Explore these meanings further as you answer the questions below. Cite Scripture in your answers.

1. How does the motif of *promise and fulfillment* link all dimensions of the Bible's teaching, in both Old and New Testaments?

2. How does the *promise-fulfillment motif* affirm the *unity of the Old and New Testaments*, especially in terms of God's intention to redeem and restore a people for himself? What role does the NT establish for Jesus of Nazareth in this purpose?

3. What is the *protoevangelium*, and where is it located in Scripture? What specifically does God lay out concerning his salvation promise–for the serpent, for the woman, and for the seed of the woman?

4. How is the *protoevangelium* "shorthand" for the entire message of the Bible, both Old and New Testaments? How does the NT reveal Jesus of Nazareth to be this divine seed commissioned to destroy the devil's work and to redeem humankind to God? Cite specific Scripture to support your answer.

5. How is the covenant God made with Abraham a *progressive revelation*, that is, a continuation of God's divine promise for a Savior first cited in the *protoevangelium*?

6. Lay out the specific promises God made to Abraham in his covenant as recorded in Genesis 12.1-3. What specifically is promised regarding the seed of Abraham and the blessings of all the families of the earth? What does Galatians 3 suggest about this promise? (Cf. Galatians 3.7-9 Know then that it is those of faith who are the sons of Abraham. [8] And the Scripture, foreseeing that God would justify the Gentiles by faith, preached the gospel beforehand to Abraham, saying, "In you shall all the nations be blessed." [9] So then, those who are of faith are blessed along with Abraham, the man of faith.)

7. How does the NT describe Jesus of Nazareth to be the seed of Abraham, the one through whom Abraham, his descendants, and the all the families of the earth would be blessed? How does this affirm the *promise-fulfillment motif* as perhaps the most valid way to understand the relationship of the OT to the New? Explain.

1

CONNECTION

Summary of Key Concepts

This lesson focuses upon the various motifs and approaches that will allow us to see the Old and New Testaments as fundamentally and intimately connected—through *progressive revelation*, the *promise-fulfillment motif*, and the complimentary relationships that the testaments have as they both come to fulfillment in the person and work of Jesus of Nazareth. Carefully review the concepts below as a mastery of these themes is essential if you are to adopt exegetical strategies that will enable you to see the unity as well as the diversity of the Old and New Testament literature.

- The relationship of the Old Testament to the New Testament can be effectively understood through the idea of *progressive revelation*, which affirms that God has revealed himself progressively and definitively throughout the history of his people, and finally through Jesus Christ

- The concept of *progressive revelation* includes God's continuous revelation of himself to us through creation, through specific manifestations and occasions, and in these last days through his Son. The OT explains and reveals the NT through the person of Christ, and both testaments focus upon God's final and full revelation of himself in Jesus Christ and his kingdom reign.

1

- Augustine's epigram (saying) nicely summarizes the relationship between the two testaments: "In the OT the NT lies hidden; in the NT the OT stands revealed." This complementary relationship is seen in how the OT provides an introduction to the NT's conclusion about Christ, the OT's anticipation of the person and work of Messiah, and the NT's identification of Jesus of Nazareth as the climax of that anticipation. Also, the OT serves as the shadow (prefiguring) of the person and work of Christ and the NT as its embodiment, and the OT is seen as the ineffective former revelation of God's salvation consummated later in the NT revelation of Jesus. Finally, what was particularized to Israel in the OT was universalized to all nations in the NT.

- The motif of *promise and fulfillment* in OT revelation affirms the promise of God for his own chosen One to redeem humankind and to destroy the devil's work, a promise fulfilled in the person of Jesus of Nazareth

- The NT provides several central texts which affirm how the OT's work is to provide compelling and definitive witness to the person of Messiah fulfilled in the person of Jesus Christ (cf. Luke 22.25-27, 44-48; Matt. 5.17-18; John 1.45; 5.39-40; Heb. 10.5-10 with Ps. 40.6-8). This witness can be seen in the history of the patriarchs, the nation of Israel, the Messianic prophecies, and the moral standards of the Law.

- The major motif that links all biblical revelation in Scripture is the *promise and fulfillment* motif. This theme affirms the unity of the Old and New Testaments, in terms of God's intention to reveal himself, to redeem his people, and to do this through the promise made to Abraham and his descendants fulfilled in the person of Jesus of Nazareth.

- The seminal text of the promise is explained in the *protoevangelium*, the first telling of the Gospel in Genesis 3.15. Here in this text God lays out the specifics of his salvation promise, including the certainty of hostility between the serpent and the woman and their respective "seeds," the bruising of the heel of the woman's seed, and the crushing of the serpents head by the seed.

- The theological implications of the *protoevangelium* are plain and profound. Namely, these include the fact that God would provide humanity with a Savior through the woman's lineage who would destroy the serpent, albeit his heel would be bruised by the serpent. In the NT, Jesus of Nazareth is revealed to be this divine seed commissioned to destroy the devil's work and to redeem humankind to God.

- Yahweh's covenant promise with Abraham serves as progressive continuation of God's divine promise for a Savior. In the covenant with Abraham, this promise is specified to be the seed of Abraham who would bring redemption and restoration not only to God's people (Abraham's descendants), but blessing to the nations of the earth as well. In the NT, Jesus of Nazareth is declared to be the seed of Abraham, the one through whom Abraham, his descendants, and the all the families of the earth would be blessed.

1

I Find My Lord in the Bible

I find my Lord in the Bible, wherever I chance to look,
He is the Theme of the Bible, the center and heart of the Book;
He is the Rose of Sharon, he is the Lily fair,
Where ever I open my Bible, the Lord of the Book is there.

He, at the Book's beginning, gave to the earth its form,
He is the Ark of shelter, bearing the brunt of the storm
The Burning Bush of the desert, the Budding of Aaron's Rod,
Where ever I look in the Bible, I see the Son of God.

The Ram upon Mount Moriah, the Ladder from earth to sky,
The Scarlet Cord in the window, and the Serpent lifted high,
The Smitten Rock in the desert, the Shepherd with staff and crook,
The face of the Lord I discover, where ever I open the Book.

He is the Seed of the woman, the Savior virgin-born
He is the Son of David, whom men rejected with scorn,
His garments of grace and of beauty the stately Aaron deck,
Yet he is a Priest forever, for he is Melchizedek.

Lord of eternal glory Whom John, the Apostle, saw;
Light of the golden city, Lamb without spot or flaw,
Bridegroom coming at midnight, for whom the virgins look.
Where ever I open my Bible, I find my Lord in the Book.

~ Author Unknown

Student Application and Implications

Now is the time for you to discuss with your fellow students your questions about your own grasp and application of the concepts of progressive revelation and the promise-fulfillment motif. What you must do is ask pointed, direct, and open questions about your own understanding and mastery of these principles, and seek the ways in which you might need to apply this material directly to your own spiritual journey today. The questions below seek to anticipate some of the particular questions you may have in light of the material you have just studied.

* What is my relationship to the Old Testament material–do I know all the books of the OT, have I read through the OT at least once, and do I have a steady habit of reading and applying the OT in my life and ministry today?

* Did you have any grasp of the principle of progressive revelation before this module of study, and if so, how did your knowledge of this actually influence the way in which you read and applied both the Old and the New Testaments?

* Do you tend to emphasize the connection and continuity between the Old and New Testament, or the differences between them? Explain.

* Do I tend to read all of the Bible with an eye toward the ways in which this text or these Scriptures might connect either *backward* to the life and revelation contained in the Old Testament, or *forward* to the life and work of Jesus of Nazareth, who is the fulfillment of the Old and full revelation of the New? How so?

* Could I have written what Augustine said: "In the OT the NT lies hidden; in the NT the OT stands revealed." Does the way I handle the Scriptures *really show* how much I believe in the unity of the OT to the New?

* In the church I attend, does the preaching and teaching reflect the connections between the Old and New Testament brought out in our discussion of the complimentary relationships between them (i.e., that the OT provides introduction to the NT's conclusion about Christ, the OT's anticipates the person and work of Messiah with the NT identifying Jesus of Nazareth as the climax of that anticipation, etc.)?

* How much do I worship and serve God with this kind of historical understanding that the motif of *promise and fulfillment* brings out? Do I focus most of my time on the past, the present, or the future in my Bible reading, meditation, and prayer?

* Do I tend to see Jesus both as the seed of the woman who will destroy the devil's work, as well as the seed of Abraham through whom all the families of the earth will be blessed? What is the primary way in which I view Jesus in light of these revelations about him?

* Do I (more often than not) affirm Jesus' teaching that he himself is the key theme and subject of all biblical revelation (cf. Luke 22.25-27, 44-48; Matt. 5.17-18; John 1.45; 5.39-40; Heb. 10.5-10 with Ps. 40.6-8)? How do I *most often* use the Bible in my life–as an affirmation of the person of Jesus or more related to my own troubles, needs, and issues? How ought we use the OT in light of Jesus' teaching about it?

CASE STUDIES

It Was Our Hebrew Bible before it Was Your Old Testament

1

Gang violence has been on the climb in your community for some time. In a show of unity and support, various religious groups have sent their religious representatives to an ecumenical panel discussion on violence, tolerance, and respect for others. As one of the panel members began to share his views about the "Old Testament" the local rabbi very warmly but firmly suggested the following: "As I know that many followers of Christ, Christian believers, are in attendance, and that it is their habit to refer to the first portion of their Bibles as the Old Testament, I would suggest that during our time together that we would refer to the Christian Old Testament as the Hebrew Bible. You see, for us, believers in Judaism, it has never been an old book; it is our *Scripture* and we refer to it as our Hebrew Scriptures. Would it be too much for us to refer to it in this way, as we dialogue together about respect, unity, and support for one another?" How would you answer the rabbi in this setting? Is this much ado about nothing, or is there something important about refusing to see the OT as merely the *old* portion of the Bible? How does viewing the "Hebrew Bible" as the "Old Testament" limit our ability to see its relevance for Christians today?

1

The OT and Equipping the Saints

2

It is quite clear that the Scriptures that Paul referred to in 2 Timothy 3, which could make God's woman or man outfitted for the work of the ministry, was the OT. The Bible of Jesus and the apostles was, in fact, our OT, and from even a cursory reading of the epistles we see that they quoted and referred to it often in their writings to new believers and emerging congregations. Unlike them, however, it is difficult to find follow-up material and discipleship curriculum where the teaching, stories, figures, and prophecies of the OT are made the heart and soul of the material. In some ways, the OT is in some sort of exile in many evangelical church settings. It is rarely read, and often even more rarely preached. A story here, a proverb there, but rarely do you find even expositors spending weeks or months in OT literature in the instruction of Christians. Obviously, this neglect has produced a kind of illiteracy of the OT in many Christians, those who have never had ongoing, systematic teaching of the OT. What should we make of this neglect of the OT in our churches—is it a product of the times, something more fundamental, or something else altogether?

A Gentilized Faith?

3 If you were not aware of it, the casual observer would take Christianity as essentially a Euro-centric faith, one that essentially began as a result of the Protestant revolt against Catholic extremes during the period of the Reformation in 16th Century Europe. And no wonder that they would suppose this, especially in evangelical settings, which tend to rarely if ever refer to the Jewish roots of the Christian faith, giving it little or no time in a Christian experience that is informed by middle class American values and trends. Unfortunately, many minority groups are growing in hostility to Christianized forms of "religion," seeing essentially the term "Christian" to be synonymous with holding deep affinity with white, middle-class, conservative perspectives and moral values. A growing movement of thinkers and scholars are referring to the need to de-Gentlize our faith, arguing that we have swung too far to interpreting Christian experience as merely an American value system with a religious twist. Obviously, many who do not find this attractive are rejecting Christian faith before even being exposed to the biblical claims about the person of Jesus of Nazareth as outlined in the Old and New Testament. How might a rediscovery of the OT (admittedly, a distinctively Hebrew book) help us mature beyond the *Gentilization* of much of the Christian faith and practice today?

1

Too Hard and Not on Point

4 A well-studied and beloved youth group leader in a growing church was recently struck by how few of the members of his youth group understood any of even the most basic stories and figures of the OT. We are not speaking of some of the lesser characters, but the main figures: Moses, Elijah, Elisha, etc. were not known, either. In an attempt to remedy this difficulty, the youth group leader started a bible teaching series entitled "Defining Moments" which would take selected key points of the OT and show how it related to Christ and his Kingdom spoken of in the NT. After a few weeks, the character of the youth group changed greatly. Some students, finding the stories and materials too hard and not real exciting, quit the group altogether, and another group has found the stories intriguing, but not relevant to where they see themselves at. A small group, however, have flourished under the teaching, and for the first time believe that they are coming to understand the OT. Pressure is growing in the church to go back to the good ol' days of teaching on contemporary issues that were easier to teach (and to hear!), but the leader has determined to finish the series, which has another three months to go. If the youth group leader asked your opinion, how would you advise him on making the OT

come alive in his group without alienating and confusing some of the "weaker brethren" complaining about it?

Restatement of the Lesson's Thesis

The relationship of the Old Testament to the New Testament can be effectively understood through the idea of *progressive revelation*, which affirms that God has revealed himself progressively and definitively throughout the history of his people, and finally through Jesus Christ. God in diverse manners and at different times made himself known to the nation of Israel in limited ways, but in these last days he has spoken to us through his Son. Jesus of Nazareth is God's final and full revelation of himself, now testified of in Scripture. As Augustine suggests: "In the OT the NT lies hidden; in the NT the OT stands revealed." The Testaments have a complementary relationship, the OT providing the introduction to the NT's conclusion about Christ, the OT as anticipation to the NT's climax about God's salvation story in Christ. Furthermore, the OT prefigures Christ's person and work fully embodied in the NT. While the OT is the ineffective former revelation of God's salvation, the NT can be seen as the consummated latter and universalized call of which the OT is particularized to the nation of Israel. The connection of the testaments can be seen in the *promise and fulfillment* motif, especially in the way the NT affirms how the OT's work is to provide compelling and definitive witness to the person of Messiah fulfilled in the person of Jesus Christ in the history of the patriarchs, the nation of Israel, the Messianic prophecies, and the moral standards of the Law.

The major motif that links all biblical revelation in Scripture is the *promise and fulfillment* motif. This theme affirms the unity of the Scriptures; God intends to reveal himself and redeem his people through the seed, the one promised to Abraham and his descendants. This seed is fulfilled in the person of Jesus of Nazareth. The seminal text in Scripture outlining the promise is the *protoevangelium*, the first telling of the Gospel in Genesis 3.15. Here God promises the certainty of hostility between the serpent and the woman and their respective "seeds," the bruising of the heel of the woman's seed, and the crushing of the serpent's head by the seed. In the NT, Jesus of Nazareth is revealed to be this divine seed commissioned to destroy the devil's work and to redeem humankind to God. Yahweh's covenant promise with Abraham serves as progressive continuation of God's divine promise for a Savior. In his covenant with Abraham, God promised to supply him a "seed" who would bring redemption and restoration to Abraham's descendants and all the nations of the earth. In the NT, Jesus of Nazareth is declared to be the seed of Abraham, the restorer and redeemer of creation and the world.

Resources and Bibliographies

If you are interested in pursuing some of the ideas of *The Promise Given*, you might want to give these books a try:

Baron, David. *Rays of Messiah's Glory: Christ in the Old Testament.* Eugene, OR: Wipf and Stock Publishers, 2001.

Clowney, Edmund P. *The Unfolding Mystery: Discovering Christ in the Old Testament.* Phillipsburg, NJ: P & R Publishing, 1991.

Drew, Charles D. *The Ancient Love Song: Finding Christ in the Old Testament.* Phillipsburg, NJ: P & R Publishing, 2000.

1

Ministry Connections

As you go through this module, probing the nature of the OT's witness to Christ, you will want to examine the ways in which these insights and perspectives can affect your own understanding and practice of ministry. How do *you* study and investigate the OT, what are *your attitudes and responses* to the OT literature, and in what way does your own *preaching and teaching* need to be impacted by a fresh and more unified understanding of the relationship of the testaments? Ask the Holy Spirit to help you identify the key ways in which you might want to make a direct practical ministry connection with the perspectives and ideas that you covered in this lesson, and ones that you can think about and pray for throughout this next week. The key to dynamic growth and innovation in ministry is being dramatically open to the Holy Spirit's promptings about growth, change, and application. Ask him to point out particular situations where you can integrate these new insights into your own personal walk and ministry.

Counseling and Prayer

Spend time in prayer for yourself and your colleagues, asking that God would enable you to grow in your knowledge and application of the biblical concepts of *progressive revelation*, of the *promise-fulfillment motif*, and of your own mastery and appreciation of the unity underlying both the Old and New Testament. Ask God to grant you a new love and insight into the Bible's revelation about the majesty and centrality of Jesus Christ, and ask him for a fresh filling of the Holy Spirit so you can prove in experience Augustine's epigram: "In the OT the NT lies hidden; in the NT the OT stands revealed." Prayer is a powerful, effective, and God-ordained way to receive his wisdom (James 1.5), never underestimate the power of prayer in your study of the Word of God. Pray fervently for yourself and for your fellow students, and ask the Lord for his generous supply and help–he is more than willing to provide it.

ASSIGNMENTS

1

Scripture Memory

Genesis 3.15 and 12.1-3

Reading Assignment

To prepare for class, please visit *www.tumi.org/books* to find next week's reading assignment, or ask your mentor.

Other Assignments

It is important that you set aside time to review the material covered in this teaching section. The module study is arranged so that you will be quizzed on the content (the video content) of this lesson *in your next class session.* Make sure that you spend time covering your notes, especially focusing on the main ideas of the lesson. Read the assigned reading, and summarize your readings with no more than a paragraph or two for each. In this summary please give your best understanding of what you think was the main point in each of the readings. Do not be overly concerned about giving detail; simply write out what you consider to be the main point discussed in that section of the book. Please bring these summaries to class next week. (Please see the "Reading Completion Sheet" at the end of this lesson.)

Looking Forward to the Next Lesson

In this first lesson we probed the relationships between the Old and New Testament. We considered the notion of progressive revelation, and how this concept helps us keep our understanding of the Old and New Testaments united in the person of Jesus Christ and his kingdom reign. We also saw how the two testaments complement each other, and how the biblical motif of *promise and fulfillment* is a helpful perspective to guide us in our study of the Old Testament. We also saw how Jesus is the seed of the woman destined to crush the serpent's head, recounted in the marvelous promise first spoken in the *protoevangelium*. We also considered the seed of Abraham cited in Yahweh's covenant promise. Jesus Christ himself is the fulfillment of both of these OT promises, destined to destroy the devil and bless all the families of the earth.

In our next lesson we will discover how the history of Israel, especially its worship in the Tabernacle with the priests, feasts, and festivals, further give witness to Jesus Christ as the fulfillment of God's promise for redemption to all humanity. We will see from OT Scripture how the major emblems of the Tabernacle, the Levitical priesthood, the sacrifices, and the feasts and festivals all find their fulfillment in the life and work of Jesus of Nazareth. In a real way, all of these personages, events, and institutions prefigure the person and work of Jesus Christ as the fulfillment of God's promise to Abraham.

Module 9: Old Testament Witness to Christ
Reading Completion Sheet

Name ________________________________

Date ________________________________

For each assigned reading, write a brief summary (one or two paragraphs) of the author's main point. (For additional readings, use the back of this sheet.)

Reading 1

Title and Author: ________________________________ Pages ________

Reading 2

Title and Author: ________________________________ Pages ________

LESSON 2

The Promise Clarified

Lesson Objectives

Welcome in the strong name of Jesus Christ! After your reading, study, discussion, and application of the materials in this lesson, you will be able to:

- Give a clear and simple definition of *type*, as an object, event, happening, image, or reality that prefigures in the OT a reality in the NT, usually focused on Jesus Christ (as its *antitype*).
- Outline the major justifications for a typological approach of the study of the Scriptures, including Jesus' and the apostles' use of the method, and the implicit connection in many of the same representations and images mentioned throughout Scripture.
- List the major aspects of biblical types: that they are historically real, they illumine the person and work of Christ, are contained in the NT, are connected to God's redemptive work in Christ, and they illumine the teaching of God on the matter they cover.
- Articulate the principles for using typology properly in biblical hermeneutics, including the need to believe that God has placed correspondences in the Bible, to focus on Christ in drawing connections between the Old and New Testaments, to concentrate on the major links suggested in the types themselves and not on the details, to appreciate the relevance of the type *through the antitype.*
- Explain how the experience of Israel, the descendants of Abraham and the people of God, represent an analogy where we can understand the larger relationship of God with all of the redeemed through Jesus Christ.
- Highlight specifically how God's deliverance of his people during the Exodus prefigures specific dimensions of God's deliverance of his people through Jesus of Nazareth; our Passover, manna, and spiritual water from the Rock.
- Demonstrate how the conquest of the nation of Canaan, the entering into the Promised Land and the establishment of Israel's kingdom reign pictures the conquest of God's enemies through Christ whom God will establish as

King and Lord forever, and the blessing of God's kingdom people, the Church, who will rule with Christ as co-regents with him.

- Show how God's restoration of his people after the captivity is a type of study of Scripture, and how the three distinct moments within Israel's history help us understand the OT essentially as a witness to Christ and his kingdom reign. These three moments are the Exodus, the conquest of Canaan and entering into the Promised Land, and the restoration of Israel from the Babylonian Captivity.

- Summarize these three moments in Israel's history as parallel to the new life given to us by faith in Christ, which is a *New Exodus*, a new deliverance from the powers which oppress us spiritually; the fight against the devil and the world by the Church in spiritual warfare which represents a *New Conquest of Canaan*, and the ministry of the Gospel of Christ as a *New Restoration of God*, leading eventually to the new heavens and new earth under the sovereign authority of Jesus Christ.

- Show how the various elements and activities associated with the Tabernacle is a type of the salvation provided in Jesus Christ, including how the Tabernacle was a copy or shadow of the true dwelling place of God in the heavenlies, a symbol of God's presence among his people, and a way for God to reveal through type the one true salvation in Jesus.

- Describe how the Tabernacle's dimensions and compartments made access available to God, so Jesus Christ makes access to God available through his blood sacrifice.

- Show how the various articles of the Tabernacle represent distinctive aspects of Jesus Christ and his work: *the Brazen Altar* represents sacrificial redemption in Christ, *the Laver* represents the cleansing we receive through the blood of Jesus Christ, *the Table of Shewbread* represents Jesus Christ as the Bread of Life, *the Golden Candlestick* represents Christ as the Light of the world, *the Altar of Incense* represents Jesus' ministry of intercession on behalf of his people, *the Veil* represents the body of Jesus torn and broken for us on Calvary, *the Ark of the Covenant* represents the communion with God we share by faith in Jesus Christ.

- Highlight the elements of the priesthood which show how Jesus Christ perfects in every way the pattern and meaning of the high priesthood of

Aaron, and yet surpasses it through the priesthood in the order of Melchizedek, whose order was eternal, unchangeable, perfect, and final.

- Give knowledge of how Jesus Christ fulfills in meaning and substance all the offerings associated with the Temple sacrifices: *the whole burnt offering* is a type of Jesus' own free will offering of himself to God; *the meal offering* is a type of Jesus' own presentation and dedication of his life and sufferings to God acceptable to him in every respect; *the peace offering* is a type of Jesus Christ himself who is our peace with God and with one another; *the sin offering* is a type of Jesus Christ who became sin for us by bearing our offense and penalty on the Cross; *the trespass offering* is a type of how Jesus is both propitiation for our sins as well as cleansing and provision for us to live a new life.

- Explain how Jesus is the *antitype* in terms of the meaning of Israel's feasts, festivals, and convocations: in *the Feast of the Passover*, Jesus is our Paschal Lamb whose blood cleanses and redeems us; in *the Feast of Unleavened Bread*, Jesus is the one who inspires our walk in holiness before him, and not in malice or evil living; in *the Feast of First Fruits*, Jesus is the first fruits of the coming harvest of new humanity to be redeemed for God; in *the Feast of Pentecost*, Jesus is the one who with the Father pours out his Holy Spirit upon the Church in this present age; in *the Feast of Trumpets*, Jesus is the one who will return and regather his people for redemption and blessing; in *the Day of Atonement*, Jesus is both the High Priest and the sacrifice offered to God in the heavenly Tabernacle for our sin; in *the Feast of Tabernacles*, Jesus is the one who will regather his people at his Second Coming for glorification and rest.

2

Devotion

Written Down for Our Instruction

1 Cor. 10.1-11 - I want you to know, brothers, that our fathers were all under the cloud, and all passed through the sea, [2] and all were baptized into Moses in the cloud and in the sea, [3] and all ate the same spiritual food, [4] and all drank the same spiritual drink. For they drank from the spiritual Rock that followed them, and the Rock was Christ. [5] Nevertheless, with most of them God was not pleased, for they were overthrown in the wilderness. [6] Now these things took place as examples for us, that we might not desire evil as they did. [7] Do not be idolaters as some of them were; as it is written, "The people sat down to eat and drink and rose up to play." [8] We must not indulge in sexual immorality as some of them did, and twenty-three thousand fell in a single day. [9] We must not put Christ to the test, as some of them did and were destroyed by serpents, [10] nor grumble, as some of them did and were destroyed by the Destroyer. [11] Now these things happened to them as an example, but they were written down for our instruction, on whom the end of the ages has come.

What is the purpose of all of the material in the OT, and precisely how does it relate to our lives today? This question is constantly being asked in churches and by pastors across the country. Relatively few people seem to be literate as Christians in the voluminous materials of the OT, and even fewer seem able to gain a handle on the *unity* of the material for our lives. While many will give a kind of respectful lip-service to the OT, it is not easy to find many who are dedicated to studying the text with an obedience spoken of in Joshua 1.8: "This Book of the Law shall not depart from your mouth, but you shall meditate on it day and night, so that you may be careful to do according to all that is written in it. For then you will make your way prosperous, and then you will have good success." Even the categorical promises of Yahweh to the one who dedicates himself to the meditation on the Law of the Lord does not seem to get a rise from many believers in their determination to master the OT. What is the source of this halting difficulty to grasp the Hebrew Bible?

Perhaps many could be given. "The OT is too large a library to master." "The OT is so filled with metaphors, symbols, allegories, parables, and unusual imagery that only an expert can grasp it." "I don't see how I would ever have the time to do it. How on earth would anyone find a way to read let alone master all of the things contained in our OT?"

Regardless of the reasons given, it is plain that there remains a kind of strange silence and eery ignorance of much of the OT in our churches today. It can be argued, though, that our OT was the Bible of Jesus and the apostles, the beloved Word of God which could not be broken to Jesus (John 10.35), the word that lives and abides forever for Peter (1 Pet. 1.25), and the God-breathed Word that equips the man or woman of God for every good work for Paul (2 Tim. 3.17). Indeed, the Word that comforted the hearts of Jesus and the apostles was our Old Testament!

Paul's instruction to the Corinthians is instructive about our study and application of the OT. Paul recited the incidents of God's deliverance of Israel in the Exodus, and alluded to Moses' "baptism" the people of Israel were placed into in the Red Sea, and the spiritual drink they received from God "from the spiritual Rock that followed them, and the Rock was Christ" (v.4). He instructed the ex-pagan Corinthians from the OT, exhorting them based on the analogy he drew between the hardheaded Israelites and the stubborn Corinthians. He warned them of the perils of idolatry, and exhorted them not to follow the example of Israel who because of their disobedience and sexual immorality twenty-three thousand fell in a single day. He recounted the Israelite's disobedience and testing of the Lord, and warned them not to put Christ to the test nor grumble as they had done, lest they suffer the same fate as they who were destroyed by serpents, and by the Destroyer. Paul ends his exhortation based on the *experience, analogy, and life lessons learned* from the Israelites, and instructed them on the *reason behind the experiences recorded in the OT*. "Now these things happened to them as an example, but they were written down for our instruction, on whom the end of the ages has come" (v. 11).

So, from Paul's own use of the OT with believers who had no orientation to it–how did he explain its function in the Church? The answer is simple and plain. *The experience of the Israelites was given as a typos (example) for us to follow and derive spiritual wisdom from, to instruct us in the ways of the Lord*, those for whom the very end of the ages has come. In a real sense, the richness and benefit of the Word of God, the OT, is rooted in its ability to coincide with our experience. There is much time between us and the history of the Israelites, but there is no difference in the relationship we have with the Lord. Their experience was written for *our instruction*; the very lessons, experiences, insights, revelations, and happenings that they endured and enjoyed are given to lead us into God's very own will and blessing for *our lives*. At the very heart of the OT is this *analogy of faith*, this connection that all of God's people have as human beings and as the cherished of the Lord.

2

Perceived in this way, the OT is demythologized from its so-called *difficult and hard-to-understand and apply* status. When we read the stories of the people of God in the OT, according to Paul, we read *our own story*, and we can avoid the horrible disciplines they received, or, alas, *learn the very same lessons* they had to learn because of our own inability to listen and respond to his voice. This connection that the people of God have regardless of the time, place, or era is the very ground on which we study and apply the OT. It is not simply the record of the happenings of the ancient people, Israel and their neighbors. In a very real sense, *it is our story*, and we can use their experience as an example, a model, a means of learning God's will and ways for our lives today.

This is how our Lord referred to the OT's messages and stories. Notice the allusion he gave to Nicodemus in speaking of salvation to humankind:

John 3.14-15 - And as Moses lifted up the serpent in the wilderness, so must the Son of Man be lifted up, [15] that whoever believes in him may have eternal life.

Going back to God's experience with his people Israel recorded in the OT, Jesus said, "*As Moses lifted up the serpent in the wilderness* [the OT experience] *so must the Son of Man be lifted up* [the NT correlation] *that whoever believes in him may have eternal life* [the contemporary application]." This analogy reveals the usefulness and absolute necessity of the OT for us today. It is the foundation that Jesus and the apostles used to explain *who we are in Christ* and what *our spiritual obligation to God is in light of it*. The OT is not the same as the *obsolete testament*! As the Word of God, it will forever be relevant and important for us, and we ought to seek the analogies so we can be "equipped for every good work" through it.

Are you ready for your lesson today, taken from the experience and truths to be learned from the history of Israel? Indeed, it was *written for our instruction.*

2

Nicene Creed and Prayer

After reciting and/or singing the Nicene Creed (located in the Appendix), pray the following prayer:

Almighty, everlasting God, who dist give thine only Son to be a High Priest of good things to come: Hereafter grant unto us, thine unworthy servants, to have our share in the company of the blessed; through the same Jesus Christ, thy Son, our Lord. Amen.

~ Lutheran Church in America.
Service Book and Hymnal of the Lutheran Church in America
Minneapolis, Minn.: Augsburg Publishing House, 1958. p. 233

Quiz

Put away your notes, gather up your thoughts and reflections, and take the quiz for Lesson 1, *The Promise Given.*

Scripture Memorization Review

Review with a partner, write out and/or recite the text for last class session's assigned memory verse: Genesis 3.15 and 12.1-3.

Assignments Due

Turn in your summary of the reading assignment for last week, that is, your brief response and explanation of the main points that the authors were seeking to make in the assigned reading (Reading Completion Sheet).

Go to the Ant, You Sluggard! Consider Her Ways and Be Wise!

1 To the uninitiated and naive reader of the Bible, it would appear obvious that it is a book of images, symbols, stories, and metaphors. Literally, on every page images of the divine are seen through the lens of the common images of human experience. Undoubtedly, the ability to communicate through the concrete images of object lessons and historical example heightens our ability to envision the truth, and not merely reason about it. The image of industry in Proverbs is the industrious insect, the ant, who provides for its needs early (Prov. 6.6ff.). The image of the Kingdom of God is a banquet thrown by a king for his subjects (Luke 14.16-24), and the Messiah illustrates the relationship between he and his followers in the relationship of a vine to its branches (John 15). The power of *the concrete and the known* to illustrate and illumine *the abstract and the unknown* could very well be the integrating principle of communication in the OT, especially in its witness to Christ through the images of the Prophet, the Priest, and the King. What do you see as the immediate benefits of God communicating about the nature of Christ through the lives and stories of individuals in the Bible? What about this method of communication (if anything) makes it more difficult to understand the nature of the Messiah through these historical examples and analogies?

2

An Old-Fashioned Method, and Prone to Error

2 The OT's focus on characters, images, symbols, and stories that point to the identity of Christ is seen in many circles as a failed method of biblical interpretation of the Scriptures. Although this method was a popular and deftly-used method in the 19th century, many modern scholars rejected it because of the many odd and weird interpretations that it produced in connection with allegories, types, and analogies. To be sure, some interpreters of types have come up with fanciful and unbiblical interpretations which neither support nor connect to the New Testament pictures of Christ. Although Jesus and the apostles often interpreted the OT in light of its direct witness to Christ through the images and types contained in it, the method of typology is rejected because of its proneness to error and abuse. What ought to be our attitude toward this method of OT interpretation, especially in light of the abuse and misuse of it by some interpreters in the past? Can we ignore it as a vital way of interpreting the OT, especially if Jesus and the apostles employed the method to interpret the revelation of Jesus of Nazareth *through* the images and characters of the OT?

What Are the Boundaries Here?

3

The Book of Hebrews in the NT for many is all the justification needed for the proper use of the typological method to discern how the OT reveals and discloses the true nature of the Messiah and his work of redemption in the world. The analogies given between the Tabernacle, the sacrifices, the priesthood, and many other OT characters and symbols reveal a true relationship between them and the person and ministry of Jesus Christ as the Messiah and the history of Israel. Jesus is seen in Hebrews, in fact, as the actual body and substance of the things which were only prefigured and seen through type and analogy in the OT. Even those who employ this method, however, are concerned with one very present problem: how does one avoid seeing connections and linkages regarding the Messiah *in every image, metaphor, and story in the OT?* In other words, does such a method give us license to probe *everything in the OT* with the intent of finding Christ in it, and if so, how do we prevent wrong and misguided interpretations of the OT all done in the spirit of seeking to identify Christ in the story, image, prophecy, or event?

2

The Promise Clarified

Segment 1: The History of God's People as Type and Analogy

Rev. Dr. Don L. Davis

Summary of Segment 1

The simple definition of *type* is "an object, event, happening, image, or reality that prefigures in the OT a reality in the NT, usually focused on Jesus Christ (as its *antitype*)." The typological approach of the study of the OT Scriptures as related to the revelation of Christ was the method employed by both Jesus and his apostles, and makes clear the Bible's own connection of many representations and images in both testaments. The major aspects of biblical types suggest that types (and their antitypes) are historically real, they illumine the person and work of Christ, true types of the OT are always contained in the NT, they are connected to God's redemptive work in Christ, and they illumine the teaching of God on the matter they cover. Using typology in biblical hermeneutics must be done properly, focusing on Christ as connections are drawn between the Old and New Testaments, appreciating the relevance of the type *through the antitype*. The experience of Israel, the descendants of Abraham and the people of God, represent an analogy which can help us understand the larger relationship of God with all of the redeemed through

Jesus Christ. Three distinctive moments in their history which illustrate this principle is their deliverance at the Exodus, the conquest of Canaan and the entering into the Promised Land, and the restoration of Israel from the Babylonian Captivity.

The experience of God's redeemed in Christ is exhibited clearly in these three moments in Israel's history: the Church's new life in Christ is their *New Exodus,* a new deliverance from the powers which oppress us spiritually; the Church's fight against the devil and the world is its *New Conquest of Canaan,* and the ministry of the Gospel of Christ represents our *New Restoration of God,* leading eventually to the new heavens and new earth under the sovereign authority of Jesus Christ.

Our objective for this segment, *The History of God's People as Type and Analogy*, is to enable you to see that:

- The simple definition of *type* is "an object, event, happening, image, or reality that prefigures in the OT a reality in the NT, usually focused on Jesus Christ (as its *antitype*)."

- The major hermeneutical justifications for a typological approach of the study of the Scriptures are that it was the method employed by both Jesus and his apostles and that the Bible itself makes in comparative study implicit connection between many of the same representations and images mentioned throughout Scripture.

- The major aspects of biblical types suggest that types (and their antitypes) are historically real, they illumine the person and work of Christ, true types of the OT are always contained in the NT, they are connected to God's redemptive work in Christ, and they illumine the teaching of God on the matter they cover.

- The principles for using typology in biblical hermeneutics include our need to believe that God has placed correspondences in the Bible, to focus on Christ in drawing connections between the Old and New Testaments, to concentrate on the major links suggested in the types themselves and not on the details, and to appreciate the relevance of the type *through the antitype.*

- The experience of Israel, the descendants of Abraham and the people of God, represent an analogy which can help us understand the larger relationship of God with all of the redeemed through Jesus Christ. Three distinctive moments in their history which illustrate this principle is their deliverance at the Exodus, the conquest of Canaan and the entering into the Promised Land, and the restoration of Israel from the Babylonian Captivity.

- God's deliverance of his people during the Exodus prefigures specific dimensions of God's deliverance of his people through Jesus of Nazareth; our Passover, Manna, spiritual water from the Rock.

- The story of Israel's conquest of the nation of Canaan, their entry into the Promised Land, and the establishment of their kingdom reign pictures the conquest of God's enemies through Christ whom God will establish as King and Lord forever, and the blessing of God's kingdom people, the Church, Christ's co-regents.

- God's restoration of his people after the Captivity is a type of Christ's future restoration of his people, and the promise of their future blessing at the Second Coming. The OT essentially is a witness to Christ and his kingdom reign.

- The experience of God's redeemed in Christ is exhibited clearly in these three moments in Israel's history: the Church's new life in Christ is their *New Exodus,* a new deliverance from the powers which oppress us spiritually; the Church's fight against the devil and the world is its *New Conquest of Canaan*, and the ministry of the Gospel of Christ represents our *New Restoration of God*, leading eventually to the new heavens and new earth under the sovereign authority of Jesus Christ.

2

I. Picturing Forth the Truth: the Role of Types and Analogies in Biblical Interpretation

Video Segment 1 Outline

The History of Adam and Humanity Recapitulated in the Person of Jesus Christ

The doctrine of recapitulation (Latin ***recapitulatio****; Greek,* ***anakephalaiosis****; a "summing up") was derived from Ephesians 1.10. It is especially associated with Irenaeus, although later authors picked up its themes. There are two principal interpretations of the meaning which Irenaeus gave to recapitulation: 1) Christians retraced the steps of Adam and humanity, an interpretation which accords with Irenaeus's presentation of Christ's career; 2) Christ comprehended* *or brought to a head in himself the whole of humanity, an interpretation which better accords with the meaning of Ephesians 1.10. Irenaeus elaborated the parallels between Adam and Christ. Adam was made of virgin soil, was tempted by Satan, and brought sin and death into the world through disobedience at the tree. Christ was born of the Virgin Mary, resisted temptation by Satan, and overcame sin by obedience to death on the cross. Irenaeus further suggested that Christ passed through all ages of life–infant, child, youth, and old man–in order to sanctify all who are born again to God through him. He became what we are in order to make us what he is. As a result of his life, death, and resurrection all that was lost in Adam is regained in Christ. The human race was given a new start, and saved humanity is gathered together as one in Christ. Christ also summed up and completed in himself the revelation of God. The doctrine of recapitulation was important in the context of the Gnostic controversy because it secured the reality of the incarnations, the unity of mankind, and the certainty of redemption.*

~ E. Ferguson. "Recapitulation." **Evangelical Dictionary of Theology.** Walter Elwell, ed. Grand Rapids: Baker Book House, 1984. pp. 916-17.

2

A. Definition of types and analogy

1. F. F. Bruce: (derived from the Greek, *typos*, meaning "seal-impression"); "a way of setting forth the biblical history of salvation so that some of its earlier phases are seen as anticipations of later phases, or some later phase as the recapitulation or fulfillment of an earlier one."

2. Moorhead: "a type is a person, event, or thing so fashioned as to resemble another."

3. J. A. Schmidt: "types are a set of pictures or object lessons by which God would teach his people about his grace and saving power."

4. D. L. Davis: "a biblical type is an object, event, happening, image, or reality that prefigures in the Old Testament a reality in the New Testament, usually focused on the person and work of Jesus Christ."

   a. Type: the mark left by a blow, a stamped image; (by analogy) a statue; [fig.] a model used of imitation or warning

   b. Antitype: [lit.] striking back, echoing; [fig.] a thing resembling another, i.e., its counterpart; a thing formed for some pattern

*Typology deals with the concept of **form** or **pattern**, to which the Greek word **typos** refers. In biblical times, **typos** referred to the **original model or prototype** of an item, and was also connected to the **copy** that resulted from it.*

B. Is a typological study of the Scriptures valid today?

2

1. It is the way the apostles studied and correlated the OT to the new revelation in Christ.

   a. Moses and the serpent in the wilderness, John 3.14-15

   b. Jonah, Queen of Sheba, and Solomon, Matt. 12.40-42

   c. Manna in the wilderness, John 6.49-51

   d. Spiritual drink from the Rock, 1 Cor. 10.1-4

2. Much abuse of this kind of interpretation has caused many to ignore the richness of this method of connecting truth between the OT and NT.

3. The Bible makes connections and analogies, having certain figures, images, and characters stand for and represent other things.

4. Seeking linkages and connections between the OT and NT can help us see how the OT bears witness to Christ and his Kingdom.

C. Aspects of biblical types

1. They are *historically real*, Rom. 5.14.

2. They *illumine* the person and work of Christ, John 3.14-15.

3. They are *contained (alluded to or mentioned in) the New Testament*, 1 Pet. 3.20-21.

4. They are *connected to God's redemptive work in Jesus Christ*, 1 Cor. 5.7.

5. They *illumine the teaching of God on the matter* (i.e., types reveal by picturing forth the truth in a richer, clearer, more concrete way), e.g., John 3.14-15.

D. Principles for using typology in biblical interpretation

1. Look for connections between the testaments: believe that the God who orders all events can create correspondences for us to behold and learn from.

2. Focus on Christ in drawing correspondences between types in the OT and NT: Jesus' own testimony suggests that correspondences of himself exist in the OT (e.g., Luke 24.25-27, 44-48).

3. Focus on the key links suggested by the types; don't focus on every little detail.

4. Remember that we can only appreciate the relevance of the type in light of the antitype.

Types as Pictures of Christ in the OT

There are many fitting pictures of Christ in the Old Testament which, properly speaking, should not be classified as types. For a type not only pictured Christ but it was a kind of implicit prediction that Christ would fulfill its function. Such were the sacrifices, the temple, the priesthood, and the feasts of the old economy. They were prefigurations that were not permanent but pointed to their perfection in Christ. But, besides these types, there are in the Old Testament many pictures which are appropriately applied to Christ. Some of these the New Testament applies to Christ and some it does not. In the former class are: 1) Jonah's three days and nights in the whale [Matt. 12.40]; 2) Solomon and his wisdom [Matt. 12.42]; 3) the "Rock" in the wilderness [1 Cor. 10.4]; 4) the "manna" from heaven [John 6.41]; 5) the "serpent" in the wilderness [John 3.14]. It is difficult to draw a distinct line this side of religious fancy in regard to pictures of Christ in the Old Testament which are not applied to him by the New Testament. On the other hand, as with typology, it would seem too restrictive to limit "pictures" of Christ to only those things in the Old Testament which the New Testament applies to Christ. It would be better, to use the general principle involved in the above list, namely, ***anything which appropriately depicts some significant aspect of Christ's Messianic mission which has some matching Messianic metaphor in the Bible*** *[emphasis mine].*

~ Norman Geisler. **To Understand the Bible Look for Jesus.** Eugene, OR: Wipf and Stock Publishers, 2002. p. 60-61.

II. Pictures of Christ in the OT History of Israel

A. The Exodus: deliverance from the powers of Egypt by the power of God

1. Viewed as a new creation where the God who controlled the seas at creation restrained the sea at the Exodus, Exod. 14.21-29

2. As Moses was God's prophetic vessel to speak to others on his behalf, so Jesus is an antitype of Moses, the revealer of God as the Living Word of God, Deut. 18.15.

3. God's overthrow of the symbols of evil and chaos, Rahab and the dragon (Job 26.12f) are applied to his victory at the Exodus.

   a. Ps. 74.12-14

   b. Ps. 89.8-10

   c. Rahab is a type of Egypt (cf. Isa. 30.7).

   d. The dragon (Leviathan) is a type of Pharaoh, Ezek. 29.3.

4. The Exodus in the New Testament

   a. The infancy of Jesus is associated with the going down of Israel into Egypt, Matt. 2.15.

b. As Moses represented God and was the builder of his people, so Jesus too is faithful as God's representative building God's people, that is, his house, Heb. 3.1-6.

c. Jesus is the Paschal Lamb of our Passover.

(1) 1 Cor. 5.7

(2) 1 Pet. 1.19

d. As Israel passed through the waters, so we have been baptized into Christ Jesus, Rom. 6.3-4.

e. As Israel received bread from heaven and water from the Rock, so we in Christ receive him as our Manna from heaven and he is our spiritual drink, 1 Cor. 10.1-4.

f. As Israel fell in the wilderness due to their own disobedience and unbelief, we are exhorted to take warning against these threats in our lives, 1 Cor. 10.11.

B. The Conquest of Canaan and the establishment of Israel's kingdom reign: engaging the powers of the world

1. As Israel engaged in fighting its enemies in Canaan, so we engage in spiritual warfare with Christ as our strength and Captain.

a. We sojourn through this barren land of the world system, 1 Pet. 2.11-12.

b. We fight against the rulers of this present darkness, Eph. 6.10-13.

c. We are to share in the suffering of this spiritual warfare as good soldiers of Jesus Christ, 2 Tim. 2.3-4.

d. The weapons of our spiritual warfare are divine and effective, 2 Cor. 10.3-6.

2. As Israel defeated their enemies and entered into God's rest, so we in Christ by faith have defeated our enemies and enter in God's Sabbath rest, Heb. 4.8-11 .

3. As God established kings on the throne of Israel, so God will establish Jesus Christ on the throne as King and Lord forever, and his people as co-regents with him.

   a. Isa. 9.6-7

   b. Luke 1.31-33

   c. 1 Pet. 2.9

   d. Rev. 1.5-6

4. The extraordinary glory of Solomon's kingdom is associated with the person of Jesus Christ himself, Matt. 12.40-42.

C. Restoration after Captivity (Isa. 40-66): the blessedness of God's people in their restored relationship with God.

Isa. 40.9 - Get you up to a high mountain, O Zion, herald of good news; lift up your voice with strength, O Jerusalem, herald of good news; lift it up, fear not; say to the cities of Judah, "Behold your God!"

Isa. 52.7 - How beautiful upon the mountains are the feet of him who brings good news, who publishes peace, who brings good news of happiness, who publishes salvation, who says to Zion, "Your God reigns."

Isa. 61.1 - The Spirit of the Lord GOD is upon me, because the LORD has anointed me to bring good news to the poor; he has sent me to bind up the brokenhearted, to proclaim liberty to the captives, and the opening of the prison to those who are bound.

1. This portion of prophetic Scripture is dramatically rich in making associations regarding the "good tidings."

2. As God promised "good tidings proclaimed" for the people of God after the return from exile, so we see this fulfilled in the NT history.

    a. John the Baptist as the voice in the wilderness, Isa. 40.3

    b. The Suffering Servant of Jehovah as the Lord Jesus himself, Luke 4.18-19

3. The outpouring of God's Spirit on his people, Joel 2.28-32 and Acts 2.16-18 (cf. Joel 2.28-32)

4. Rebuilding of Zion and the establishment of God's glory among his people as a type of the Church's waiting on God's building of the New Jerusalem, Heb. 11.13-16

Conclusion

- » Three biblical type scenes help us understand the OT essentially as a witness to Christ and his kingdom reign.
- » God's deliverance of his people at the Exodus, the conquest of Canaan and entering into the Promised Land, and the restoration of Israel from the Babylonian Captivity–these all parallel God's work in Christ spoken of in the NT.

Segue 1

Student Questions and Response

Please take as much time as you have available to answer these and other questions that the video brought out. In the last section we saw how the experience of Israel represents a redemptive analogy which helps us understand the larger relationship of God with all of the redeemed through Jesus Christ. Three distinctive moments in their history illustrate this principle: their deliverance at the Exodus, the conquest of Canaan and the entering into the Promised Land, and the restoration of Israel from the Babylonian Captivity. What we must seek to understand is both the *method* of how these analogies work, and the *message* of how they make more plain for us the work of Christ on behalf of his Church today. Review the key concepts covered in the first section by answering the questions below.

2

1. What is the definition of *type*? Correspondingly, what is the definition of *antitype*, and how are they related to one another? Why is the focus on Jesus Christ so important in discovering types and antitypes in our understanding of the OT's witness to him?
2. What are the major hermeneutical justifications for a typological approach of the study of the OT? How does the fact that Jesus and his apostles used this approach in interpreting the OT strengthen *our interest in and application of* it in our study of the OT?
3. What are the characteristics and aspects of a type in the OT? Why are these important to identify in a *proper use* of typology?
4. Why is it important for us to believe that *God has placed correspondences* in the Bible between the experiences and happenings of the OT people and Christ in order to use the typological method? What place ought Christ to take as we seek to draw connections between the Old and New Testament events? Why is it always necessary to appreciate the relevance of a study of a biblical type *through the antitype*? Explain.

5. In what ways does the experience of Israel represent an analogy which can help us understand the larger relationship of God with all of the redeemed through Jesus Christ?

6. How does God's deliverance of his people during the Exodus prefigure specific dimensions of God's deliverance of his people through Jesus of Nazareth today? Be specific.

7. What is the relationship between the history of Israel's conquest of the nation of Canaan and their entry into the Promised Land with God's conquest of the devil and his minions today through Christ?

8. In what sense is God's restoration of his people after the Captivity a type of Christ's future restoration of his people, and the promise of their future blessing at the Second Coming? Explain.

9. Explain briefly how the three moments in Israel's history in the Exodus, the conquest of Canaan, and the restoration of his people after Captivity are the Church's *New Exodus, New Conquest of Canaan*, and *New Restoration of God*, leading eventually to the new heavens and new earth under the sovereign authority of Jesus Christ.

The Promise Clarified

Segment 2: Jesus as Fulfillment of the Tabernacle, Priesthood, Sacrifices, and Festivals

Rev. Dr. Don L. Davis

Summary of Segment 2

In a real sense, the Tabernacle was a copy or shadow of the true dwelling place of God in the heavenlies, a symbol of God's presence among his people, and a way for God to reveal through type the one true salvation in Jesus. The description of the Tabernacle's dimensions and compartments (e.g., the Outer Court, the Holy Place, and the Holy of holies) all illustrate the principle of *access to God*, and in the same way the Tabernacle provided this access, so Jesus Christ makes access to God final and perfect, available to all by faith through his blood sacrifice. The various articles of the Tabernacle represent distinctive aspects of Jesus Christ and his work. The high priesthood and its sacrifices are a type of the perfect high priesthood of Jesus Christ which is perfectly better than the pattern of Aaron's priesthood, being of the order of Melchizedek's, whose priestly order was eternal, unchangeable, perfect, and final. Moreover, Jesus Christ fulfills in his life and sacrifice the meaning of all the offerings associated with the Temple sacrifices, and he serves as the *antitype* of the types included in Israel's feasts, festivals, and convocations. Indeed, the OT's witness to Christ is comprehensive and compelling.

Our objective for this segment, *Jesus as Fulfillment of the Tabernacle, Priesthood, Sacrifices, and Festivals*, is to enable you to see that:

- The various elements and activities associated with the Tabernacle are a type of the salvation provided in Jesus Christ. In a real sense, the Tabernacle was a copy or shadow of the true dwelling place of God in the heavenlies, a symbol of God's presence among his people, and a way for God to reveal through type the one true salvation in Jesus.

- The description of the Tabernacle's dimensions and compartments (e.g., the Outer Court, the Holy Place, and the Holy of holies) all illustrate the principle of *access to God*, and in the same way the Tabernacle provided this access, so Jesus Christ makes access to God final and perfect, available to all by faith through his blood sacrifice.

- The various articles of the Tabernacle represent distinctive aspects of Jesus Christ and his work: *the Brazen Altar* represents sacrificial redemption in Christ, *the Laver* represents the cleansing we receive through the blood of Jesus Christ, *the Table of Shewbread* represents Jesus Christ as the Bread of Life, the *Golden Candlestick* represents Christ as the Light of the world, *the Altar of Incense* represents Jesus' ministry of intercession on behalf of his people, *the Veil* represents the body of Jesus torn and broken for us on Calvary, *the Ark of the Covenant* represents the communion with God we share by faith in Jesus Christ.

- The high priesthood and its sacrifices are a type of the perfect high priesthood of Jesus Christ which is perfectly better than the pattern of Aaron's priesthood, being of the order of Melchizedek's, whose priestly order was eternal, unchangeable, perfect, and final.

- Jesus Christ fulfills in his life and sacrifice the meaning of all the offerings associated with the Temple sacrifices: *the whole burnt offering* is a type of Jesus' own free will offering of himself to God; *the meal offering* is a type of Jesus' own presentation and dedication of his life and sufferings to God acceptable to him in every respect; *the peace offering* is a type of Jesus Christ

2

himself who is our peace, with God and with one another; *the sin offering* is a type of Jesus Christ who became sin for us by bearing our offense and penalty on the Cross; *the trespass offering* is a type of how Jesus is propitiation for our sins as well as cleansing and provision for us to live a new life.

- Jesus is the antitype of the types included in Israel's feasts, festivals, and convocations: in *the Feast of the Passover*, Jesus is our Paschal Lamb whose blood cleanses and redeems us; in *the Feast of Unleavened Bread*, Jesus is the one who inspires our walk in holiness before him, and not in malice or evil living; in *the Feast of First Fruits*, Jesus is the first fruits of the coming harvest of new humanity to be redeemed for God; in *the Feast of Pentecost*, Jesus is the one who with the Father pours out his Holy Spirit upon the Church in this present age; in *the Feast of Trumpets*, Jesus is the one who will return and regather his people for redemption and blessing; in *the Day of Atonement*, Jesus is both the High Priest and the sacrifice offered to God in the heavenly Tabernacle for our sin; in *the Feast of Tabernacles*, Jesus is the one who will regather his people at his Second Coming for glorification and rest.

The Tabernacle Is a Symbol of the Messiah

The OT tabernacle is full of meaning because it is a symbol of the Messiah and his salvation. The book of Hebrews gives much instruction concerning the tabernacle. . . . The earthly tabernacle was a copy or a shadow of the true dwelling place of God in heaven (Heb. 8.5; 9.24). It showed what God was like and what was needed to deal with sin. In this way it symbolized what the Messiah was to do for our salvation. We may say that it "foreshadowed" the Messiah and his work. It was like a shadow of the Messiah cast backward in time into the OT period. The shadow was always inferior to the reality. The earthly tabernacle was made of earthly things, and could never equal the splendor or holiness of God in heaven. The earthly sacrifices of bulls and goats could never equal the blood of Christ, who cleansed us from sin forever. The shadow was not itself the reality, but a pointer to Christ who was the reality. Yet the shadow is also like the reality. And the shadow even brought the reality to bear on people in the Old Testament. As they looked ahead through the shadows, longing for something better, they took hold of the promises of God that he would send the Messiah.

~ Vern Poythress. **The Shadow of Christ in the Law of Moses.**
Phillipsburg, NJ: P & R Publishing, 1991. pp. 10-11.

Video Segment 2 Outline

I. The Tabernacle of God: a Type of Jesus Christ

Jesus Christ fulfills all the types within the earthly Tabernacle of the Lord in the wilderness (including all replicas of the Tabernacle in the Temple).

A. General truths regarding the Tabernacle

1. The Tabernacle was a copy or a shadow of the true dwelling place of God in the heavenlies.

   Heb. 8.5 - They serve a copy and shadow of the heavenly things. For when Moses was about to erect the tent, he was instructed by God, saying, "See that you make everything according to the pattern that was shown you on the mountain."

   Heb. 9.24 - For Christ has entered, not into holy places made with hands, which are copies of the true things, but into heaven itself, now to appear in the presence of God on our behalf.

   a. No physical place can actually be the dwelling place of God; Solomon's Temple was a larger replica of the same structure and truths.

   b. God dwells with us in various ways.

      (1) He dwells in heaven in the midst of his holy angels and ministering spirits.

      (2) He dwells in the people of God through the Holy Spirit, Eph. 2.19-22.

      (3) He indwells in the person of the Holy Spirit each individual believer, Eph. 1.13.

      (4) The Tabernacle looks forward to the final dwelling place of the Lord with humankind, the New Jerusalem, Heb. 11.16; 12.22 cf. Rev. 21-22.

2

c. Various names were given to the Tabernacle.

(1) Tent, Exod. 39.32,33, 40

(2) The Sanctuary, Exod. 25.8

(3) Tabernacle, Lev. 1.1

(4) Tabernacle of the Congregation, Exod. 27.21; Num. 1.1; Deut. 31.14

(5) Tabernacle of the Lord, 1 Kings 2.28

(6) Tabernacle of Testimony, Exod. 38.21

(7) Tabernacle of Witness, Num. 17.7, 8

2. The Tabernacle is a symbol of God's dwelling place with his people, Exod. 25.8-9.

a. God is holy and inaccessible, except through the means by which he outlines and determines.

b. This theme of God dwelling with his people was fulfilled in the incarnation of Jesus Christ, John 1.14.

c. As the Tabernacle was situated in the midst of Israel, so Jesus lives in the midst of his people, until the very end of the age.

Deut. 23.14 - Because the LORD your God walks in the midst of your camp, to deliver you and to give up your enemies before you, therefore your camp must be holy, so that he may not see anything indecent among you and turn away from you.

Matt. 18.20 - For where two or three are gathered in my name, there am I among them.

Matt. 28.20 - . . . teaching them to observe all that I have commanded you. And behold, I am with you always, to the end of the age.

Rev. 1.13 - . . . and in the midst of the lampstands one like a son of man, clothed with a long robe and with a golden sash around his chest.

3. The Tabernacle is a way for God to reveal through type the one true way of salvation.

   a. Approach to God through atonement by blood sacrifice, Lev. 17.11 cf. Heb. 9.21-22

   b. Christ's sacrifice is based on the pattern of the type prefigured in the sacrificial system of Israel and the Tabernacle, Heb. 9.23-24.

B. Description of the Tabernacle's dimensions (God himself was the architect, who gave the specifications directly to Moses, Exod. 25.9.)

1. Three compartments, the Outer Court, the Holy Place, and the Holy of Holies

2. The entire Outer Court (which surrounded the Holy Place and the Holy of holies) was 150 feet by 75 feet.

3. Curtains formed a fence around the courtyard of the Tabernacle, made of "fine linen" (cf. Exod. 27.9) about five cubits high (approx. 7.5 feet), supported by 60 pillars of brass, resting on sockets of brass with connected rods made of silver.

4. In the center of the outer court was an enclosure, divided into two compartments (the entire enclosure measured 45 feet by 15 feet; it was 15 feet high).

   a. The inner room of the enclosure (about 15 feet square) was called the Most Holy Place, or Holy of holies. *Only the high priest could enter into this room once a year (where the Ark of the Covenant was kept) and never without blood.*

   b. The outer room of the enclosure (about 30 by 15 feet) was called the Holy Place. *Only priests could enter into this place in their turn (where the table of shewbread, the lampstand, and the altar of incense were kept).*

   c. These two rooms were separated by a special curtain or veil, as was the Holy Place and Outer Court yard.

5. The gate was at the east end of the court with only one access in it, Exod. 27.16-17 *(Christ alone is the only way into relationship with the Father, John 14.6).*

6. *As the Tabernacle made access to God available (albeit in a restricted manner), so Jesus Christ made access to God available to all through his shed blood on the Cross*, Heb. 10.19-20.

2

The Tabernacle as an Expression of God's Holy Character

The tabernacle expresses another side to the character of God, namely, that he is holy and inaccessible. The altar, several coverings and two sets of curtains bar the way into his presence. No one can enter into the inner room (the Most Holy Place) except the high priest, and even then he does so only once a year in a special ceremony, during which he is protected from his sin and from the accusation of the law by the blood that he sprinkles on the mercy seat (Lev. 16). Death is threatened to transgressors of God's holiness (Exod. 19.12-13, 21-25). Even the priests may suffer death if they do not honor God (Num. 10.1-2; Lev. 22.9; 16.2; Exod. 30.21). They are especially in danger of death as they approach the inner rooms of the tabernacle. The high priest must take special care not even to see the atonement cover when he performs his actions in the Most Holy Place (Lev. 16.13). By these means the Lord shows the preciousness of the love between the Father and the Son. The tabernacle symbolism points to Christ.

~ Vern Poythress. **The Shadow of Christ in the Law of Moses.** Phillipsburg, NJ: P & R Publishing, 1991, pp. 12.

C. Articles of furniture represent the person of Jesus Christ

1. *The Brazen Altar* represents redemption and salvation in Jesus Christ.

   a. Exod. 27.1-8: made of shittim wood, overlaid with brass

   b. Place of sacrifice (all five offerings were made on this altar)

   c. A type of redemption in Christ (where the Innocent bore the sin debt of the guilty) as a ransom for many, Mark 10.45; cf. John 1.29; Heb. 9.12-14

2. *The Laver* represents our cleansing through Jesus Christ (1 John 1.5-7; Eph. 5.25-26).

   a. Exod. 30.17-21: a basin of brass, set on a pedestal or stand, called the foot

b. Made of brass (from the women's mirrors), Exod. 38.8

c. Cleansing for fellowship, both through the Word of God and the blood of Christ, cf. John 15.3 with 1 John 1.7

John 15.3 - Already you are clean because of the word that I have spoken to you.

1 John 1.7 - But if we walk in the light, as he is in the light, we have fellowship with one another, and the blood of Jesus his Son cleanses us from all sin.

3. *The Table of Shewbread* represents Jesus Christ as the Bread of life, John 6.48.

2

a. Exod. 25.23-30: made of shittim wood, overlaid with gold, standing on the north side of the Holy Place

b. A type of Christ who is the Bread of Life, John 6.48-51

c. Twelves loaves placed in two rows on the table (could they represent sufficient nourishment for each of God's tribes [cf. the Church of God is represented as a loaf, see 1 Cor. 10.7])

4. *The Golden Candlestick* represents Jesus Christ as our Light

a. Exod. 25.31-40: this piece of furniture is also called the Lamp of God, see 1 Sam. 3.3.

b. Made of fine beaten gold. No measurements are given for the candlestick. Six branches and the main stem or shaft.

c. Given to give light to the Holy Place at night (cf. Exod. 30.7-8)

d. Represents Christ as the Light of the World, John 8.12; John 1.9 (cf. Isa. 42.6)

Isa. 42.6 - I am the LORD; I have called you in righteousness; I will take you by the hand and keep you; I will give you as a covenant for the people, a light for the nations.

John 1.9 - The true light, which enlightens everyone, was coming into the world.

John 8.12 - Again Jesus spoke to them, saying, "I am the light of the world. Whoever follows me will not walk in darkness, but will have the light of life."

5. *The Altar of Incense* represents the ministry of intercession constantly given on our behalf by Jesus Christ.

   a. Exod. 30.1-7: made of shittim wood, overlaid with gold.

   b. Sweet incense was offered on it daily by the High Priest, Exod. 30.7-8.

   c. A curse was pronounced on any who would use it for any other purpose than worship, Exod. 30.37-38.

   d. Represents Jesus Christ, our intercessor, Heb. 7.25; he prays for us, John 17.9

6. *The Veil* of the Temple represents the body of Jesus Christ torn and broken for us.

   a. Made of the same materials as the hanging of the gate but had cherubim embroidered in it

   b. Supported by four pillars, made of acacia wood overlaid with gold

   c. Represents the death of our Lord Jesus, Heb. 10.19-20 (i.e., only way to the Holy of holies [John 10.7-9], its rending a type of the death of Christ, Isa. 53.10)

   d. This is my body which is broken for you, Matt. 26.26.

7. *The Ark of the Covenant* represents communion with God, the presence of God abiding with us as a result of our faith in Christ.

   a. Exod. 25.10-16: a chest (Hebrew word for ark is "chest"), made of wood, covered with pure gold inside and out

   b. Four golden rings at the corners, two on each side, through which staves of wood covered with gold were used to bear it along

   c. Its contents

      (1) Unbroken tablets of the Covenant, the Law

      (2) The golden pot of manna

      (3) Aaron's rod that budded in the wilderness

d. At rest: the pillar of cloud rested over it [Num. 9.15], on the march, it was in the midst of his people (6 tribes before and 6 in the rear) with *two exceptions*:

(1) The march from Sinai (cf. Num. 10.31-33)

(2) When crossing the Jordan (it was nearly a mile ahead), Josh. 3.3-4

e. Represents a type of the very throne of God, only accessible through the *veil*, that is, the death of Christ's body, Heb. 10

D. *The Tabernacle represents a type of Jesus Christ, his person, his ministry, his death and resurrection, and the life of fellowship with God and others that he provides to those who believe.*

2

II. The Priesthood of the Tabernacle: a Type of Jesus Christ

Christ perfects in every way the pattern and meaning of the priesthood of Aaron, and introduces a priesthood superior to Aaron's, one after the order of Melchizedek.

A. The classes and stations of priesthood

1. The High Priest

2. The priests

3. The Levites

B. The calling of the priests

1. The High Priest (Exod. 28.1), called of the Lord, a type of Jesus Christ

   a. Taken from among the people, Heb. 5.1

   b. Ordained by God to represent humankind in things pertaining to the Lord, Heb. 5.1

   c. Called of God himself, Heb. 5.4-6

   d. Needed to be able to sympathize with the people in their weakness and sin

      (1) Heb. 5.2

      (2) Heb. 2.17-18

      (3) Heb. 4.15-16

2. Priests were the sons of Aaron, Num. 3.1-4.

3. Levites called by God to serve with Aaron and his sons, Num. 3.5-6, 17

C. The pattern of Aaron versus the perfection of Jesus Christ (Norman Geisler)

The Pattern of Aaron	The Perfection of Jesus Christ
Entered into the earthly Tabernacle	Entered into the heavenly Tabernacle (Heb. 6.19)
Entered once a year to make sin offering	Entered one time for all (Heb. 9.25-26)
Entered beyond the veil	Tore the veil of his own body (Heb. 10.20)
Offered many sacrifices	Offered himself as sacrifice (Heb. 10.11-12)
Offered for his own sin	Offered only for our sin (Heb. 7.27)
Offered the blood of bulls and goats	Offered his own blood (Heb. 9.12)

D. Aaron versus Melchizedek: Jesus is a priest after the order of Melchizedek.

1. Whereas Aaron's priesthood and its consecration is temporal, *Christ's priesthood (after Melchizedek) is eternal*, Heb. 7.21-23.

2. Whereas Aaron's priesthood is fallible and subject to sin, *Christ's eternal priesthood is sinless*, Heb. 7.26.

3. Whereas Aaron's priesthood is changeable, *Christ's priesthood is unchangeable*, Heb. 7.24.

4. Whereas Aaron's priesthood had to make sacrifices continually to God, *Christ's priesthood is final*, Heb. 9.12, 26.

5. Whereas Aaron's mediation was imperfect, *Christ's priestly mediation was absolutely perfect*, Heb. 2.14-18.

6. Whereas Aaron's sacrifices were insufficient and ineffective to take away sin, *Christ's priestly ministry was all-sufficient*, Heb. 10.11-12.

7. Whereas Aaron's intercession on behalf of the people could never fully prevail for the seeker, *Christ's priesthood prevails for the seeker in every case*, Heb. 7.25.

III. The Sacrifices of the Tabernacle: Christ as the Fulfillment of the OT Sacrifices

Jesus Christ fulfills in meaning and substance all the offerings associated with the Temple sacrifices.

A. The Whole Burnt Offering

1. Type: Lev. 1; wholly consumed upon the altar as God's meat; an offering given as a sweet smelling savor to God, when the worshiper comes for acceptance of his own voluntary will, not to make an atonement for sin but as an offering for life, Lev. 1.4,9.

2. *Antitype: Jesus Christ gave himself of his own free will wholly to God to live according to God's holy will, demonstrating in all he did and was his moral perfection and commitment to God and his law, Heb. 9.14.*

B. The Meal Offering

1. Type: Lev. 2.; a sweet smelling savor offering not of the life, but of the fruits, offered as a dedication to the Lord

2. *Antitype: Jesus Christ presented and dedicated his life and sufferings to God, acceptable to him in every way (Matt. 3.16-17; Heb. 5.7 with John 4.34).*

C. The Peace Offering

1. Type: Lev. 3; 7.11-21, 29-34; a sweet smelling savor offering to the Lord; the offerer kills it, and the offerer, God, and the priest are fed by it (cf. Lev. 7.15, 31-34); offered as a thanksgiving or as a vow.

2. *Antitype: Jesus Christ himself is our peace, the peace of our lives before God and peace in life with God (Heb. 4.1ff.; Eph. 2.14).*

D. The Sin Offering

1. Type: Lev. 4.1-35; 5.6-13; an offering not for acceptance, but for the sake of atoning for evil; the offerer brought it not so much because he had done evil, but that he himself was evil; the offering had to be without blemish, Lev. 4.28, 32.

2. *Antitype: Jesus Christ became sin for us, he was charged with our offense, and identifies with our sin; he himself bore the penalty for our offense (Heb. 10.12; 1 John 2.2).*

E. The Trespass Offering

1. Type: Lev. 5.1-5, 14-19; 6.1-7; distinct from the sin offering; focus is upon the trespass that the offerer did, thus involved restitution to the injured parties.

2. *Antitype: Jesus Christ not only provides propitiation (satisfaction of God's anger against our sin) but also cleansing and provision (enabling us as offenders to receive help, cleansing, and strength to transcend our trespass) (cf. Heb. 10.20 with 1 John 1.7 and 1 Cor. 10.13).*

2

IV. Jesus Is the Fulfillment of All the Holy Days in Israel's Feast and Festival Celebrations, Remembrances, and Convocations.

Jesus Christ fulfills the meaning behind all of the festal ceremonies which made up the festive holidays of the nation of Israel.

A. Feast of the Passover

1. Type: Lev. 23.4-5; Exod. 12.1-14; celebration April 14; remembrance of the deliverance from Egypt

2. *Antitype: Jesus is our paschal lamb, who cleanses us by his blood and nourishes us as we feed upon him, 1 Cor. 5.7; 1 Pet. 1.19.*

B. Feast of Unleavened Bread

1. Type: Lev. 23.6-8; Exod. 12.15-20; April 15; remembrance of the bread eaten in haste in Israelite's departure from Egypt

2. *Antitype: we are to walk holy in Jesus Christ, not with malice or evil living but according to holiness in him, 1 Cor. 5.7-8.*

C. Feast of the First Fruits

1. Type: Lev. 23.9-14; April; the feast of ingathering which occurred at the turning of the year, where all males must come before the Lord, where a sheaf of the first fruits of the harvest was offered, and a lamb sacrificed

2. *Antitype: As a celebration of the first fruits of the harvest, this feast points to the resurrection of Christ, who arose the first day of the week, and is the first fruits of those who sleep [have died] in him, 1 Cor. 15.22-23.*

D. Feast of Pentecost

1. Type: Lev. 23.15-20; June (or 50 days after the Feast of First Fruits)– the culmination of the Feast of Weeks, whose offering represented the first products of the harvest, Exod. 34.22; Deut. 16.10

2. *Antitype: the outpouring of the Holy Spirit of Jesus Christ on the believers, which resulted in the birth of the Church, Acts 1.5 cf. 2.4.*

E. The Feast of Trumpets

1. Type: Lev. 23.23-25; September 1; a celebration of solemn rest, with a memorial proclaimed with a blast of trumpets in a holy convocation, accompanied by an offering by fire to the Lord

2. *Antitype: this celebration is a type of Christ's return and the regathering of Israel by Jesus Christ (cf. Matt. 24.29-31; Ezek. 37.11-14; Jer. 16.14-15).*

F. The Day of Atonement

1. Type: Lev. 23.26-32; September 10; where the high priest made atonement for Israel, Zech. 13.1

2. *Antitype: this represents Christ's offering of himself as a sacrifice for our sin on Calvary, as well as his offering of himself in the heavenly Tabernacle for our sin (cf. Rom. 11.26).*

G. The Feast of Tabernacles

1. Type: Lev. 23.33-43; September 15-22 [week long celebration]

2. *Antitype: this celebration typifies Israel's regathering and rest with Jesus Christ at his Second Coming (cf. Zech. 14.16-21; Amos 9.13-15).*

Conclusion

» The OT provides a comprehensive witness to Christ and his Kingdom in the OT priestly and sacrificial system.

» Jesus is the substance and fulfillment of the Tabernacle, the Levitical Priesthood, the Sacrifices, and the feasts and festivals.

» In a real way, all of these personages, events, and institutions prefigure the person and work of Jesus Christ as the fulfillment of God's promise to Abraham.

» In all of Israel's history and worship, if we look with the mind of the Spirit, we will see the Lord Jesus Christ, the center of the Scriptures, our dear Redeemer and Savior.

Segue 2

Student Questions and Response

The Three Errors of Typology to Avoid

There are three dangers, however, which must be avoided: limiting the type, and therefore not using it. Exaggerating the type, and therefore overusing it. Imagining the type, and therefore misusing it.
~ J. Boyd Nicholson from the forward to *Harvest Fields.*

The following questions were designed to help you review the material in the second video segment. The OT pictures forth the coming of Messiah in powerful images of priesthood, Tabernacle, sacrifice, and festival. Indeed, we saw how the OT provides a comprehensive witness to Christ and his Kingdom in Israel's priestly and sacrificial system. Jesus is the antitype for the sacrifice and redemption prefigured in the actions of the Tabernacle and the priesthood, the numerous sacrifices as well as the feasts and festivals of its worship and celebration. In this sense, the OT's very soul (its key characters, events, and institutions) all together prefigure the person and work of Jesus of Nazareth. This segment included a broad overview of some of these ideas, so be careful to review the material through the questions below. Seek to trace your own understanding of these types and antitypes through the Scriptures (for future reference).

1. In what sense is the OT Tabernacle a type of the salvation provided in Jesus Christ? In what sense can we say that it was a copy or shadow of the true dwelling place of God in the heavenlies?

2. In what way does the description of the Tabernacle's dimensions and compartments (e.g., the Outer Court, the Holy Place, and the Holy of holies) illustrate the principle of *access to God*? How was that access limited in the Tabernacle system? In contrast to its antitype, how is the access we now have to Jesus Christ *different from* the access provided by the Tabernacle?

3. In what way does *the Brazen Altar* represent sacrificial redemption in Christ, *the Laver* represent the cleansing we receive through the blood of Jesus Christ, *the Table of Shewbread* represent Jesus as the Bread of Life, and *the Golden Candlestick* represent Christ as the Light of the world?

4. Explain how *the Altar of Incense* pictures forth the ministry of Jesus as our intercessor before the Father. How does the *Veil* of the Tabernacle represent his broken body upon the Cross?

5. In what way does the Ark of the Covenant in the Holy of holies represent our own communion with God that all believers share in Jesus Christ?

6. Compare the elements of the priesthood of Aaron, Melchizedek, and Jesus Christ.

7. Compare and contrast the various Tabernacle sacrifices and how Jesus Christ fulfills in his life and sacrifice the meaning of all of them: the whole

2

burnt offering, the meal offering, the peace offering, the sin offering, and the trespass offering.

8. How does Jesus serve as the *antitype* of the types included in Israel's feasts, festivals, and convocations: the Feast of the Passover, the Feast of Unleavened Bread, the Feast of First Fruits, the Feast of Pentecost, the Feast of Trumpets, the Day of Atonement, and the Feast of Tabernacles.

9. How does all of this evidence show that the fundamental witness of the OT, in all of its personages, events, and institutions, prefigures the person and work of Jesus Christ as the coming Messiah?

CONNECTION

2

Summary of Key Concepts

This lesson focuses the role of typological interpretation in the OT, and its usefulness to help us decipher the OT's witness to Jesus Christ. Three biblical type scenes help us understand the OT essentially as a witness to Christ and his kingdom reign. God's deliverance of his people at the Exodus, the conquest of Canaan and entering into the Promised Land, and the restoration of Israel from the Babylonian Captivity all parallel God's work in Christ spoken of in the NT. Also, the OT provides a comprehensive witness to Christ and his Kingdom in the OT Tabernacle, priestly, and sacrificial system. Jesus is the substance and fulfillment of the Tabernacle, the Levitical priesthood, the sacrifices, and the feasts and festivals. All of these personages, events, and institutions prefigure the person and work of Jesus Christ. Review these and related concepts covered in this lesson below.

- The simple definition of *type* is "an object, event, happening, image, or reality that prefigures in the OT a reality in the NT, usually focused on Jesus Christ (as its *antitype*)."

- The major hermeneutical justifications for a typological approach of the study of the Scriptures are that it was the method employed by both Jesus and his apostles, and that the Bible itself makes in comparative study implicit connection between many of the same representations and images mentioned throughout Scripture.

- The major aspects of biblical types suggest that types (and their antitypes) are historically real, they illumine the person and work of Christ, that true types of the OT are always contained in the NT, they are connected to

God's redemptive work in Christ, and they illumine the teaching of God on the matter they cover.

- The principles for using typology in biblical hermeneutics include our need to believe that God has placed correspondences in the Bible, to focus on Christ in drawing connections between the Old and New Testaments, to concentrate on the major links suggested in the types themselves and not on the details, and to appreciate the relevance of the type *through the antitype.*

- The experience of Israel, the descendants of Abraham and the people of God, represents an analogy which can help us understand the larger relationship of God with all of the redeemed through Jesus Christ. Three distinctive moments in their history which illustrate this principle is their deliverance at the Exodus, the conquest of Canaan and the entering into the Promised Land, and the restoration of Israel from the Babylonian Captivity.

- God's deliverance of his people during the Exodus prefigures specific dimensions of God's deliverance of his people through Jesus of Nazareth, our Passover, manna, spiritual water from the Rock.

- The story of Israel's conquest of the nation of Canaan, their entry into the Promised Land, and the establishment of their kingdom reign pictures the conquest of God's enemies through Christ whom God will establish as King and Lord forever, and the blessing of God's kingdom people, the Church, Christ's co-regents.

- God's restoration of his people after the captivity is a type of Christ's future restoration of his people, and the promise of their future blessing at the Second Coming. The OT essentially is a witness to Christ and his kingdom reign.

- The experience of God's redeemed in Christ is exhibited clearly in these three moments in Israel's history: the Church's new life in Christ is their *New Exodus*, a new deliverance from the powers which oppress us spiritually, the Church's fight against the devil and the world is its *New Conquest of Canaan*, and the ministry of the Gospel of Christ represents our *New Restoration of God*, leading eventually to the new heavens and new earth under the sovereign authority of Jesus Christ.

- The various elements and activities associated with the Tabernacle are a type of the salvation provided in Jesus Christ. In a real sense, the Tabernacle was a copy or shadow of the true dwelling place of God in the heavenlies, a symbol of God's presence among his people, and a way for God to reveal through type the one true salvation in Jesus.

- The description of the Tabernacle's dimensions and compartments (e.g., the Outer Court, the Holy Place, and the Holy of holies) illustrate the principle of access to God, and in the same way the Tabernacle provided this access, so Jesus Christ makes access to God final and perfect, available to all by faith through his blood sacrifice.

- The various articles of the Tabernacle represent distinctive aspects of Jesus Christ and his work: *the Brazen Altar* represents sacrificial redemption in Christ, *the Laver* represents the cleansing we receive through the blood of Jesus Christ, *the Table of Shewbread* represents Jesus Christ as the Bread of Life, *the Golden Candlestick* represents Christ as the Light of the world, *the Altar of Incense* represents Jesus' ministry of intercession on behalf of his people, *the Veil* represents the body of Jesus torn and broken for us on Calvary, and *the Ark of the Covenant* represents the communion with God we share by faith in Jesus Christ.

- The high priesthood and its sacrifices are a type of the perfect high priesthood of Jesus Christ which is perfectly better than the pattern of Aaron's priesthood, being of the order of Melchizedek's, whose priestly order was eternal, unchangeable, perfect, and final.

- Jesus Christ fulfills in his life and sacrifice the meaning of all the offerings associated with the Temple sacrifices: *the whole burnt offering* is a type of Jesus' own free will offering of himself to God; *the meal offering* is a type of Jesus' own presentation and dedication of his life and sufferings to God acceptable to him in every respect; *the peace offering* is a type of Jesus Christ himself who is our peace with God and with one another; *the sin offering* is a type of Jesus Christ who became sin for us by bearing our offense and penalty on the Cross; *the trespass offering* is a type of how Jesus is propitiation for our sins as well as cleansing and provision for us to live a new life.

- Jesus is the *antitype* of the types included in Israel's feasts, festivals, and convocations: in *the Feast of the Passover*, Jesus is our Paschal Lamb whose blood cleanses and redeems us; in *the Feast of Unleavened Bread*, Jesus is the one who inspires our walk in holiness before him, and not in malice or evil living; in *the Feast of First Fruits*, Jesus is the first fruits of the coming harvest of new humanity to be redeemed for God; in *the Feast of Pentecost*, Jesus is the one who with the Father pours out his Holy Spirit upon the Church in this present age; in *the Feast of Trumpets*, Jesus is the one who will return and regather his people for redemption and blessing; in *the Day of Atonement*, Jesus is both the High Priest and the sacrifice offered to God in the heavenly Tabernacle for our sin; in *the Feast of Tabernacles*, Jesus is the one who will regather his people at his Second Coming for glorification and rest.

Student Application and Implications

Now is the time for you to discuss with your fellow students your questions about the clarification of the promise covered in lesson two. Review the relationship of these truths to your own life and ministry in the questions below. Perhaps they will trigger specific concerns and questions for you as well.

2

* Have you ever done a typological study of the OT before? When, and what was the result of it? Were you convinced that it might be helpful in understanding the NT *through* these stories and images?

* How would those with whom you fellowship now take to a typological approach to the OT? Do your spiritual leaders ever teach, preach, or instruct with this approach? If not, why not?

* What difference does it make to you that the typological approach was the method that Jesus and his apostles used to understand the NT? Should we limit this method of study to them, because of its ability to be abused?

* Do you know the aspects of biblical types (and their antitypes) well enough that you would be able to use this approach in one of your own studies? If not, which of the aspects are still either unclear or unknown to you?

* Why would it be absolutely important to use the time-tested rule of biblical interpretation "Interpret the Scriptures with Scripture" when employing this particular method? What if someone suggested that something was a type, and you could not find its *antitype* in the NT–what then?

* Are there other distinctive moments in Israelite history which might be explored as a type of God's deliverance of his people through Jesus of

Nazareth in our lives today? Would it be wrong to read *the entire OT* with this principle in mind? Why or why not?

* How far can one go as we seek to explore the ways in which the Tabernacle, the priesthood and its sacrifices, and the feasts and festivals are a type of the salvation provided in Jesus Christ? In other words, how much of the detail can be proven to link up with the NT view of Christ?

* Must one be an expert in the OT in order to do this *properly*? Wouldn't this be a risky method for a person who *jumped quickly to conclusions*, i.e., someone who *failed to check their observations against what the NT is teaching about Christ?*

* Some say that using the OT in such a way forces us to *ignore the OT* as a book with a message *on its own terms*, and not merely as a witness to Christ. Is this a fair argument about this approach?

* If one were to seek to preach and teach the OT in this way, how would they go about doing it–where would you start? Explain.

2

CASE STUDIES

Exodus and Liberation Theology

1

It is clear that the most important OT story for liberation theology is the Exodus event. Liberation theology is that 20th century theological discipline and perspective that addresses, highlights, and considers the religious implications of the poor and the oppressed as it is correlates with Christian faith. With a deep and passionate burden to articulate the meaning of the life and struggle of the poor and oppressed to the revelation of God in Jesus Christ, liberation theologians interpret the OT with special reference to the Exodus as the model of all of God's saving activity. God chooses the broken, despised, and enslaved people of Israel as his own peculiar possession, and liberates them personally through his direct intervention over the oppressive and unrepentant Pharaoh and Egyptians. The focus for many liberation theologians here is not on the picture this story provides for a promised Messiah who would liberate his people through his blood sacrifice as the true Passover, but rather on God rescuing a real people from its oppression and poverty in the here and now. Evangelicals are rightly squeamish about this kind of emphasis on social and political liberation, especially since many liberation theologians employ Marxist theory to formulate their theological vision. How does liberation theology's use of Exodus show that we must be careful how we employ historical materials to undergird our theological vision today?

Warfare Not a Politically Correct Image

The images of warfare in the OT many agree provide us with keen insight into the witness of the Messiah as God's warrior, the divine seed who will crush the head of the serpent and bring in God's Kingdom in power and glory at the end of time. In a world torn by violence, civil strife, war, genocide, and unbelievable cruelty, many thoughtful Christians find any appeal to images of war as unhelpful and unclear. In the current era of international strife and armed conflict, these believers reason that any focus on images of war and violence only obscure the heart of the Christian message—the unfailing love of God in Christ. Those who believe that images of spiritual warfare are both integral and necessary to understand this role of the Messiah in the OT argue just the opposite. They claim that the Bible is full of strategic military metaphors applied to God's people, and the reality of evil and satanic deception and interference make it unavoidable to ignore them. Given the fact that much of the OT history is understood through the lens of warfare, Yahweh against his enemies and those of his people, and the prophecies of the Messiah as God's warrior to come, how are we to rightly interpret the images of warfare as they apply to the OT witness to the Christ?

2

Living as Priests . . . Literally!

The images of the priesthood and their ministry are dominant and everywhere present in the OT. The fact that the Messiah would be a priest after Melchizedek is a central argument in the NT book of Hebrew's understanding of the OT. Furthermore, the people of God in the NT are perceived as a royal priesthood, each member being given the unique and gracious role of an intercessor and advocate for others before the Lord as servants and care givers (cf. 1 Pet. 2.9-10). While many see this language of the priesthood as illustrative only, others believe that the images of the OT applied to Christ and believers today are *invitations to a new kind of persona and identity.* In other words, rather than a small group of clergy seeing themselves as priests, this view would hold that all believers have been made priests of the Most High God, as members of his people. For them, this is not mere figurative language but the concrete expression of our true identity in Christ. As Jesus is *literally* our High Priest before God and our Father, so we are members of a *royal priesthood* and ought to act, minister, and pray accordingly. To what extent are the types of Christ (and their extensions to his people as in this example of the priesthood) to be taken literally, and to serve as the basis of our true identity and walk in Christ? Are they mere object lessons, or true expressions of spiritual reality?

The Absolute Seriousness of Having Fun in the Lord

4

Those who study the ceremonies, celebrations, feasts, and festivals of Israel have often seen interconnections between them and the person and work of Jesus of Nazareth in his revelation of the Father and redemption of his people. These events in Israel's experience and history speak of the one who actually *is the Passover,* is the one who *brings atonement* on the day of redemption of Jesus' death on the cross, and so on. The fact that the redemption of Jesus is embodied in these annual celebrations of God's redemption of his people has prompted a new generation of the Church to embrace the notion of festival and feast as a spiritual discipline that grows out of a true application of the OT witness to Christ. Some segments of the evangelical church are seeking to find ways to celebrate *spiritually* in the way God commanded his people in the OT. They argue that if in fact the occasions were prefigurings of the work of Jesus, what they celebrated in *shadow* ought to now be celebrated in *substance.* Jesus has come, died, and been raised from the dead. Along with the Lord's Supper, we ought to celebrate and feast in the same way his people did of old. These Christians are not arguing that we are under the law; no, Christ has redeemed us from the law and its condemnation, they believe. Rather, they are suggesting that, in full knowledge of our freedom in Christ, we ought to develop liturgies, litanies, and celebrations that recognize the work of Christ in such a way that we take festival and fun as absolutely serious work. What do you think of this growing movement among evangelicals in the Church—are they taking the idea of festival and feast too far—or not far enough?

2

Restatement of the Lesson's Thesis

The simple definition of *type* is "an object, event, happening, image, or reality that prefigures in the OT a reality in the NT, usually focused on Jesus Christ (as its *antitype*)." The typological approach of the study of the OT Scriptures as related to the revelation of Christ was the method employed by both Jesus and his apostles, making clear the Bible's own connection of many representations and images in both testaments. The major aspects of biblical types suggest that types (and their antitypes) are historically real, they illumine the person and work of Christ, that true types of the OT are always contained in the NT, they are connected to God's redemptive work in Christ, and they illumine the teaching of God on the matter they cover. Using typology in biblical hermeneutics must be done properly, focusing on Christ as connections are drawn between the Old and New Testaments, appreciating the relevance of the type *through the antitype.* The experience of Israel, the descendants of Abraham and the people of God, represent an analogy which can help us understand the larger relationship of God with all of the redeemed through Jesus Christ. Three distinctive moments in their history which illustrate this principle is their deliverance at the Exodus, the conquest of Canaan and the entering into the Promised Land, and the restoration of Israel from the Babylonian Captivity.

The experience of God's redeemed in Christ is exhibited clearly in these three moments in Israel's history: the Church's new life in Christ is their *New Exodus*, a new deliverance from the powers which oppress us spiritually, the Church's fight against the devil and the world is its *New Conquest of Canaan*, and the ministry of the Gospel of Christ represents our *New Restoration of God*, leading eventually to the new heavens and new earth under the sovereign authority of Jesus Christ.

In a real sense, the Tabernacle was a copy or shadow of the true dwelling place of God in the heavenlies, a symbol of God's presence among his people, and a way for God to reveal through type the one true salvation in Jesus. The description of the Tabernacle's dimensions and compartments (e.g., the Outer Court, the Holy Place, and the Holy of holies) illustrate the principle of *access to God*, and in the same way the Tabernacle provided this access, so Jesus Christ makes access to God final and perfect, available to all by faith through his blood sacrifice. The various articles of the Tabernacle represent distinctive aspects of Jesus Christ and his work. The high priesthood and its sacrifices are a type of the perfect high priesthood of Jesus Christ which is perfectly better than the pattern of Aaron's priesthood, being of the order of Melchizedek's, whose priestly order was eternal, unchangeable, perfect, and final. Moreover, Jesus Christ fulfills in his life and sacrifice the meaning of all the offerings associated with the Temple sacrifices, and he serves as the *antitype* of the types included in Israel's feasts, festivals, and convocations. Indeed, the OT's witness to Christ is comprehensive and compelling.

2

Resources and Bibliographies

If you are interested in pursuing some of the ideas of *The Promise Clarified*, you might want to give these books a try:

Conner, Kevin J. *Interpreting the Symbols and Types*. rev. ed. Portland, OR: City Christian Publishing; 1999.

Goldsworthy, Graeme. *Preaching the Whole Bible As Christian Scripture: The Application of Biblical Theology to Expository Preaching*. Grand Rapids: Wm. B. Eerdmans Publishing Company, 2000.

Kaiser, Walter C., Jr. *Preaching and Teaching from the Old Testament*. Grand Rapids: Baker Academic Books, 2003.

Wilson, Walter L. *A Dictionary of Bible Types*. Peabody, MS: Hendrickson Publishers, 1999.

Ministry Connections

Now is the time to try to nail down this high theology to a *real practical ministry connection,* one which you will think about and pray for throughout this next week. This can be from any corner of your walk and life. Concentrate on which key insight or principle covered in this lesson may be of help to you specifically in a ministry application. What in particular is the Holy Spirit suggesting to you in regard to your own handling and interpretation of the Old Testament as it relates to your life and your ministry? What particular situation comes to mind when you think about how God might want to equip you better to represent him through this material and your interaction with it? Seek the face of the Lord, and ask for his direction in your application of these truths.

Counseling and Prayer

E. M. Bounds comments on the absolute necessity of fervent prayer for the man or woman of God in ministry:

> *The preacher that prays indeed puts God into the work. God does not come into the preacher's work as a matter of course or on general principles, but he comes by prayer and special urgency. That God will be found of us in the day that we seek him with the whole heart is as true of the preacher as of the penitent. A prayerful ministry is the only ministry that brings the preacher into sympathy with the people. Prayer as essentially unites to the human as it does to the divine. A prayerful ministry is the only ministry qualified for the high offices and responsibilities of the preacher. Colleges, learning, books, theology, preaching cannot make a preacher, but praying does. The apostles' commission to preach was a blank till filled up by the Pentecost which praying brought. A prayerful minister has passed beyond the regions of the popular, beyond the man (sic) of mere affairs, of secularities, of pulpit attractiveness; passed beyond the ecclesiastical organizer or general into a sublimer and mightier region, the region of the spiritual. Holiness is the product of his work; transfigured hearts and lives emblazon the reality of his work, its trueness and substantial nature. God is with him. His ministry is not projected on worldly or surface principles. He is deeply stored with and deeply schooled in the things of God. His long, deep*

communings with God about his people and the agony of his wrestling spirit have crowned him as a prince in the things of God. The iciness of the mere professional has long since melted under the intensity of his praying.

~ E. M. Bounds. **Power Through Prayer.** (electronic ed.).
Oak Harbor, WA: Logos Research Systems, Inc., 1999.

Bounds captures the need for ongoing, focused prayer in order to master these weighty truths of the Word of God. "A prayerful minister has passed beyond the regions of the popular, beyond the man (*sic*) of mere affairs, of secularities, of pulpit attractiveness; passed beyond the ecclesiastical organizer or general into a sublimer and mightier region, *the region of the spiritual.*" It is essential that you seek to penetrate beyond mere *information* to *spiritual insight*. Only as you pray for yourself and your fellow students can you glean this insight. Take time to lift one another up; ask for wisdom, clarity, courage, boldness, and discipline as you seek to understand these root meanings of the OT for the sake of being a more effective disciple, and a more equipped minister of the Gospel.

2

Scripture Memory

Luke 24.44-48

Reading Assignment

To prepare for class, please visit *www.tumi.org/books* to find next week's reading assignment, or ask your mentor.

Other Assignments

Please read carefully the assignments above, and as last week, write a brief summary for them and bring these summaries to class next week (please see the "Reading Completion Sheet" at the end of this lesson). Also, now is the time to begin to think about your ministry project, as well as decide your Scripture text for your exegetical project. These are weighty decisions, for these assignments possess great weight in the figuring of your final grade for this course. Therefore, do not delay in determining either your ministry or exegetical project. The sooner you select, the more time you will have to prepare!

Looking Forward to the Next Lesson

In this lesson we have seen the power of typological and analogical study of the OT, and how it can enhance our understanding of the life and ministry of Christ presented in the NT. We considered three biblical type scenes which help us understand the OT essentially as a witness to Christ and his kingdom reign, that is the Exodus, the conquest of Canaan and entering into the Promised Land, and the restoration of Israel from the Babylonian Captivity. We also looked at how the OT provides a comprehensive witness to Christ and his Kingdom in the OT sacrificial system. Jesus is the substance and fulfillment of the Tabernacle, the Levitical priesthood, the sacrifices, and the feasts and festivals. All of these institutions, offices, and events prefigure the person and work of Jesus Christ as the fulfillment of God's promise for Messiah.

In our next lesson we will explore further aspects of OT story and narrative, character types, and how many point toward and illustrate the work of Jesus in the NT. We will look at the offices of the prophet, priest, and king in OT history, and see how the most significant characters in each role all serve as a type of Christ: Moses as a type of the prophetic role, Melchizedek as a type of Christ in his priestly order, and David as a type of Christ in his role as King of God's people. We will also explore the issue of *special character types*, which deserve special mention because of their significance in understanding Christ's role as head of humanity, redeemer of his kinsmen, and warrior in God's conquest. These characters represent the persons of Adam, Joseph, and Joshua. A survey of their lives reveals a deep linkage between their journeys and the life and ministry of our Lord Jesus Christ, making God's promise for redemption and restoration personal and visible for all to see.

Module 9: Old Testament Witness to Christ
Reading Completion Sheet

Name ______________________________

Date ______________________________

For each assigned reading, write a brief summary (one or two paragraphs) of the author's main point. (For additional readings, use the back of this sheet.)

Reading 1

Title and Author: ______________________________ Pages __________

Reading 2

Title and Author: ______________________________ Pages __________

The Promise Personalized

Lesson Objectives

Welcome in the strong name of Jesus Christ! After your reading, study, discussion, and application of the materials in this lesson, you will be able to:

- Recognize and articulate the importance of character types in the stories and journeys of Israel: how they provide us with a full and rich presentation of the truth about Christ, spurring great interest in the craftsmanship of the OT stories, causing us to worship God because of the richness of his salvation plan, and enabling us to see the Bible as a whole, especially the connections between the testaments.
- Lay out the elements of a character-type study, including getting a general outline of the character's life, searching for links and resemblances between the character and Jesus as the antitype, avoiding over-concentration on details that fail to connect the type to its antitype, and seeking to expand one's knowledge of the antitype *through* the understanding of the type.
- Recognize the benefits of character-type investigations: gain an increased knowledge of the Scriptures, learn to communicate the Word to others at higher levels of interest, relevance, and entertainment, regain a sense of wonder at the inspiration of the Scriptures, and discover a more comprehensive picture of Jesus Christ through the types.
- Give knowledge of how the character types in the OT point to and illustrate the ministry of Jesus Christ in the NT in his roles as prophet, priest, and king. While Christ is illumined in the character types, the nature of his own roles is infinitely greater in both glory and significance.
- Show how Moses, the Prophet of the Lord, is an OT character type of Jesus Christ, who as an infant was sought by a king, was hidden in Egypt for a time for his protection, was sent by God to deliver God's people and God's message, was rejected at his own "first coming," chose a Gentile bride during the period of his rejection, and learned obedience through suffering. Show further how he mediated a covenant between the people and God, reflected the glory of the Father (by contrast), and was messenger of the Lord, both to God's people and his enemies.

3

- Outline how Melchizedek, the Priest of the Most High God, is an OT character type of Jesus Christ, whose name resonates with the title of Christ (King of righteousness, King of peace), who was both a priest and a king, who possessed no genealogy, who was called the Priest of the Most High God, who received tithes from God's people, who blessed faithful Abraham, and whose priesthood is eternal and unchanging.

- Articulate how David, the King of Israel, is an OT character type of Jesus Christ, who was born in Bethlehem, grew in lowly reputation, was chosen and anointed by God to rule over God's people Israel, who was a shepherd (risking his life for his sheep), was sent to his brothers who derided him, and who as God's warrior defeated God's enemy who had oppressed God's people. Articulate further how prophetic promises were given regarding his future reign, how God made a covenant with him that the Kingdom would never depart from his heart, and how his reign was an administration of justice and equity to all the people.

- Show how special cases of character types in the OT deserve special mention because of their significance in understanding Christ's role as head of humanity, redeemer of his kinsmen, and warrior in God's conquest. These characters represent the person of Adam, Joseph, and Joshua.

- Detail the various aspects of Adam, the Source of humankind, as an OT character type of Jesus Christ by contrast. Show how both Adam and Jesus are the source and head of all those connected to them by birth and rebirth, with Adam as the head of the old creation, and Christ of the *new creation*, Adam being of the earth, Christ as the *Lord from heaven*, Adam being made a living soul, and Christ a *life-giving Spirit*. As in Adam all die, in Christ all are made alive, and as Adam brought pride and disobedience into the world, so the righteousness of Christ justifies those who believe in him.

- Lay out how Joseph, redeemer of his kinsman, is an OT character type of Jesus, beloved of his father, sent by his father to his kinsman, hated by his brothers who plotted to kill him, rejected by his brothers the "first time," and was sold for "blood money" (pieces of silver). Further show how he was imprisoned with two criminals (one who "died" and the other "lived"), was considered dead but lived as one alive to the Gentiles. Show how he was raised from the dungeon and exalted to a place of authority, and power, and took a Gentile bride. Finally, show how, like Christ, he gave all honor to the king, and delivered all glory and treasure into the king's hand, brought his people to repentance and self-knowledge, was reconciled to his kinsman and received back into fellowship, and was acknowledged to be the savior of his people and their ruler.

- Give evidence of how Joshua, the captain of the Lord's armies is an OT character type of Christ, his name resonates with Jesus' name (Joshua=Jehovah is salvation; Jesus=Jehovah saves), he alone was chosen by God to lead the people into the Promised Land, his commitment was to utterly destroy God's enemies in Canaan, and he was accompanied by a special manifestation of the presence of the Lord throughout his fight with God's enemies. Show, too, how he subordinated himself to the leading of God, dying to his own will, how his warfare was rooted in his relationship with Yahweh, leading God's people personally into battle, fighting alongside them in combat against God's enemies, and won complete victory, dividing the spoils among those who fought beside him in the battle.
- Explain how the roles of prophet, priest, and king, are the special character types of Adam, Joseph, and Joshua are seen in the life of Jesus. While such roles and types are tremendously helpful in providing our OT witness to Christ, they give comprehensive not exhaustive pictures of the life and ministry of Christ. Only by linking the *prefiguring in the OT* to the *revelation of Christ in the NT* do we get the fullest picture and meaning of these roles and types together in the life and ministry of Jesus.

3

Devotion

As with Him, So with Me

Matt. 12.38-42 - Then some of the scribes and Pharisees answered him, saying, "Teacher, we wish to see a sign from you." [39] But he answered them, "An evil and adulterous generation seeks for a sign, but no sign will be given to it except the sign of the prophet Jonah. [40] For just as Jonah was three days and three nights in the belly of the great fish, so will the Son of Man be three days and three nights in the heart of the earth. [41] The men of Nineveh will rise up at the judgment with this generation and condemn it, for they repented at the preaching of Jonah, and behold, something greater than Jonah is here. [42] The queen of the South will rise up at the judgment with this generation and condemn it, for she came from the ends of the earth to hear the wisdom of Solomon, and behold, something greater than Solomon is here.

There are picture puzzles in many children's books which are designed to fool their little eyes. Pictures of items, animals, and things are hidden within a picture of an ordinary scene. They are warned that they are there, but often times, the little ones are not able to see them. Once they are pointed out, how silly we feel that we didn't see them in the first place!

How are we to understand the life and ministry of Jesus Christ–what is the best way to grasp the *meaning of what he came to do*?

Such a question always lies at the heart of doing real spiritual business with God. God has revealed his Son in the record of his work in the OT; the pictures are there, it simply requires a readiness and preparedness to see it.

Our answer regarding the *meaning* of the life and work of Jesus of Nazareth is given the greatest import in the NT. Jesus seems, in every situation depicted in the Gospel, to be aware of *who he is* and *what he is called to do in the world*. This sense of identity and purpose affected every conversation, every encounter, every situation he found himself in. The apostolic testimony is clear: he had no need that anyone teach him about human beings, for he knew perfectly what their intentions and thoughts were (cf. John 2.25).

In our text in Matthew 12, Jesus encounters some of the scribes and Pharisees who, in answer to Jesus' own testimony about his unique inauguration of the Kingdom of God into this present age, followed up his testimony with a request for a sign: "Teacher, we wish to see a sign from you." Jesus answers them back, as if knowing that the intention and motive of their desire had nothing to do with his own testimony about himself. In verses 39-40 we read his answer to them: "An evil and adulterous generation seeks for a sign, but no sign will be given to it except *the sign of the prophet Jonah.* [40] For just as Jonah was three days and three nights in the belly of the great fish, so will the Son of Man be three days and three nights in the heart of the earth."

Jesus links his own work before the Jewish authorities to the *sign of the prophet Jonah*. In the same way Jonah was three days and three nights in the belly of the great fish, Jesus says, so he will be three days and three nights in the heart of the earth. Jesus here interprets his own identity and ministry in light of a special character type in the OT. This habit of referring to himself *in the context of an OT character or account*, points carefully to a right use of the OT to provide a witness to the person and work of Christ. In the case of this text the sign was truly a sign of *judgment*. Their inability to recognize his identity through the plain acts of Messianic power and his prophetic teaching made the necessity of a sign unnecessary. The hard hearted nature of those who rejected his open revelation of his true identity led him to say that only the sign of Jonah would be given. D. A. Carson refers to the judgment involved in this entire allusion in his commentary on the Matthew text:

> *Jesus' refusal of any special sign produced to order is based on a broader concept of his authority as one greater than Jonah or Solomon (cf. v 6 for the same argument in relation to the temple and its priests). If even pagans could recognize God's presence in those great men of the OT, why could not this (Jewish) generation accept the authority of the one in whom all those strands of authority (prophet, priest, king, wise man) found their fulfilment? To reject the call of such a spokesman could lead only to judgment.*
>
> ~ D. A. Carson. **New Bible Commentary: 21st Century Edition.** (Electronic ed. of the 4th ed.). (Mt 12:38). Downers Grove, IL: InterVarsity, 1997.

In every way, the life and ministry of Jesus was made plain to these leaders, yet, because of the hardness of their hearts, they refused to accept his clear testimony and demonstration of his true identity as Messiah. Jesus here shows the true nature of his role as Messiah, and gives us insight into the nature of his relationship to the OT. Not only does Jesus' life and ministry *correspond* to the events of these characters in the OT, he *fulfills* and *transcends* them by nature of the superiority of his revelation juxtaposed to theirs. Jesus is greater than the prophet Jonah, although there is a correspondence between his life and ministry and Jonah's time spent in the belly of the great fish. Jesus is greater than Solomon, although Solomon's wisdom and glory resonates with the coming Kingdom and glory of Jesus in his full consummation of the reign of God to come.

There is a resonance, a correspondence, a connection between the person of Jesus and the great characters and personages in the OT. Jesus can say and say truly that "*just as Jonah* was three days and three nights in the belly of the great fish, *so will the Son of Man* be three days and three nights in the heart of the earth." The contours of Jonah's experience point to, expand, and fill out the meaning of Jesus *as the Son of Man*, his favorite title and the one which speaks most directly to his divinity and role as the coming ruler and king of the world (cf. Dan. 2.44-45; 7.13-14).

H. L. Wilmington has compiled a list for those who want to explore the significance of Jonah and other character types, who desire to see the interconnection with the characters of the OT and the event of Jesus' life and ministry:

3

1. *Adam: his headship over a new creation, Gen. 1.28; Rom. 5.17–19; 1 Cor. 15.22, 45, 47; Heb. 2.7–9*
2. *Noah: his saving life, Gen. 6.13–14, 17–18; 1 Pet. 3.18–22*
3. *Abraham: his fatherhood, Gen. 22.7–8; Matt. 26.36, 42–43*
4. *Melchizedek: his priestly ministry, Gen. 14.18–20; Ps. 110.4; Heb. 5–8*
5. *Isaac: his death, Gen. 22.2, 8, 10; Matt. 26.36, 42–43*
6. *Joseph: most perfect type of Christ in the Old Testament*
    a. *Hated without a cause, Gen. 37.4, 8; John 15.25*
    b. *Ridiculed, Gen. 37.19; Luke 22.63*
    c. *Plotted against, Gen. 37.20; John 11.53*
    d. *Stripped of his robe, Gen. 37.23; John 19.23–24*
    e. *Sold for silver, Gen. 37.28; Matt. 26.14–16*
    f. *Lied about, Gen. 39. 14; Matt. 26.61*
    g. *Placed in captivity with two guilty men, Gen. 40.1–3; Luke 23.32–33*
    h. *Unrecognized by his own, Gen. 42.8; John 1.11*
7. *Moses: his prophetical ministry, Deut. 18.15–18; Heb. 3.5–6*
8. *Joshua: his victorious life, Josh. 1.3, 5–6, 8–9; John 10.17–18; 19.30*
9. *David: his kingly ministry, 2 Sam. 7.1–17; Mark 11.10; Rev. 5.5; 22.16*
10. *Solomon: his wisdom, 1 Kings 3.11–13; Luke 4.22; John 7.46*
11. *Elijah: his forerunner, Isa. 40.3–4; Matt. 17.11–12*
12. *Elisha: his miracles, 2 Kings 2.9; John 3.2*
13. *Jonah: his resurrection, Jon. 1.17; Matt. 12.40; 16.4; Luke 11.29*
14. *Jeremiah: his sorrows, Jer. 3.20; 5.1–5; 8.20–22; 9.1; 10.19; 11.19*
15. *Daniel: his acceptance by the Father, Dan. 9.23; 10.11, 19; Matt. 3.17; 17.5*
16. *Ezekiel: his parables, Ezek. 17.2; 20.49; Matt. 13.3*

17. *Ezra: his zeal for the Scriptures, Neh. 8; Matt. 21.42; 22.29; Mark 12.10, 24; Luke 4.21; 24.27; John 10.35*

18. *Nehemiah: his zeal for the Holy City, Neh. 1–2; Matt. 23.37–39; Luke 19.41*

~ H. L. Willmington. **Willmington's Book of Bible Lists.** Wheaton, IL: Tyndale House, 1987.

This list of characters reinforces our understanding of the connection between Jesus and the lives of the OT saints as *prefigurations* of his own ministry as Lord and Messiah. The allusion to Jonah, therefore, is Jesus' understanding that critical aspects of his life and ministry *are seen in the historical events of Jonah and his time spent in the belly of the fish.* Those of Nineveh will rise up at the judgment with this generation and condemn it, because they repented at *Jonah*, and in Christ, someone infinitely greater than Jonah was before them. The amazed and astonished queen of the South (Sheba), likewise, will condemn it, for, as Jesus says, "she came from the ends of the earth to hear the wisdom of Solomon, and behold, something greater than Solomon is here." Jesus is greater than both Jonah and Solomon; yet, in a fundamental way, to *read the stories of Jonah and Solomon is to gain insight into the very nature of the Messiah himself*, whom we now know to be the living and risen Savior, Jesus Messiah, of Nazareth.

3

Those who truly have eyes *that see* and ears *that hear* will see this hidden yet significant under-story and plot that connects all of the personages, institutions, offices, and histories included in the OT. In a very real sense, Jesus' testimony about the Word of God is true, and must be affirmed in all of our study of the OT:

> John 5.39-40 - You search the Scriptures because you think that in them you have eternal life; and it is they that bear witness about me, [40] yet you refuse to come to me that you may have life.

The Lord is there, testifying, witnessing, revealing the glory of Christ throughout the OT history of Israel, in the characters of its key figures, in the prophet's foretellings of Messiah, in the tabernacle, sacrifices, the priesthood, and grand events. What we must pray for is a spirit soft enough and a heart clear enough that we do not "miss the forest for the trees," rather that we see history and not see *His Story*. For those with eyes to see, we know that "as with them, so with him."

Nicene Creed and Prayer

After reciting and/or singing the Nicene Creed (located in the Appendix), pray the following prayer:

> *Almighty and everlasting God, whose will it is to restore all things in your well-beloved Son, the King of Kings and Lord of Lords: mercifully grant that the peoples of the earth, divided and enslaved by sin, may be freed and brought together under his most gracious rule; who lives and reigns with you and the Holy Spirit, one God, now and for ever. Amen.* (Episcopal Church, 236)
>
> ~ Episcopal Church. **The Book of Common Prayer and Administrations of the Sacraments and Other Rites and Ceremonies of the Church, Together with the Psalter or Psalms of David.** New York: The Church Hymnal Corporation, 1979. p. 236.

Quiz

Put away your notes, gather up your thoughts and reflections, and take the quiz for Lesson 2, *The Promise Clarified.*

Scripture Memorization Review

Review with a partner, write out and/or recite the text for last class session's assigned memory verse: Luke 24.44-48.

3

Assignments Due

Turn in your summary of the reading assignment for last week, that is, your brief response and explanation of the main points that the authors were seeking to make in the assigned reading (Reading Completion Sheet).

CONTACT

Jesus of Nazareth, the Prophet

One of the clearest ways in which the OT provides witness to Christ is his linkage to the ministry role of Moses, the prophet of the Lord. Moses himself states that the Lord would raise up from among the people of Israel an anointed prophet *just like himself* whom the people would hear, and whom they would follow (cf. Deut. 18.15ff.). Indeed, the apostles make the connection of this prediction with Jesus of Nazareth, whose revelation of the Father is unique, complete, and exhaustive (see John 14.7ff.). In many evangelical churches today, the role of prophecy as a spiritual gift, a living dynamic presence in the body of believers, and as a *charismata* that ought to be sought and used in the assembly is diminished. Likewise, the role and function of Jesus as prophet is rarely mentioned in many churches today. Frankly, Moses is *contrasted* to Christ more than he is seen as the *precursor* to Christ, let alone as a *type* of Christ. Why do you think that in many churches the role and function of the prophet is so seldom spoken of or highlighted? How does this absence of emphasis affect our ability to understand the OT office of the prophet as a clear and compelling witness to Jesus of Nazareth, as a prophet, God's last and true prophet, in the midst of his people?

Types of Christ: Intriguing, but not Very Practical

2 With the devotional use of the Bible in the last 40-50 years, the ordinary use of the Bible is as a *handbook for ethical living*. In fact, many preachers have abandoned approaches like typology precisely for the reason that they think it is simply *impractical*. What is the *practical* use of knowing that Jesus has a linkage to the Brazen Altar of the Tabernacle? What difference will it make in the life of a believer, they argue, to simply know that Jesus is the *manna* from heaven for us like the *manna* fed the people in the wilderness? In this day of controversial contemporary issues such as abortion, euthanasia, political corruption, and economic injustice, these argue that we need homilies and sermons dealing with these and other similar hard-hitting contemporary issues, not rummaging around the OT to find types of Christ in the Bible! For them, they see no way that using the OT to understand how it points to Christ as *practical for one's spiritual journey*. Many find this argument compelling—what about you? Why might it be absolutely important to study Jesus in the lives of David, Moses, or Melchizedek, and how might the study of types *actually be very practical for one's life and ministry?*

3

Retrieving Our Sense of the Wonder of the Word

3 For many, the use of the OT has become either a chore or a task that they have given up on altogether. It is such a complex library of diverse literature, they feel it is nigh impossible to master it, let alone find it helpful and practical in their lives. They argue that while some pieces are more helpful than others, most of it is difficult to understand. Filled with frustration at the inability to understand much of it, and somewhat guilty for their negligence in reading it, many Christians surrender to the idea that the OT is too difficult to comprehend, and they settle on reading the portions that make "immediate sense," the Psalms and Proverbs, and some of the narrative material. The study of typology and analogy suggests that the OT *has profound depth and wisdom* especially for those willing to pursue it according to its own *structure and logic*. If Jesus is right in saying that the OT Scriptures were

written to testify of him (e.g., John 5.39-40), then it is possible to discover a new level of intimacy and mystery of the Bible as we explore the OT with its primary purpose of displaying Jesus in mind. By means of prefiguring, typology, analogy, and prophecy, we can discover the OT's purpose by focusing on the way in which it communicates through images, stories, characters, symbols, metaphors, and prophecies the promise of the Messiah and his work revealed plainly in the NT. Why is it important to use Christ's and the apostles' own method to *recover the sense of the wonder of the Word of God* in the OT if we are to appreciate its *true value as a preparation and anticipation of Messiah?*

CONTENT

The Promise Personalized

Segment 1: Character Types of the Prophet Ministry, Priesthood, and Kingship of Jesus

Rev. Dr. Don L. Davis

3

Summary of Segment 1

The OT provides a solid and convincing witness to the life and ministry of Jesus through its character types of key figures in the history of Israel. Character types provide us with a full and rich presentation of the truth about Christ, spur great interest in the craftsmanship of the OT stories, cause us to worship God because of the richness of his salvation plan, and enable us to see the Bible as a whole, especially the connections between the testaments. This form of study requires careful attention: we must create a general outline of the character's life, search for links and resemblances between the character and Jesus as the antitype, avoid over-concentration on details that fail to connect the type to its antitype, and seek to expand one's knowledge of the antitype *through* the understanding of the type. Such studies help us gain an increased knowledge of the Scriptures, learn to communicate the Word to others at higher levels of interest, relevance, and entertainment, rediscover our wonder at the inspiration of the Scriptures, and discover a more comprehensive picture of Jesus Christ through the types. Some of the most important character types in the OT point to and illustrate the ministry of Jesus Christ in the NT in his roles as a prophet, priest, and king in the persons of Moses, Melchizedek, and David respectively. While Christ is illumined in the character types, the nature of his own roles is infinitely greater in both glory and significance.

Our objective for this segment, *Character Types of the Prophet Ministry, Priesthood, and Kingship of Jesus Christ*, is to enable you to see that:

- The OT provides a solid and convincing witness to the life and ministry of Jesus through its character types of key figures in the history of Israel. Character types provide us with a full and rich presentation of the truth about Christ, spur great interest in the craftsmanship of the OT stories, cause us to worship God because of the richness of his salvation plan, and enable us to see the Bible as a whole, especially the connections between the testaments.

- The elements of a proper character-type study highlight the need to be careful and circumspect in our use of them to provide a witness to Christ. We must create a general outline of the character's life, search for links and resemblances between the character and Jesus as the antitype, avoid over-concentration on details that fail to connect the type to its antitype, and seek to expand one's knowledge of the antitype *through* the understanding of the type.

- The benefits of character-type investigations for creating continuity between the Old and New Testaments are enormous. They include our gaining an increased knowledge of the Scriptures, learning to communicate the Word to others at higher levels of interest, relevance, and entertainment, regaining a sense of wonder at the inspiration of the Scriptures, and discovering a more comprehensive picture of Jesus Christ through the types.

- Some of the most important character types in the OT point to and illustrate the ministry of Jesus Christ in the NT in his roles as a prophet, priest, and king in the persons of Moses, Melchizedek, and David respectively. While Christ is illumined in the character types, the nature of his own roles is infinitely greater in both glory and significance.

- Moses, the Prophet of the Lord, is an OT character type of Jesus Christ demonstrated in key aspects of his life. His life coincides with Jesus in that he was as an infant that was sought by a king, hidden in Egypt for a time for his protection, was sent by God to deliver God's people and God's message, and was rejected at his own "first coming." In a sense, Moses (like Christ) chose a Gentile bride during the period of his rejection, and learned obedience through suffering. He also mediated a covenant between the people and God, reflected the glory of the Father (by contrast), and was messenger of the Lord, both to God's people and his enemies.

- Melchizedek, the Priest of the Most High God, is an OT character type of Jesus Christ, whose name resonates with the title of Christ (King of righteousness, King of peace), who was both a priest and a king, and who possessed no priestly lineage or genealogy. Like Christ, he was called the Priest of the Most High God, received tithes from God's people, blessed faithful Abraham, and his priestly order is both eternal and unchanging.
- David, the King of Israel, is an OT character type of Jesus Christ. Like the Lord Jesus, David was born in Bethlehem, grew in lowly reputation, and was chosen and anointed by God to rule over God's people Israel. Like Christ, David was a shepherd (risking his life for his sheep), was sent to his brothers who derided him, and who, as God's warrior, defeated God's enemy who had oppressed God's people. Also, promises were given regarding his future reign—God made a covenant with him that the Kingdom would never depart from his house, and his reign would be an administration of justice and equity to all the people.

3

I. The Study of Character Types and the OT Witness to Jesus Christ and His Kingdom

Video Segment 1 Outline

Is Jesus' and the Apostles' Bible Study Method Different than Ours?

After more than twenty years of teaching the grammatical-historical hermeneutic, I can see only one problem with it: it doesn't appear to be the way the biblical writers always did it! When we examine how the biblical writers used previously written Scripture, we see that they seemed to "discover" meaning there that, judged by its original context, can hardly be imagined to have been in the mind of the original author. This problem is especially evident in the way the New Testament authors used Old Testament passages to prove that Jesus Christ fulfilled prophecy (or to make some theological point.)

~ James DeYoung and Sarah Hurty. **Beyond the Obvious.** Gresham, OR: Vision House Publishing, 1995. p. 24.

A. Importance of character types

1. They show how the stories and characters of Israel provide us with a rich and full presentation of the truth about Christ, 1 Cor. 10.1-6.

2. They cause us to look with greater interest and intensity at the OT narratives and characters.

3. They cause us to worship God and marvel at the richness of God's plan and the unity of his biblical revelation, Matt. 12.39-41.

4. They enable us to transcend overly atomistic treatments of Bible study; they encourage us to look for the interconnections between the testaments even in its most basic images and stories.

3

B. Elements of character type study

What of Typology as a Valid, Important Method of Bible Interpretation?

[Typology] is a genuine approach widely practiced in the New Testament. For example, the furniture of the tabernacle and other matters associated with it and the temple (the altar and sacrifices, the veil, the golden cover of the ark of the covenant) are all types of Christ and of the heavenly realm (see Hebrews 9). When we come to typology, we must avoid being too broad or too narrow in our interpretation. We can be too broad if we find typology everywhere. We can be too narrow if we reject typology as an exegetical method on the basis of the claim that it is not consistent with a literal meaning which embraces one meaning, found by means of grammatical-historical study. . . . Yet we believe that typology is not to be divorced from exegesis, even though it cannot be fully "regulated hermeneutically, but takes place in the freedom of the Holy Spirit." It very much involves a deeper meaning and was readily practiced by the Bible in its exegetical method (see 1 Corinthians 10; Romans 5).

~ James DeYoung and Sarah Hurty. **Beyond the Obvious.** Gresham, OR: Vision House Publishing, 1995. p. 74.

1. Get a grasp of the general outline of the character type's life and work.

2. Look for links and resemblances between the character (the type) and Jesus Christ (as antitype).

3. Seek to understand the unknown through the known (i.e., use the type to enrich your understanding of the antitype).

4. Avoid seeking to connect every detail of the type to Christ as the antitype; concentrate on essential correspondences between the two.

5. In the end, focus on how the antitype is explained, illustrated, and better comprehended *through* the type.

Can or Should We Use the Method of Jesus and the Apostles in Our Study of the New Testament?

To the question whether we can reproduce the exegesis of the New Testament, [S. L.] Johnson answers: Unhesitatingly the reply is yes, although we are not allowed to claim for our results the infallibility of the Lord and His apostles. They are reliable teachers of biblical doctrine and they are reliable teachers of hermeneutics and exegesis. We not only can reproduce their exegetical methodology, we must if we are to be taught their understanding of the Scriptures.
~ James DeYoung and Sarah Hurty. *Beyond the Obvious.* Gresham, OR: Vision House Publishing, 1995. p.265.

3

C. Benefits of character type study

1. Increased joy and knowledge in study of the Scriptures

2. Easier to communicate with others at higher levels of interest and entertainment

3. Wonder at the inspiration of the Scriptures

4. More comprehensive picture of Jesus Christ through the study of the types

Moses, Melchizedek, and David: Types of Jesus Christ as Prophet, Priest, and King

II. Moses, the Prophet of the Lord (a Type of Christ)

A. Aspects of his *prophetic ministry* that resonate with Christ

1. As an infant, his life was sought by a king.

   a. Moses, Exod. 1.22

   b. Jesus, Matt. 2.3-8

2. His infant life was hidden in Egypt for a time for his protection.

   a. Moses, Exod. 2.2-3

   b. Jesus, Matt. 2.13-15

3. Sent by God to deliver God's captive people

   a. Moses, Exod. 3.10-12

   b. Jesus, Luke 4.18-19

4. Rejected by his own at his first coming

   a. Moses, Exod. 2.11-15

   b. Jesus, John 1.11

5. Chose a Gentile bride during the period of his rejection

   a. Moses, Exod. 2.16-21

   b. Jesus, Eph. 5.30-32

6. Learned obedience through suffering

   a. Moses, Heb. 11.24-26

   b. Jesus, Heb. 5.8

7. Mediated a covenant between the people and God, Heb. 8.5-6

8. Reflected the glory of the Father in his person (by contrast)

   a. Moses, 2 Cor. 3.12-14

   b. Jesus, 2 Cor. 4.6

9. Was a messenger of the Lord, both to God's people as well as to his enemies

   a. Moses, Deut. 18.15

   b. Jesus, Heb. 3.2-6

B. Implications for our understanding of the OT's witness to Christ and his Kingdom

   1. Moses' ministry of being God's prophet and messenger are fulfilled in the person of Christ.

   2. Christ is in a final sense the last true messenger and prophet of God.

   3. Christ's ministry is superior to Moses' in every respect, most namely in the fact that Jesus himself is the Word of the Lord made flesh.

III. Melchizedek, the High Priest of God (a Type of Christ)

Gen. 14.18-20 - And Melchizedek king of Salem brought out bread and wine. (He was priest of God Most High.) [19] And he blessed him and said, "Blessed be Abram by God Most High, Possessor of heaven and earth; [20] and blessed be God Most High, who has delivered your enemies into your hand!"

A. Aspects of his *priestly ministry* that resonate with Christ

   1. His name resonates with the person and ministry of Christ (King of righteousness, King of peace), Heb. 7.2.

2. Jesus is not only a high priest, but a coming king who will rule, just like Melchizedek, Isa. 9.6-7.

3. As Melchizedek possessed no priestly genealogy, neither does the priestly ministry of Jesus Christ.

   a. Melchizedek, Heb. 7.3

   b. Jesus, Heb. 7.14-17

4. Melchizedek was called Priest of the Most High God, and so is Christ, Heb. 5.5-6.

5. He received tithes from Abraham, and so Jesus received offerings from his followers, Matt. 26.7-11.

6. As Melchizedek blessed faithful Abraham, so Christ blesses his people.

   a. John 1.16

   b. Eph. 1.6

   c. Eph. 4.7

7. The unchangeable nature of his priesthood (his priesthood is forever), Heb. 7.21-25

B. Implications for our understanding of the OT's witness to Christ and his Kingdom

1. Melchizedek's order of priesthood of the Most High God is fulfilled in the person of Christ.

2. Christ is, in a final sense, the High Priest of God serving in the Tabernacle made without hands in the heavenlies.

3. Christ's ministry is analogous to Melchizedek's, especially in the sense that both Melchizedek's and Christ's priestly ministries are far superior to the Aaronic priesthood.

IV. David, the King of God's People (a Type of Christ)

3

A. Aspects of his *kingship* that resonate with Christ

1. Bethlehem was his place of birth.

a. David, 1 Sam. 17.12

b. Jesus, Luke 2.11

2. Both were born in lowly reputation.

a. David, 1 Sam. 18.23

b. Jesus, Luke 2.7

3. He was chosen and anointed by God to rule over God's people Israel.

    a. David, 1 Sam. 16.12

    b. Jesus, Matt. 3.16-17

4. He was a shepherd, risking his life for the sheep.

    a. David, 1 Sam. 17.32-36

    b. Jesus, John 10.11

5. He was sent to his brothers, who derided and rejected him.

    a. David, 1 Sam. 17.28

    b. Jesus, John 7.3-5

6. As a warrior of the Lord, he defeated the enemy of God who had brought shame and fear upon the people.

    a. David, 1 Sam. 17.49-51

    b. Jesus, Heb. 2.14-15

7. Prophetic promises were given him regarding his reign and the promise of his future.

    a. David, 2 Sam. 7.12-16

    b. Jesus, Isa. 9.6-7

8. God made a covenant with him that the kingdom would never depart from his house, and his dominion would be an everlasting dominion.

    a. David, 2 Sam. 7.16

    b. Jesus, Luke 1.31-33

9. His reign was an administration of justice and equity to all the people.

    a. David, 2 Sam. 8.15

    b. Jesus, Jer. 23.5-6

B. Implications for our understanding of the OT's witness to Christ and his Kingdom

    1. David's kingship over the people of Israel is a type which has been fulfilled in the person of Christ.

2. Christ is, in a final sense, the King over the Kingdom of God, the heir to David's promises and the rightful authority to rule over the coming Kingdom.

3. Christ's kingship is superior to David's in that Christ's kingly duties touch God's ultimate reign over all peoples and nations, and will have no end of its blessing, justice, and freedom.

Conclusion

» The OT character types point directly to Jesus' roles as a prophet (Moses, prophet of the Lord), as the high priest of God (Melchizedek, priest of God and king of Salem), and King over the Kingdom (David, king of Israel).

Segue 1

Student Questions and Response

Please take as much time as you have available to answer these and other questions that the video brought out. In this section we looked carefully at the role of character types in helping us understand the OT's witness to the person and work of Christ. The OT character types point directly to Jesus' roles as a prophet (Moses, prophet of the Lord), as the high priest of God (Melchizedek, priest of God and king of Salem), and King over the Kingdom (David, king of Israel). To comprehend the way in which the OT character gives a living and vital picture of the person of Christ is a major element in the correct and fruitful use of the OT. Review the basic principles associated with this method through the questions below.

1. What is a character type, and where do we find them in our study of the OT? What connection do these types have to the life and ministry of Jesus? What are some of the major benefits of gaining expertise in the study of character types of key figures in the history of Israel, as it relates to the person of Jesus? Explain.

2. If one is to use this form of OT study in a proper way, what are the elements which must be attended to? When we identify a character of the OT which seems to have resonance with the revelation of Jesus in the NT, why is it then important to search for links and resemblances between the character and Jesus as antitype? How do we do this?

3. Why is it necessary always to avoid over-concentration on minor details in a character-type study that would fail to connect the type to its antitype, and seek to expand one's knowledge of the antitype *through* the understanding of the type?

4. What are perhaps the three most important character types in the OT which illustrate the ministry of Jesus Christ in his roles as a prophet, priest, and king? Who are the persons (characters) associated with these three roles which best outline the person of Christ for us?

5. Why must we always study the character type in light of the *antitype, and not the other way around?* Why is Christ's identity as the anointed one infinitely greater in both glory and significance than any type or role discovered in the OT (see Hebrews 1.1-4)?

6. Explain some of the ways in which Moses can be said to be an OT character type of Jesus Christ. How is this connection and linkage demonstrated in the specific experiences, encounters, and events in the key aspects of his life? What are the implications of these linkages for our understanding Moses as a type of Christ in terms of Jesus role as a prophet of the Lord?

7. Articulate how Melchizedek can be referred to as a OT character type of Jesus Christ. How is this connection and linkage demonstrated in the specific experiences, encounters, and events in the key aspects of his life? What are the implications of these linkages for our understanding Melchizedek as a type of Christ in terms of Jesus' role as priest of the Lord? How do Psalm 110 and the book of Hebrews support this claim?

8. Compare and contrast the ways in which David can be said to be an OT character type of Jesus Christ. How is this connection and linkage demonstrated in the specific experiences, encounters, and events in the key aspects of his life? What are the implications of these linkages for our understanding David as a type of Christ in terms of Jesus' role as king of the Kingdom of God?

9. Why is such a method (such as character types) an essential tool for understanding the ways in which the OT provides a clear witness to the life and ministry of Jesus of Nazareth?

10. Read and discuss Ada Habershon's quotation on the study of types (below). In light of your study in this lesson, how ought we to proceed in our use of types in our study of the NT?

The Study of Types Critical to NT Mastery

There are many passages in the New Testament which we cannot understand without having become in some measure familiar with the types. The epistle to the Hebrews is almost entirely made up of references to the Old Testament: as the substance, Christ, is proved to be better than the shadows–better than Moses, than Joshua, than Abraham, than Aaron, than the first Tabernacle, than the Levitical sacrifices, than the whole cloud of witnesses in the picture gallery of faith; and lastly, His blood is proved to be better than the blood of Abel.

We sometimes forget that the writers of the New Testament were students of the Old Testament; that it was their Bible, and that they would naturally allude again and again to the types and shadows, expecting their readers also to be familiar with them. If we fail to see these allusions, we lose much of the beauty of the passage, and cannot rightly understand it. . . .

[The study of types] gives us a sure antidote for the poison of the so-called "higher criticism." If we acknowledge the Divine intention of every detail of the types, even though we may not understand all their teaching, and if we believe there is a lesson in every incident recorded, the attacks of modern criticism will not harm us. We may not be clear enough to understand what the critics say, or to answer their criticisms; but if our eyes have been opened to see the beauty of the types, the doubts which such writers suggest will not trouble us, and we shall have a more profitable occupation than reading their works. When so much of this destructive criticism is about, we cannot do better than urge all–even the youngest Christians–to take up the typical study of God's Word; for though He has hid these things from the wise and prudent, He reveals them unto babes.

~ Ada R. Habershon. **Study of the Types**.
Grand Rapids: Kregel Publishing, 1997. pp. 19, 21.

3

The Promise Personalized

Segment 2: Special Character Types: Adam, Joseph, and Joshua

Rev. Dr. Don L. Davis

Summary of Segment 2

Certain characters in the OT deserve our special exegetical attention because of their critical theological significance in helping us comprehend Christ's role as head of humanity, redeemer of his kinsmen, and warrior in God's conquest. These characters represent the persons of Adam, Joseph, and Joshua. Adam, as the federal head and source of humankind, is a special OT character type of Jesus Christ, by way of contrast, that is, how he is different from the Lord who is also the federal head and source of the new redeemed humanity. Joseph, the redeemer of his kinsman, is perhaps the most prolific and "on-point" OT character type of Jesus. In ways that are both wondrous and moving, Joseph's experience links and connects with the life and ministry of Jesus Christ. Joshua, the captain of the Lord's armies, is an OT character type of Christ whose spiritual warfare resonates with Messiah's role as the warrior of God. While the character roles of prophet, priest, and king, and the special character types of Adam, Joseph, and Joshua are tremendously helpful in providing our OT witness to Christ, they give comprehensive not exhaustive pictures of the life and ministry of Christ. Only by linking the *prefiguring in the OT* to the *revelation of Christ in the NT* do we get the fullest picture and meaning of these roles and types together in the life and ministry of Jesus.

Our objective for this segment, *Special Character Types: Adam, Joseph, and Joshua*, is to enable you to see that:

- Certain characters in the OT deserve our special exegetical attention because of their critical theological significance in helping us comprehend Christ's role as head of humanity, redeemer of his kinsmen, and warrior in God's conquest. These characters represent the person of Adam, Joseph, and Joshua.
- Adam, as the federal head and source of humankind, is a special OT character type of Jesus Christ, by way of contrast, that is, how he is different from the Lord who is also the federal head and source of the new redeemed humanity.
- In every way, both Adam and Jesus are the source and federal heads of all those connected to them by birth and rebirth respectively. As Adam is the head of the old creation, so Christ is the head of the *new creation*, and as

3

Adam's being was "of the earth," so Christ, by contrast, is the *Lord from heaven.* While Adam was made a living soul, Christ Jesus was made a *life-giving Spirit*. As in Adam all die, so in Christ all are made alive, and as Adam brought pride and disobedience into the world, so Christ, through his righteousness, is the source of righteousness and justifies all those who believe in him.

- Joseph, the redeemer of his kinsman, is perhaps the most prolific and "on-point" OT character type of Jesus. In ways that are both wondrous and moving, Joseph's experience links and connects with the life and ministry of Jesus Christ.

- In virtually every way, Joseph's life story coincides with the experience of the Messiah. He was beloved of his father, sent by his father to his kinsman, hated by his brothers who plotted to kill him, rejected by his brothers the "first time," and was sold for "blood money" (pieces of silver). Furthermore, Joseph (like Christ) was imprisoned with two criminals (one who "died" and the other "lived"), was considered dead for a long time but lived "as one alive" to the Gentiles. Joseph, like the Messiah, was raised from the dungeon and exalted to a place of authority and power, and took a Gentile bride. Finally, like Christ, he gave all honor to the king, and delivered all glory and treasure into the king's hand, brought his people to repentance and self-knowledge, was reconciled to his kinsman and received back into fellowship, and was acknowledged to be the savior of his people and their ruler.

- Joshua, the captain of the Lord's armies, is an OT character type of Christ whose spiritual warfare resonates with Messiah's role as the warrior of God.

- In numerous ways, the events and happenings of Joshua's life connect with the Messiah's life. Joshua's name resonates with Jesus' name (Joshua=Jehovah is salvation; Jesus=Jehovah saves), and he alone was chosen by God to lead the people into the Promised Land. He possessed an absolute commitment to utterly destroy God's enemies in Canaan, and was accompanied by a special manifestation of the presence of the Lord throughout his fight with God's enemies. Like the Messiah, Joshua subordinated himself to the leading of God, dying to his own will, his warfare was rooted in his relationship with Yahweh, leading God's people personally into battle, fighting alongside them in combat against God's enemies. Joshua won complete victory, dividing the spoils among those who fought beside him in the battle.

- While the character roles of prophet, priest, and king, and the special character types of Adam, Joseph, and Joshua are tremendously helpful in providing our OT witness to Christ, they give comprehensive not exhaustive pictures of the life and ministry of Christ. Only by linking the *prefiguring in the OT* to the *revelation of Christ in the NT* do we get the fullest picture and meaning of these roles and types together in the life and ministry of Jesus.

Video Segment 2 Outline

I. Adam, the Head and Source of Humankind (a Type of Christ)

A. Aspects of his *headship* that resonate with Christ

1. The headship of the first and second Adam: a type by contrast and distinction

a. Both Adam and Jesus are the source and head of all who are connected with them (as those who represent a family of human beings who participate and are connected to their actions), Rom. 5.14 - Yet death reigned from Adam to Moses, even over those whose sinning was not like the transgression of Adam, who was a type of the one who was to come.

b. Both Adam's and Jesus' descendants share in the results of their actions.

2. Adam is largely a *type by contrast*, that is, Adam and Christ both represent a kind of headship that is different.

3. As Adam is the head of the old creation, so Christ is the head of God's new creation.

3

a. Adam, Gen. 1.28

b. Jesus

(1) 2 Cor. 5.17-18

(2) Gal. 6.14-15

4. Whereas Adam was of the earth, Christ is the Lord from heaven.

a. Adam, Gen. 2.7

b. Jesus, 1 Cor. 15.47

5. Whereas Adam was made a living soul, so Christ (as the *second Adam*) was made a life-giving Spirit.

a. Adam, Gen. 2.7

b. Jesus, 1 Cor. 15.45

6. Whereas in Adam all die, so in Christ shall all be made alive.

a. Adam, Rom. 5.12

b. Jesus

(1) John 10.10

(2) 1 Cor. 15.22

7. As Adam through his callous pride brought sin into the world, so Christ is the one who takes away the sin of the world.

   a. Adam, Rom. 5.12-14

   b. Jesus

      (1) Matt. 20.28

      (2) 1 Cor. 15.3

      (3) 2 Cor. 5.21

      (4) Gal. 1.4

8. Whereas through Adam's disobedience all were condemned, so through the righteousness of Christ all who believe are justified, Rom. 5.18-21.

3

B. Implications for our understanding of the OT's witness to Christ and his Kingdom

1. Adam is a negative type of headship which illustrates and illumines Melchizedek's order of priesthood of the Most High God as fulfilled in the person of Christ.

2. Christ's headship of God's new creation offers a fuller and final picture of what Adam's role was intended to accomplish.

3. "The second Adam won more for humanity than the first Adam lost." Christ's position of headship has resulted in an untold treasure of blessing for those who unite to him by faith.

II. Joseph: Redeemer of His Kinsman (a Type of Christ)

A. Aspects of his *sonship* that resonate with Christ

1. He was beloved of his father.

   a. Joseph, Gen. 37.3

   b. Jesus, Matt. 3.17

2. He was sent to his kinsman by his father.

   a. Joseph, Gen. 37.13

   b. Jesus, John 3.16

3. He was hated by his brothers, who plotted together to kill him.

   a. Joseph, Gen. 37.4-8

   b. Jesus, John 15.24

4. He was rejected by his brothers the first time.

   a. Joseph, Gen. 37.19-20

b. Jesus, Matt. 27.22-23

5. He was sold for "blood money" (pieces of silver).

a. Joseph, Gen. 37.28

b. Jesus, Matt. 26.14-16

B. Aspects of his *suffering* that resonate with Christ

1. He was imprisoned with two criminals, one who "died" and the other who "lived."

3

a. Joseph, Gen. 40.1-3

b. Jesus, Luke 23.32

2. He was considered dead to Israel for a long time, but lived as one alive to the Gentiles.

a. Joseph lived in Egypt separated from the company and fellowship of his family and father.

b. Jesus came to his own the first time, and they refused to receive him as he was, but rejected him as their own.

(1) Acts 7.51-52

(2) John 1.11

3. He was raised from the dungeon and exalted to a place of authority and power.

    a. Joseph, Gen. 41.39-44

    b. Jesus, Phil. 2.9-11

4. Took a Gentile bride

    a. Joseph, Gen. 41.45

    b. Jesus, Eph. 5.25

C. Aspects of his *saving reign* that resonate with Christ

1. He gives all honor to the king, and delivers all glory and treasure into the king's hands.

    a. Joseph, Gen. 47.14-20

    b. Jesus, 1 Cor. 15.24

2. He brings his people to repentance and self-knowledge.

    a. Joseph, Hos. 5.15 (cf. Gen. 45.1-11)

b. Jesus, Rev. 1.7

3. He is reconciled to his kinsman, and received back into fellowship with them.

a. Joseph, Gen. 45.1-11

b. Jesus, Zech. 12.10

4. He is acknowledged to be the savior of his people and their ruler.

a. Joseph

(1) Gen. 45.5-8

(2) Gen. 50.20

b. Jesus

(1) Acts 3.13-15

(2) Acts 3.26

D. Implications for our understanding of the OT's witness to Christ and his Kingdom

1. Joseph is perhaps the clearest and most compelling type of Jesus Christ in the Scriptures.

3

2. Joseph's story paints a wonderful picture of the relationship between Jesus Christ and his own Jewish kin people.

3. The story of Joseph's own willingness to bear unjust sufferings and cruelty for others typifies our Lord's deep suffering on behalf of all who believe.

III. Joshua: Captain of the Lord's Armies (a Type of Christ)

A. Aspects of his *calling and conquest* that resonate with Christ

1. His own name resonates with Christ (Joshua = Jehovah is salvation), the same meaning of Yeshua (Jesus).

a. Joshua, Heb. 4.8 (Notice the allusion to salvation in Rahab's pleas to the spies at Jericho, cf. Josh. 2.13-14)

b. Jesus, Matt. 1.21

2. He alone was chosen by God to lead God's people into the Promise Land.

a. Joshua, Josh. 1.1-5

b. Jesus

(1) Matt. 3.16-17

(2) Acts 2.22-24

3

3. His commitment was to utterly destroy God's enemies in Canaan.

   a. Joshua

      (1) Deut. 20.17

      (2) Josh. 6.21

   b. Jesus

      (1) 1 John 3.8

      (2) Col. 2.15

      (3) Heb. 2.14

4. He was accompanied by a special manifestation of the presence of the Lord throughout his fight against God's enemies.

   a. Joshua,The "Commander of the Army of the Lord": theophany, Josh. 5.13-15

   b. Jesus (all his warfare was accompanied by the unlimited power of the Holy Spirit)

      (1) John 3.34-35

      (2) John 15.26

   c. Definition: those unsought, temporary manifestations of God the Son in human form whereby God communicated to humankind prior to the coming of Jesus Christ

d. Some of the theophanies in the OT

(1) God's appearance to Abraham at Mamre, Gen. 18.1-33

(2) Jacob's wrestling with the angel, Gen. 32.24-32

(3) Confrontation with Balaam, Num. 22.22-35

(4) The Commander of the Army of the Lord, Josh. 5.13-6.5

(5) Appearance to Gideon, Judg. 6.11-23

(6) Appearance to Gideon's wife, Manoah, Judg. 13.3-23

(7) The "son of man" in the experience of the three Hebrew boys, Dan. 3.25

e. These manifestations of the Son of God were real, divinely determined revelations of God for individuals. They were irregular in manifestation, short in duration, varied in form, and included both audible and visible evidence of his presence.

f. These manifestations are manifestations of God the Son during the *OT era only.*

5. He subordinated himself to the leading of God, dying in every way to his own leadership and will.

a. Joshua, Josh. 24.15

b. Jesus, Phil. 2.5-8

6. His warfare was rooted in his relationship with Yahweh, and he led God's people personally into battle that was relentless and difficult.

   a. Joshua, Josh. 1.9

   b. Jesus, Luke 4.18-19

7. He was the captain of the Lord's armies, fighting alongside them in combat against God's enemies.

   a. Joshua, Josh. 8.10-11

   b. Jesus

      (1) Matt. 28.20

      (2) John 14.18-19

      (3) Acts 18.9-10

      (4) 2 Tim. 4.17

8. The victory he won was complete, and he was able to divide up the spoils of battle with those who engaged the enemy.

   a. Joshua, Josh. 14.1

   b. Jesus, Eph. 4.7-8

B. Implications for our understanding of the OT's witness to Christ and his Kingdom

1. Joshua as the Captain of the order of the Lord typifies the role of Jesus Christ as Commander-in-chief of the forces of God against the devil.

2. Through his death, resurrection, and ascension, Jesus Christ has been raised to the point of victorious conqueror, who is leading the Church into greater levels of victory and conquest.

   a. Gen. 3.15

   b. Ps. 68.18

   c. Isa. 53.12

   d. Luke 10.18

   e. Luke 11.22

   f. Heb. 2.14

3. Christ's ministry as our Commander is superior to Joshua's warfare; as Joshua defeated the armies of the Amalekites (cf. Exod. 17.8-16), so the true Joshua will defeat the armies of the nations at his coming (Rev. 19), before he ushers in his reign of freedom and peace in a new heavens and earth.

Conclusion

- » The OT provides us with a look at certain character types which give solid witness to Christ and his soon-to-be-consummated kingdom reign.
- » By giving careful attention to the lives of Adam, Joseph, and Joshua, we more clearly understand Jesus' identity as Head of a new humanity, as Savior and Redeemer of his kinsmen, and as a Mighty warrior in God's conquest.
- » Studying the types of Scripture can open up to us a whole new understanding of the glory and majesty of the one of whom the whole Bible speaks, Jesus of Nazareth, the Son of the Living God.

Segue 2

Student Questions and Response

The following questions were designed to help you review the material in the second video segment. We saw in this section how the OT, in providing us with a credible witness to the person of Christ, pictures forth the Messiah in certain character types which enable us to see aspects of the Messianic ministry more poignantly and clearly. Three of these special characters are Adam, Joseph, and Joshua. As we investigate the dimensions of their lives and experiences more closely, we can see Jesus' own identity as Head of a new humanity, as Savior and Redeemer of his kinsmen, and as our Mighty warrior in God's conquest. Being able to properly and rigorously study these types can provide us with a new appreciation of the unity of the Scriptures, as well as a whole new understanding of the glory and majesty of Jesus of Nazareth, the Son of the Living God. Review these character types in the questions below.

3

1. What rules apply in connection to certain characters in the OT and the way in which they help us comprehend Christ's role as head of humanity, redeemer of his kinsmen, and warrior in God's conquest? Who are the characters that coincide with these dimensions?
2. Which of these special characters is mentioned in the NT, and which are not? Does their lack of direct association in the NT preclude them from being *legitimate character types* to help reveal the nature and work of Messiah? Explain.
3. What does it mean to suggest that Adam acts as "federal head and source of humankind" in ways similar yet different than the person of Christ? What

does it mean to say that Adam is a special OT character type of Jesus Christ, *by way of contrast*?

4. Compare and contrast the ways in which Adam and Christ are seen in Scripture. How does this comparison help us to understand better the role and function of Jesus as our federal head and source of the new redeemed humanity?

5. Why do scholars suggest that Joseph, the redeemer of his kinsman, is perhaps the most prolific and "on-point" OT character type of Jesus? What do all the linkages between Joseph's life and that of Christ's suggest about the nature of the unity and continuity of the OT and the NT in bearing a *single coherent message* about Christ and his coming Kingdom? What does it suggest about the *inspiration of Scripture*?

6. Compare and contrast the ways in which Joseph's experiences and encounters coincide with the personal journey of Jesus of Nazareth, the Messiah of God. How do the specific points of linkable connections help us to understand better the role and function of Jesus as the kinsman redeemer of his people?

7. In what sense can we say that Joshua's life and calling connects with Jesus' own life as an OT character type of Christ whose spiritual warfare resonates with Messiah's role as the warrior of God?

8. Compare and contrast some of the ways in which Joshua and Christ are seen to both represent God as his appointed warriors, both as victorious warriors over the foes of God, and the divider of the spoils among God's people. How does this comparison help us to understand better the role and function of Jesus as our captain in spiritual warfare today, the one who ultimately will reign victorious as King of kings, and Lord of lords?

9. Why do the character types, both those of the role of prophet, priest, and king, and the special character types of Adam, Joseph, and Joshua only provide *comprehensive* and not *exhaustive* pictures of the life and ministry of Christ? Why must we be careful to link the *prefiguring characters in the OT* to the *full revelation of Christ in the NT* in order to get the fullest picture of the Messiah?

10. Read and discuss F. F. Bruce's insights on the typological relationship between the two testaments below. What does this suggest about our ongoing study of the OT, especially in regard to its witness to Christ?

What Is the Typological Relationship Between the Old and the New Testament?

The typological relation between the two Testaments was summed up in Augustine's epigram: 'In the OT the NT lies hidden; in the NT the OT stands revealed.' In the NT the Christian salvation is presented as the climax of the mighty works of God, as the 'antitype' of his 'typical' mighty works in the OT. The Christian salvation is treated as a new creation, a new exodus, a new restoration from exile.

New creation. *'It is the God who said, 'Let light shine out of darkness,' who has shone in our hearts to give the light of the knowledge of the glory of God in the face of Christ' (2 Cor. 4.6). The Fourth Gospel perhaps provides the clearest instance of creation typology, with its exordium 'In the beginning ...' echoing the opening words of Genesis: the divine Word which called the old creation into being has now become flesh to inaugurate a new creation. Those who are 'in Christ', according to Paul, constitute a 'new creation' (2 Cor. 5.17; Gal. 6.15). Paul and the seer of Patmos join in seeing the curse of the primordial fall reversed by the redemptive work of Christ (Rom. 8.19–21; Rev. 22.1–5). The gospel establishes 'new heavens and a new earth in which righteousness dwells' (2 Pet. 3.13; cf. Rev. 21.1).*

New exodus. *The exodus typology is particularly pervasive in the NT. Matthew seems to view the infancy of Jesus as a recapitulation of the early experiences of Israel, which went down to Egypt and came up again (Matt. 2.15). John, by the chronology of his Gospel and otherwise, implies that Christ is the antitypical Passover lamb (cf. John 19.14, 36). Peter's language points in the same direction (1 Pet. 1.19), while Paul makes the thought explicit: since 'Christ, our paschal lamb, has been sacrificed', the ensuing festival should be celebrated by his people 'with the unleavened bread of sincerity and truth' (1 Cor. 5.7-8). As the Israelites passed through the Sea of Reeds, so Christians have been baptized into Christ; as the Israelites received bread from heaven and water from the rock, so Christians have their distinctive 'supernatural food and drink' (1 Cor. 10.1–4). As, despite all those blessings, the Exodus generation died in the wilderness because of*

3

*unbelief and disobedience and so failed to enter the promised land, Christians for their part are exhorted to take warning lest they fall (1 Cor. 10.5–12; cf. Heb. 3.7–4.13; Jude 5). For these things befell the Israelites 'as a warning (**typikos**), but they were written down for our instruction, upon whom the end of the ages has come' (1 Cor. 10.11). This typology has an intensely ethical and paraenetic emphasis.*

New restoration. *The very word 'gospel' (**euangelion**) and its cognates are probably derived by the NT writers from their occurrences in Is. 40–66 to denote the 'good tidings' of return from Exile and rebuilding of Zion (Isa. 40.9; cf. 52.7; 61.1). No stretch of OT prophecy has provided such a fertile 'plot' of gospel* **testimonia,** *from the 'voice' of Isaiah 40.3 through the ministry of the Servant in Isaiah 42–53 to the new heavens and new earth of Isaiah 65.17; 66.22.*

~ F. F. Bruce. "Typology." **The New Bible Dictionary**. 3rd ed. D. R. W. Wood, ed. (electronic ed.). Downers Grove, IL: InterVarsity Press, 1996. pp. 1214-1215.

CONNECTION

3

Summary of Key Concepts

This lesson focuses upon the role of character types, both in terms of the roles of Jesus as prophet, priest, and king in Moses, Melchizedek, and David respectively, as well as special character types of Adam, Joseph, and Joshua. These links with the experience and calling of the Messiah are remarkable and encouraging; these connections provide a comprehensive store of knowledge about the person of Christ all *prefigured in the lives and experiences of characters in the OT.* Review these concepts thoroughly through the principles listed below.

- The OT provides a solid and convincing witness to the life and ministry of Jesus through its character types of key figures in the history of Israel. Character types provide us with a full and rich presentation of the truth about Christ, spur great interest in the craftsmanship of the OT stories, cause us to worship God because of the richness of his salvation plan, and enable us to see the Bible as a whole, especially the connections between the testaments.

- The elements of a proper character-type study highlight the need to be careful and circumspect in our use of them to provide a witness to Christ. We must create a general outline of the character's life, search for links and resemblances between the character and Jesus as the antitype, avoid over-concentration on details that fail to connect the type to its antitype, and seek to expand one's knowledge of the antitype *through* the understanding of the type.

- The benefits of character-type investigations for creating continuity between the Old and New Testaments are enormous. They include our gaining an increased knowledge of the Scriptures, learning to communicate the Word to others at higher levels of interest, relevance, and entertainment, regaining a sense of wonder at the inspiration of the Scriptures, and discovering a more comprehensive picture of Jesus Christ through the types.

- Some of the most important character types in the OT point to and illustrate the ministry of Jesus Christ in the NT in his roles as a prophet, priest, and king in the persons of Moses, Melchizedek, and David respectively. While Christ is illumined in the character types, the nature of his own roles is infinitely greater in both glory and significance.

- Moses, the Prophet of the Lord, is an OT character type of Jesus Christ demonstrated in key aspects of his life. His life coincides with Jesus in that he was as an infant that was sought by a king, hidden in Egypt for a time for his protection, was sent by God to deliver God's people and God's message, and was rejected at his own "first coming." In a sense, Moses (like Christ) chose a Gentile bride during the period of his rejection, and learned obedience through suffering. He also mediated a covenant between the people and God, reflected the glory of the Father (by contrast), and was messenger of the Lord, both to God's people and his enemies.

- Melchizedek, the Priest of the Most High God, is an OT character type of Jesus Christ, whose name resonates with the title of Christ (King of righteousness, King of peace), who was both a priest and a king, and who possessed no priestly lineage or genealogy. Like Christ, he was called the Priest of the Most High God, received tithes from God's people, blessed faithful Abraham, and his priestly order is both eternal and unchanging.

- David, the King of Israel, is an OT character type of Jesus Christ. Like the Lord Jesus, David was born in Bethlehem, grew in lowly reputation, and was chosen and anointed by God to rule over God's people Israel. Like Christ, David was a shepherd (risking his life for his sheep), was sent to his brothers who derided him, and who, as God's warrior, defeated God's enemy who had oppressed God's people. Also, promises were given regarding his future reign—God made a covenant with him that the kingdom would never depart from his house, and his reign would be an administration of justice and equity to all the people.

- Certain characters in the OT deserve our special exegetical attention because of their critical theological significance in helping us comprehend Christ's role as head of humanity, redeemer of his kinsmen, and warrior in God's conquest. These characters represent the person of Adam, Joseph, and Joshua.

- Adam, as the federal head and source of humankind, is a special OT character type of Jesus Christ, by way of contrast, that is, how he is different from the Lord who is also the federal head and source of the new redeemed humanity.

- In every way, both Adam and Jesus are the source and federal heads of all those connected to them by birth and rebirth respectively. As Adam is the head of the old creation, so Christ is the head of the *new creation*, and as Adam's being was "of the earth," so Christ, by contrast, is the *Lord from heaven*. While Adam was made a living soul, Christ Jesus was made a *life-giving Spirit*. As in Adam all die, so in Christ all are made alive, and as Adam brought pride and disobedience into the world, so Christ, through his righteousness, is the source of righteousness and justifies all those who believe in him.

- Joseph, the redeemer of his kinsman, is perhaps the most prolific and "on-point" OT character type of Jesus. In ways that are both wondrous and moving, Joseph's experience links and connects with the life and ministry of Jesus Christ.

- In virtually every way, Joseph's life story coincides with the experience of the Messiah. He was beloved of his father, sent by his father to his kinsman, hated by his brothers who plotted to kill him, rejected by his brothers the "first time," and was sold for "blood money" (pieces of silver). Furthermore, Joseph (like Christ) was imprisoned with two criminals (one who "died" and the other "lived"), was considered dead for a long time but lived "as one alive" to the Gentiles. Joseph, like the Messiah, was raised from the dungeon and exalted to a place of authority and power, and took a Gentile bride. Finally, like Christ, he gave all honor to the king, and delivered all glory and treasure into the king's hand, brought his people to repentance and self-knowledge, was reconciled to his kinsman and received back into fellowship, and was acknowledged to be the savior of his people and their ruler.

- Joshua, the captain of the Lord's armies, is an OT character type of Christ whose spiritual warfare resonates with Messiah's role as the warrior of God.
- In numerous ways, the events and happenings of Joshua's life connect with the Messiah's life. Joshua's name resonates with Jesus' name (Joshua=Jehovah is salvation; Jesus=Jehovah saves), and he alone was chosen by God to lead the people into the Promised Land. He possessed an absolute commitment to utterly destroy God's enemies in Canaan, and was accompanied by a special manifestation of the presence of the Lord throughout his fight with God's enemies. Like the Messiah, Joshua subordinated himself to the leading of God, dying to his own will, his warfare was rooted in his relationship with Yahweh, leading God's people personally into battle, fighting alongside them in combat against God's enemies. Joshua won complete victory, dividing the spoils among those who fought beside him in the battle.
- While the character role of prophet, priest, and king, and the special character types of Adam, Joseph, and Joshua are tremendously helpful in providing our OT witness to Christ, they give comprehensive not exhaustive pictures of the life and ministry of Christ. Only by linking the *prefiguring in the OT* to the *revelation of Christ in the NT* do we get the fullest picture and meaning of these roles and types together in the life and ministry of Jesus.

3

Student Application and Implications

Now is the time for you to discuss with your fellow students your questions about the nature of character types and your own study of them. Again, what we are seeking here is candid self-assessment on whether or not you have actually applied this knowledge or skill within your own walk and life. Try to unearth your particular questions in light of the material you have just studied, and use the questions below to "prime the pump" for your own issues and concerns.

* What is your theological comprehension of Jesus' roles as prophet, priest, and king? Have you ever studied the lives of Moses, Melchizedek, or David *in light of how they might make more plain for you* the person and work of Christ? Explain.

* When is the last time you heard a sermon on any of these character types or offices of Christ? What were the major points included? How did those insights influence and affect your study of these concepts here?

* Do you know how to study characters in the Bible? If you were going to start, how would you proceed?

* This kind of study of the OT forces you to look for clues about Messiah in the actual persons and characters in the text. Why is this such *a good way* to investigate the OT's witness to Christ, i.e., looking for Christ in the very history of the lives of the people of God? Explain your answer.

* How would you know that you have found a character that might be deemed as a character type of Christ? What kind of criteria would we need to look for and apply in order to have "pretty high confidence" that a character was a type of Christ, either directly (like Joseph) or by contrast (like Adam)?

* This method of study (character types) also asks you to look "beyond the obvious" in the stories of the key characters in the OT, and to look specifically for possible linkages between their lives and the life of Christ. Would you say you are skilled at this? Why or why not? How would you suppose that someone would become more skilled at this kind of perspective and practice?

* In such a *spiritual exercise and study*, what role does prayer and fasting play in this kind of study?

* Does this kind of study "move you," that is, what is your *emotional reaction* to seeing the life and ministry of Jesus so *visibly portrayed* in the lives and histories of different characters in the OT? What does this suggest to you about the nature of the Bible, and it focus on providing witness to the Son of God?

Second Adam, a Life-Giving Spirit

In making connection between OT characters and the person of Christ, the role of theology becomes a major factor. For instance, the Jehovah's Witnesses will admit, as they must, that the Bible makes an explicit connection between the person of Adam in the OT and Jesus in the New. Although they recognize the connection between the two, their own theological bias makes it difficult for them to properly interpret *the way in which they are linked.* Denying the bodily resurrection of Jesus, they interpret the text in 1 Corinthians 15 as meaning that Jesus was raised as a *spirit being*, that his physical body is still dead, and that the corporeal nature of his resurrection "body" does not exist. Obviously, such a view contradicts the plain teaching of the NT, and the reporting of the apostles on the *literal resurrection of Jesus' body.* Those doubting the usefulness of character types use this obvious error as evidence that typology and analogy, if used at all, must be done with the strictest of care. What do you make of the Jehovah's Witness interpretation? Is their view a common use of typology, or is it the exception to the rule? Can one use character types of Christ and not fall prey to the kind of theological mistake the Witnesses make, and if so, how does one do it?

Only the Ones Mentioned in the Bible, Please!

2

Those who are concerned about the use of the OT in a way that points to Christ will admit that both Jesus and the apostles actually used the Bible in the way. While this is admitted, they say that such a method could be used fruitfully to show how the OT bears witness to Christ in a typological way *if and only if* we limit our use of the types to the ones *mentioned in the NT.* They argue that the typological hermeneutic of the OT is so prone to error, abuse, and misinterpretation that it may only be justified in cases where the NT authenticates the links and connections made by the interpreter. While such a rule might make those doubtful of typology and analogy somewhat more assured of its right use, this limitation does severely constrict the use of the OT. For instance, the character of Joseph is perhaps the clearest and most moving type of Christ in the OT, and yet we find none of the NT authors exploring its richness and depth. Would we be excluded from using Joseph as a type of Christ because the NT does not mention or interpret it? Can you think of a way to change the rule to make it more "user friendly" when it comes to our use of the types of the OT and their relationship to the NT?

Jesus, Our Representative Head?

3

Sometimes, our use of analogies or types in the OT can lead to fundamental misinterpretations about their meaning in the NT. For instance, in conservative theological circles, Adam and Jesus are both seen as the *federal heads* of their respective "races," Adam of the sinful and doomed race apart from God's mercy, and Jesus as the firstborn of the new human race who will inherit eternal life. While the theological implications of this are clearly discussed by Paul in Romans 5, some have understood the idea of federal headship as saying that they personally were not responsible for their own sin, but only because of their association with Adam. Because Adam disobeyed God, and we are associated and connected to Adam's sin by birth and inheritance, our sinfulness comes from our *connection with Adam* more than our own *moral rebellion in our hearts.* Why would such a view of the linkage between the human race and Adam be untrue? How does the interpretation of Paul of the relationship between Adam and Christ in Romans 5 and 1 Corinthians 15 help us *properly explore and understand* the link and connection between the two? What lessons can we learn about typology and analogy from Paul's use of the connection here?

The Best (and the Worst) of Urban Preaching?

4

The styles between those who preach and teach in urban congregations over and against middle class churches is plain enough. Some of the best presenters of the OT are urban preachers, and most of them use *the OT's own metaphors, symbols, stories, and images* as the heart of their sermonizing. Some of the city's best preachers are those who have tended to so focus on the analogical and typological method that they are considered too fluid by their more conservative kindred. They have tended to focus on stories, taking liberties in exploring linkages with the lives of those in the stories and those today, and often use exegetical and homiletical styles that take seriously their audiences *identification with image and story.* Sometimes, in trying to find linkages with the OT figures, they see connections that are not *explicitly present.* Of course, the claim is that Jesus is seen in their preaching of the stories of the OT, and they continue to explore the images and types of the OT with great liberty and flexibility. These preachers are the heroes of some, and used as negative examples by others, usually those who preach "safe" sermons, usually in non-urban settings. Admittedly, many of the "new jack preachers" are nonetheless hugely popular, entertaining, and effective with urban audiences. What do you make of this use of the OT to communicate the person and work of Christ? Ought we to join this new generation of preachers, or brand their use as somewhat reckless? What does their popularity with the urban audiences suggest about our use of image, symbol, type, and analogy in our preaching and teaching among the poor in the city?

Restatement of the Lesson's Thesis

The OT provides a solid and convincing witness to the life and ministry of Jesus through its character types of key figures in the history of Israel. Character types provide us with a full and rich presentation of the truth about Christ, spur great interest in the craftsmanship of the OT stories, cause us to worship God because of the richness of his salvation plan, and enable us to see the Bible as a whole, especially the connections between the testaments. This form of study requires careful attention: we must create a general outline of the character's life, search for links and resemblances between the character and Jesus as the antitype, avoid over-concentration on details that fail to connect the type to its antitype, and seek to expand one's knowledge of the antitype *through* the understanding of the type. Such studies help us gain an increased knowledge of the Scriptures, learn to communicate the Word to others at higher levels of interest, relevance, and entertainment, rediscover our wonder at the inspiration of the Scriptures, and discover a more comprehensive picture of Jesus Christ through the types. Some of the most important character types in the OT point to and illustrate the ministry of Jesus Christ in the NT in his roles as a prophet, priest, and king in the persons of Moses, Melchizedek, and David respectively. While Christ is illumined in the character types, the nature of his own roles is infinitely greater in both glory and significance.

Certain characters in the OT deserve our special exegetical attention because of their critical theological significance in helping us comprehend Christ's role as head of humanity, redeemer of his kinsmen, and warrior in God's conquest. These characters represent the person of Adam, Joseph, and Joshua. Adam, as the federal head and source of humankind, is a special OT character type of Jesus Christ by way of contrast, that is, how he is different from the Lord who is also the federal head and source of the new redeemed humanity. Joseph, the redeemer of his kinsman, is perhaps the most prolific and "on-point" OT character type of Jesus. In ways that are both wondrous and moving, Joseph's experience links and connects with the life and ministry of Jesus Christ. Joshua, the captain of the Lord's armies, is an OT character type of Christ whose spiritual warfare resonates with Messiah's role as the warrior of God. While the character roles of prophet, priest, and king, and the special character types of Adam, Joseph, and Joshua are tremendously helpful in providing our OT witness to Christ, they give comprehensive not exhaustive pictures of the life and ministry of Christ. Only by linking the *prefiguring in the OT* to the *revelation of Christ in the NT* do we get the fullest picture and meaning of these roles and types together in the life and ministry of Jesus.

Resources and Bibliographies

If you are interested in pursuing some of the ideas of *The Promise Personalized*, you might want to give these books a try:

Barrett, Michael. *Beginning at Moses: A Guide to Finding Christ in the Old Testament*. Greenville, SC: Ambassador-Emerald International, 1999.

Borland, James A. *Christ in the Old Testament: Old Testament Appearances of Christ in Human Form*. Rev. and expanded ed. Ross-shire: Mentor, 1999.

Habershon, Ada R. *Study of the Types*. Grand Rapids: Kregel Publishing, 1997.

Longman, Tremper, III. *Immanuel in Our Place: Seeing Christ in Israel's Worship*. Phillipsburg, NJ: P & R Publishing, 2001.

Robertson, O. Palmer. *The Christ of the Prophets*. Phillipsburg, NJ: P & R Publishing, 2004.

------. *Christ of the Covenants*. Phillipsburg, NJ: P & R Publishing, 1981.

Ministry Connections

Seeking to relate these truths to your own ministry through your church represents the core of this teaching. How might God want you to change or alter your ministry approach based on your learning of how to do character types—to meditate on the lives of these great personages, and to glean insight into God's purpose and plan through them? How might you set aside time to become better skilled at this kind of study, and how might the Holy Spirit outfit you so you can better communicate the wonder of these truths to those who are members of your family and church? Ask the Lord, the Spirit, what he is specifically calling you to do about these truths. Plan to spend good time this week meditating on a character type, and ask the Lord to provide you with opportunity to share your findings with others. Be prepared to come back next week ready to share your insights with the other learners in your class.

Counseling and Prayer

The relationship between our ability to understand and apply God's Word and ongoing prayer and intercession is closely linked. Our comprehension and application of the Scriptures will be enhanced in every way if we commit the things we are learning to prayer, and ask the Holy Spirit to make our own what has surfaced through our study of God's Word. E. M. Bounds again recognizes this linkage carefully:

Prayer opens the way for the Word of God to run without let or hindrance, and creates the atmosphere which is favorable to the word accomplishing its purpose. Prayer puts wheels under God's Word, and gives wings to the angel of the Lord "having the everlasting Gospel to preach unto them that dwell on the earth, and to every nation, and kindred, and tongue, and people." Prayer greatly helps the Word of the Lord.

~ E. M. Bounds. **The Necessity of Prayer.**
Oak Harbor, WA: Logos Research Systems, Inc., 1997.

"Prayer greatly helps the Word of the Lord." To this we say, yes and amen! Select one of your classmates who will commit you to prayer, the burdens and applications on your heart, and ask them to lift up your requests to God throughout the week. Of course, your instructor is extremely open to walking with you on this, and your church leaders, especially your pastor, may be specially equipped to help you answer any difficult questions arising from your reflection on this study. Be open to God and allow him to lead you as he determines.

3

Scripture Memory

Deuteronomy 18.15-19

Reading Assignment

To prepare for class, please visit *www.tumi.org/books* to find next week's reading assignment, or ask your mentor.

Other Assignments

As usual, make sure that you set aside time to review the material in this lesson. Many difficult and deep concepts were shared here; do not leave your study to the last minute. Also, you ought to come with your reading assignment sheet containing your summary of the reading material for the week. By now, too, you must have *selected the text* for your exegetical project, and turn in *your proposal* for your ministry project.

Looking Forward to the Next Lesson

In this lesson we have carefully considered the way in which OT character types can provide us with insight into the work of Jesus Christ, especially in his roles as a prophet (in the person of Moses), as priest of the Most High God (in the person of Melchizedek, king of Salem), and as anointed king (in the person David, king of Israel). We also explored the lives of Adam, Joseph, and Joshua, through which we more clearly understood Jesus' identity as Head of a new humanity, as Savior and Redeemer of his kinsmen, and as Mighty warrior in God's conquest.

In our next lesson, we will explore both the nature and scope of OT Messianic prophecy as it relates to providing us with a clear OT witness to Christ and his Kingdom. We will look at some general characteristics about the nature and importance of OT Messianic prophecy, and then cover quickly the outline of OT Messianic predictions which are repeated in the NT. We will look at predictions fulfilled in Jesus Christ concerning his birth, his person and life, his death, his resurrection, and coming glory. We will also consider how God has extended the promise and blessings of Abraham to the Gentiles, to all who believe in Jesus Christ as Messiah. Through the OT witness to Christ, we gain real insight into God's design to include the nations in his redemptive purpose; the one who eventually will deliver Zion has also determined to save out of the world a people who will forever belong to him. Amen!

Module 9: Old Testament Witness to Christ
Reading Completion Sheet

Name ______________________________

Date ______________________________

For each assigned reading, write a brief summary (one or two paragraphs) of the author's main point. (For additional readings, use the back of this sheet.)

Reading 1

Title and Author: ______________________________ Pages __________

Reading 2

Title and Author: ______________________________ Pages __________

LESSON 4

The Promise Universalized

Lesson Objectives

Welcome in the strong name of Jesus Christ! After your reading, study, discussion, and application of the materials in this lesson, you will be able to:

- Define the term for Messiah in the Greek *messias*, the Aramaic form of the Hebrew *mashiach*, which means "to anoint"; *Christos* is the equivalent NT terminology meaning "anointed one."
- Provide a general overview of the basic characteristics of OT Messianic prophecy, including its focus on the deliverance of God's people, its strong use of figurative language, its predictions in the "prophetic perfect" tense (as if they were already accomplished), and their lack of easy-to-understand timetables as to their precise fulfilment. The main characteristic is its linkage of the testaments to Jesus Christ as the fulfillment of its prophetic descriptions.
- Outline the lineage of the Messiah as given in the OT literature, which includes the seed of the woman in Genesis, of the line of Seth, the seed of Abraham, the lineage of Isaac, through the house of Jacob, of the tribe and clan of Judah, through Boaz, Obed, Jesse and David, down to the person of Jesus of Nazareth.
- Show how OT Messianic prophecy is key to understanding the OT witness to Christ: it is the way that Jesus and the apostles applied the OT to his life, these prophecies illumine our understanding of the way Jesus used the OT, they directly connected the testaments (in the way Augustine suggested, that the OT is revealed in the NT), and finally, that Jesus of Nazareth fulfills the prophetic predictions of the expected Messiah.
- Give a brief sketch of the main points included in the OT Messianic prophecies which give witness to Christ and his Kingdom, including prophecies about his birth at Bethlehem, his prophetic forerunner, and his identity as Immanuel.
- Include in the sketch the main prophetic predictions about Messiah's person and life, i.e., his introduction by the coming "voice in the wilderness," his divine status as Wonderful, Counselor, Mighty God,

Everlasting Father, and Prince of peace, his anointing as the Servant of Yahweh, and his anticipated Kingship and reign. Further, the sketch should include his role as the cornerstone of God's salvific work, his role as light for the Gentiles, and his role as prophet priest and king.

- Articulate the major elements concerning the *Passion* of Christ, i.e., the suffering and death of Messiah, including (but not limited to) his brutal treatment and death, his vicarious (substitutionary) wounding and bruising for the sins of the world, his great agony, his betrayal, his feet and hands being pierced, his false trial and verdict, and his death.

- Lay out the major texts and their content regarding his resurrection, including Peter's sermon at Pentecost and Paul's preaching at Antioch, as well as the predictions made in the Gospels of his resurrection.

- Provide a general outline of some of the OT Messianic texts which predict the coming glory of Messiah, including the exaltation of Messiah as the King of glory, the terrifying judgment upon God's enemies, his return for his people, the majesty, beauty, and glory of creation's transformation that will occur under his reign, and the everlasting and universal dominion that will be given to him.

- Show how God has extended the promise and blessings of Abraham to the Gentiles, to all who believe in Jesus Christ as Messiah.

- Give evidence of the three movements in the NT's use of OT Messianic prophecy, including 1) Jesus' explanation of the OT predictions about himself, 2) the apostles' commentary on Jesus' meaning in the NT writings, especially in the preaching of the book of Acts, and 3) the Church's application of the apostles' commentary of Jesus' understanding of the OT.

- Detail how the promise was universalized to all nations by the inclusion of Gentile salvation in the Messianic hope, including the revealed mystery of Gentiles as fellow heirs of the covenant and heirs of salvation, and the prophetic clues given that pointed to Gentile salvation (e.g., the seed of the woman destroying the serpent, all the families of the earth being blessed in Abraham, and how the Messiah would be a light to all the Gentiles).

- Show how the various strands of OT Messianic prophecy were progressively understood by the apostles to represent God's salvation for all peoples, including the outpouring of the Spirit on all flesh, and full inclusion of Gentiles as fellow heirs of the Abrahamic promise.

- List some of the key ways OT Messianic prophecies were used by the apostles in the Acts and the Epistles, including the outpouring of the Spirit on all flesh, the rejection of Messiah by the builders (Jewish generation), Jesus as light for the Gentiles, the rebuilding of the tent of David including Gentile salvation, and the Messianic blindness of God's people (the Jews) due to their hardness of heart. Also, they mention the global proclamation of the Gospel, the provoking of the Jews to jealousy, and the blessing of Abraham on the Gentiles.
- Summarize the OT Messianic prophecy regarding the Gentiles as God not only fulfilled his promise for salvation to Abraham, but his inclusion of Gentiles in that salvation promise.

Devotion

You Are Not My People - But You Shall Be!

Hos. 1.1-10 - The word of the Lord that came to Hosea, the son of Beeri, in the days of Uzziah, Jotham, Ahaz, and Hezekiah, kings of Judah, and in the days of Jeroboam the son of Joash, king of Israel. [2] When the Lord first spoke through Hosea, the Lord said to Hosea, "Go, take to yourself a wife of whoredom and have children of whoredom, for the land commits great whoredom by forsaking the Lord." [3] So he went and took Gomer, the daughter of Diblaim, and she conceived and bore him a son. [4] And the Lord said to him, "Call his name Jezreel, for in just a little while I will punish the house of Jehu for the blood of Jezreel, and I will put an end to the kingdom of the house of Israel. [5] And on that day I will break the bow of Israel in the Valley of Jezreel." [6] She conceived again and bore a daughter. And the Lord said to him, "Call her name No Mercy, for I will no more have mercy on the house of Israel, to forgive them at all. [7] But I will have mercy on the house of Judah, and I will save them by the Lord their God. I will not save them by bow or by sword or by war or by horses or by horsemen." [8] When she had weaned No Mercy, she conceived and bore a son. [9] And the Lord said, "Call his name Not My People, for you are not my people, and I am not your God." [10] Yet the number of the children of Israel shall be like the sand of the sea, which cannot be measured or numbered. And in the place where it was said to them, "You are not my people," it shall be said to them, "Children of the living God."

Perhaps nothing hurts psychologically as much as the feel of not belonging to anyone, of not fitting in, of being spurned, and treated as an outsider. There is

4

something about this condition that is poignant and painful; being a stranger and having no place is one of the most difficult situations to endure. Unfortunately, many millions live with this sense of not belonging and having no family or community every day. This has become the age and the time of alienation and lack of connection.

One of the significant issues in OT theology is the subject of Gentile inclusion in the salvific promises of God. What is the place of Gentiles in God's salvation plan? Are they a footnote on the page of God? Were they ever considered an integral part of God's plan to redeem the world? How are we to understand the nations and their role in God's great desire to destroy the devil, overthrow the curse, and redeem to himself a people who would live in his recreated heavens and earth?

Hosea was a prophet in the years of the some of the notable kings of Judah, and during the reign of Jeroboam, the king of Israel. His first assignment from Yahweh was to take a wife of "whoredom" and have "children of whoredom" because the land had committed spiritual adultery against the Lord. Hosea took Gomer, and had children by her, all living visual aids of the Lord's relationship with his people. His firstborn was called *Jezreel* (associated with punishment), his second daughter was called *No Mercy* (for the Lord would have no mercy on his people). His third child, a son, was named *Not My People*, for the children of Israel were declared to not be his people. Yet, in the tender mercies of the Lord, the number of children would be innumerable, and "Not my people" would come to be called "Children of the living God."

What a stark and powerful picture of the Lord's judgment on his unjust and idolatrous people. Yet, in the prophetic application of this text to the Church, Paul reads the same text and expands its meaning to Gentiles, to those who by virtue of their alienation from the covenants of God, were not considered to be the people of God.

> Rom. 9.22-26 - What if God, desiring to show his wrath and to make known his power, has endured with much patience vessels of wrath prepared for destruction, [23] in order to make known the riches of his glory for vessels of mercy, which he has prepared beforehand for glory- [24] even us whom he has called, not from the Jews only but also from the Gentiles? [25] As indeed he says in Hosea, "Those who were not my people I will call 'my people,' and her who was not beloved I will call 'beloved.'" [26] "And in the very place where it was said to them, 'You are not my people,' there they will be called 'sons of the living God.'"

Paul here says that the plan of God for redeeming a remnant of humanity for himself, even those among the Gentiles, was ingredient in the plan all along. We have already seen that the Gospel was spoken first in the *protoevangelium* in Genesis 3.15, and renewed in the covenant to Abraham in Genesis 12.1-3, which included the promise of the blessing of the nations through Abraham's seed. Here in this text, the prophetic Word is expanded from its context only to Israel and applied to the Gentiles as well. Those who were not the people of God, not beloved, not cherished and without hope in the world—through the promise of Messiah, even these would be called "children of the living God." Israel remains the people of God, but, the love and mercy of God is extended to the Gentiles. The mystery unveiled is that our God is in fact the God of the Jew and the Gentile, and Gentiles are to be considered fellow-heirs in the great salvation of God in Messiah.

Are the Jews not to be considered the people of God any longer then? George Eldon Ladd clearly argues no to this question:

> *In the old dispensation, Israel was the people of God. Israel's rejection of her Messiah leads Paul to the question, 'Has God rejected his people?' (Rom. 11.1). No further qualifier is necessary to designate Israel as God's people. Paul devotes a long discussion to the problem of Israel (Rom. 9-11) in the course of which he makes it clear that the Church is God's new people. This is most vividly expressed in the use of quotations from Hosea. The prophet speaks of the present apostasy of Israel and her eschatological salvation. Hosea was directed to name one of his sons 'Not my people,' for apostate Israel was no longer God's people and he was not their God (Hos. 1.9). However, in the day of salvation, this situation will be changed; they will be called "sons of the living God" (Hos. 1.10). "And I will say to Not my people, 'You are my people;' and he shall say, 'Thou are my God'" (Hos. 2.23). In Hosea these prophecies clearly refer to Israel, but Paul applies them to the church, which consists of both Jews and Gentiles (Rom. 9.24). This does not mean that the title laos is taken from Israel, but that another people is brought into being along with Israel on a different basis. That Israel in some real sense remains the people of God is seen in Paul's affirmation that the Jewish people are still a "holy" people (Rom. 11.16), a people belonging to God. The fate of the Jews is seen in the light of the whole history of Heilsgeschichte. If the patriarchs-the first fruits and the root-are holy, so is the whole people. They are still "beloved for the sake of their forefathers, for the gifts and the call of God are irrevocable" (Rom. 11.28f.).*

~ George Eldon Ladd. **A Theology of the New Testament.** Grand Rapids: Eerdmans Publishing Company, 1974. pp. 537-38.

4

The Bible is clear that salvation is of the Jews, and that we Gentiles, are included by the mercy and grace of God. A few representative passages should suffice to show this emphasis:

Rom. 9.3-5 - For I could wish that I myself were accursed and cut off from Christ for the sake of my brothers, my kinsmen according to the flesh. [4] They are Israelites, and to them belong the adoption, the glory, the covenants, the giving of the law, the worship, and the promises. [5] To them belong the patriarchs, and from their race, according to the flesh, is the Christ who is God over all, blessed forever. Amen.

Eph. 2.11-13 - Therefore remember that at one time you Gentiles in the flesh, called "the uncircumcision" by what is called the circumcision, which is made in the flesh by hands- [12] remember that you were at that time separated from Christ, alienated from the commonwealth of Israel and strangers to the covenants of promise, having no hope and without God in the world. [13] But now in Christ Jesus you who once were far off have been brought near by the blood of Christ.

John 4.21-22 - Jesus said to her, "Woman, believe me, the hour is coming when neither on this mountain nor in Jerusalem will you worship the Father. [22] You worship what you do not know; we worship what we know, for salvation is from the Jews."

It is clear: the salvation promise was given to Abraham and his descendants, and Gentiles are not of that lineage. Nevertheless, now, through faith in Jesus of Nazareth, Israel's Messiah, even though we were once far away, without hope, and lost in the world as Gentiles we are brought near to God through the blood of Christ. Through him and him alone, we are no longer on the outside but are fellow heirs of the salvation to come with all those who believe, who now together, whether Jew or Gentile, are part of the one true Church of the living God (Gal. 3.28; Col. 3.11). And all this by the grace and mercy of the great God and Savior Jesus Christ.

Not My People have become *Children of the living God*. Isn't it great to belong?

Nicene Creed and Prayer

After reciting and/or singing the Nicene Creed (located in the Appendix), pray the following prayer:

> *O Immanuel, our Sovereign and Lawgiver, desire of the nations and Savior of all: Come and save us, O Lord our God. Come, Lord Jesus.*
>
> ~ Presbyterian Church (U.S.A.) and Cumberland Presbyterian Church. The Theology and Worship Ministry Unit. **Book of Common Worship.** Louisville, Ky.: Westminister/John Knox Press, 1993. p. 167.

Quiz

Put away your notes, gather up your thoughts and reflections, and take the quiz for Lesson 3, *The Promise Personalized.*

Scripture Memorization Review

Review with a partner, write out and/or recite the text for last class session's assigned memory verse: Deuteronomy 18.15-19.

Assignments Due

Turn in your summary of the reading assignment for last week, that is, your brief response and explanation of the main points that the authors were seeking to make in the assigned reading (Reading Completion Sheet).

4

Prophecies and "Double Fulfillment"

The OT contains dozens of Messianic prophecies that point to the future coming of an anointed one of the Lord who would destroy the devil's work, end the curse, regather and glorify his people, and usher in a Kingdom of righteousness which would never be defeated or overthrown. Often these prophecies are given in the context of an actual historical event, and the prophecy, which appears to be future, was actually fulfilled in the lifetime of the prophet himself. For instance, Psalm 78.1-3 - "Give ear, O my people, to my teaching; incline your ears to the words of my mouth! [2] I will open my mouth in a parable; I will utter dark sayings from of old, [3] things that we have heard and known, that our fathers have told us." This text appears to be a simple saying of David about the way in which he intends to speak to the people of Israel the promises and statutes of the Lord. The NT, however, ascribes this text to Christ, to the way in which he spoke parables to the people as he shared the Good News of the Kingdom with them (cf. Matt. 13.34). What appears here seems to be a "double fulfillment;" the saying is fulfilled both in the time of David as well as in the life and ministry of Jesus. What do you make of this principle? Does it make sense that the Scriptures could have both a contemporary meaning for the people at the time they heard it as well as a future fulfillment in the life of Messiah?

A New Grammatic Tense: "the Prophetic Perfect"

2

One of the curious and special features of OT prophecy is that the predictions are often written in what scholars have come to call the "prophetic perfect" tense. This means that at the time they were recorded these prophecies were written as if they had already been accomplished. For instance, the Messianic prophecy in Isaiah 53 graphically portrays the suffering of Messiah (Isaiah 53.3-5 - He was despised and rejected by men; a man of sorrows, and acquainted with grief; and as one from whom men hide their faces he was despised, and we esteemed him not. [4] Surely he has borne our griefs and carried our sorrows; yet we esteemed him stricken, smitten by God, and afflicted. [5] But he was wounded for our transgressions; he was crushed for our iniquities; upon him was the chastisement that brought us peace, and with his stripes we are healed). At the time of Isaiah's writing, the Messiah would not appear for another six centuries, yet he writes as though it has already occurred. Why is this "prophetic perfect" sense so important in reading and understanding the nature of prophecy in general, especially in reading and understanding Messianic prophecy in particular?

4

Gentile Pride or Equal Status?

3

Today, many people would think that Christianity is essentially a Gentile religion. In all of its major denominations and traditions, Gentile culture, theologies, customs, and practices dominate. Although all traditions recognize the Jewish roots of the ancient Christian heritage, one would be hard-pressed to find modern day American Christians who are greatly informed about these roots, let alone find anything in this Jewish pre-heritage that might need to be kept front and center in normal Christian faith. For many Christians today, for all intents and purposes, Christianity is wholly and completely a Gentile faith; many evangelicals themselves find more affinity with the Reformers or some modern teacher or preacher than the Jewish ground of all genuine faith. While Jesus can say without equivocation that "salvation is from the Jews" (John 4.22), many Christians have serious reservations in believing and practicing this perspective. What do you make of these phenomena? How does our modern-day Gentilization of the faith actually limit our ability to fully appreciate and appropriate the whole counsel of God, especially our OT literature?

The Promise Universalized

Segment 1: Old Testament Messianic Predictions Fulfilled

Rev. Dr. Don L. Davis

Summary of Segment 1

The term for Messiah in the Greek is *messias*, the Aramaic form of the Hebrew *mashiach*, which means "to anoint"; *Christos* is the equivalent NT terminology meaning "anointed one." The OT Messianic prophecy includes a handful of basic characteristics, including its focus on the deliverance of God's people, its strong use of figurative language, its predictions in the "prophetic perfect" tense (as if they were already accomplished), and their lack of easy-to-understand timetables as to their precise fulfilment. The main characteristic is its linkage of the testaments to Jesus Christ as the fulfillment of its prophetic descriptions. The key to tracing the Messiah's *family lineage* is following the clues from the beginning of Messianic prophecy, which includes the seed of the woman in Genesis, the promise of God's dwelling in the tents of Seth, the seed of Abraham, the lineage of Isaac through the house of Jacob, of the tribe and clan of Judah, through Boaz, Obed, Jesse and David, down to the person of Jesus of Nazareth. In many ways, tracing the themes in OT Messianic prophecy is key to understanding the OT witness to Christ. It is the way that Jesus and the apostles applied the OT to his life—these prophecies illumine our understanding of the way Jesus used the OT, they directly connect the testaments (in the way Augustine suggested, that the OT is revealed in the NT), and finally, they show that Jesus of Nazareth fulfills the prophetic predictions of the expected Messiah. The main points included in the OT Messianic prophecies cover his birth, his suffering and death, his resurrection, and his coming glory. In every way, the clear testimony of OT Messianic prophecy is that Jesus of Nazareth is the Messiah, providing a solid witness about his life, ministry, and coming Kingdom.

4

Our objective for this segment, *Old Testament Messianic Predictions Fulfilled*, is to enable you to see that:

- The term for Messiah in the Greek is *messias*, the Aramaic form of the Hebrew *mashiach*, which means "to anoint"; *Christos* is the equivalent NT terminology meaning "anointed one."
- The OT Messianic prophecy includes a handful of basic characteristics, including its focus on the deliverance of God's people, its strong use of figurative language, its predictions in the "prophetic perfect" tense (as if they were already accomplished), and their lack of easy-to-understand timetables as to their precise fulfilment. The main characteristic is its linkage of the testaments to Jesus Christ as the fulfillment of its prophetic descriptions.
- The key to tracing the Messiah's *family lineage* is following the clues from the beginning of Messianic prophecy, which includes the seed of the woman in Genesis, the promise of God's dwelling in the tents of Seth, the seed of Abraham, the lineage of Isaac through the house of Jacob, of the tribe and clan of Judah, through Boaz, Obed, Jesse and David, down to the person of Jesus of Nazareth.
- In many ways, tracing the themes in OT Messianic prophecy is key to understanding the OT witness to Christ. It is the way that Jesus and the apostles applied the OT to his life—these prophecies illumine our understanding of the way Jesus used the OT, they directly connect the testaments (in the way Augustine suggested, that the OT is revealed in the NT), and finally, they show that Jesus of Nazareth fulfills the prophetic predictions of the expected Messiah.
- The main points included in the OT Messianic prophecies covering his birth include prophecies about the prophetic forerunner, his birthplace at Bethlehem, and his identity as the human-divine son Immanuel.
- The main OT Messianic prophetic predictions were about his person and life, i.e., his introduction by the coming "voice in the wilderness," his divine status as Wonderful, Counselor, Mighty God, Everlasting Father, and Prince of peace, his anointing as the Servant of Yahweh, and his anticipated kingship and reign. Prophecies of Messiah's life also include his role as the cornerstone of God's salvific work, his role as light for the Gentiles, and his role as prophet, priest, and king.

- OT Messianic prophecies also address the *passion* of Christ, his suffering and death, and among them mention is made of his betrayal, his false trial and verdict, his brutal treatment and death, his vicarious (substitutionary) wounding and bruising for the sins of the world, his crucifixion, his great agony on the cross, his death, and his burial.
- The major OT texts quoted in the NT concerning Messiah's resurrection are usually included in the Gospel accounts and their predictions of it, as well in the apostolic preaching in Acts, especially in Peter's sermon at Pentecost and Paul's preaching at Antioch.
- A general outline of some of the key OT Messianic texts should include predictions of the coming glory of Messiah, including his exaltation and vindication as Yahweh's King of glory, his terrifying judgment upon God's enemies, his return for and regathering of his people, the majesty, beauty, and glory of creation's transformation that will occur under his reign, and the everlasting and universal dominion that will be given to him.

Video Segment 1 Outline

I. General Observations Regarding Messianic Prophecy as it Relates to the OT Witness to Christ

Jesus Interprets Prophecy in Terms of His Own Life and Work

It may in fact have been one of the unique contributions of Jesus that he took key themes from OT prophecy (calls to covenant faithfulness, divine disclosure of the meaning and significance of historical events, anticipations of God's work in history to bring about his purposes) and some of the key themes of intertestamental apocalyptic (the concept of two ages, predictions of final judgment and vindication, divine visitations by an exalted Son of man, revelations granted to special seers), saw himself as the fulfiller of both, and fused them into the concept of a kingdom which was already and not yet present. Luke 17.20–37, for example, gives evidence of both aspects in Jesus' concept of the kingdom.

~ Timothy J. Geddert. "Apocalyptic Teaching."
The Dictionary of Jesus and the Gospels.
J. B. Green, ed. (electronic ed.)
Downers Grove, IL: InterVarsity Press, 1997. p. 24.

4

A. Definitions of Messiah

1. Messiah is derived from the Greek *Messias* (which is a transliteration of the Aramaic form of the Hebrew *mashach*, which means "to anoint").

2. NT equivalent terminology: *Christos* ("anointed one")

3. Anointing in the OT

   a. Kings were anointed (e.g., Saul, 1 Sam. 24.6; David, 2 Sam. 19.21).

   b. "Anointed one" translated *Messiah* in Dan. 9.25-26 was in common use by the Jews at the time close to the birth of Jesus.

4. Messianic prophecy linked to *eschatological hope* (the expectation that Israel had that God would send an anointed one who as King and Priest would deliver from sin and end oppression)

B. Characteristics of OT Messianic prophecy

1. The language of Messianic prophecy is anchored in the hope for deliverance, Isa. 9.6-7.

2. Messianic prophecy is filled with figurative language, Isa. 11.

3. The predictions are often written in what scholars call the "*prophetic perfect*" tense (i.e., prophecy is written as if it is already accomplished), e.g., Isa. 53.

4. Messianic prophecy does not often give easy-to-understand timetables as to its precise fulfillment, cf. Luke 4.18-19 with Isaiah 61.1-3.

5. OT Messianic prophecy links the testaments together for *Jesus Christ is the fulfillment of its predictions and descriptions.*

6. The lineage of Messiah is well outlined in the OT promise, which is fulfilled *in the person of Jesus.*

    a. Messiah will be the seed of the woman, Gen. 3.15.

    b. In the line of Seth, Gen. 4.25

    c. Through the family of Noah, Genesis 6-9

    d. The seed of Abraham, Gen. 12.1-3

    e. In the lineage of Isaac, Gen. 17.19

    f. Through Jacob, Gen. 28.14

    g. Of the tribe and clan of Judah, Gen. 49.10

    h. Through Boaz, Obed, Jesse and David, 2 Sam. 7.12-13

i. Down to the person of Jesus, the true Messiah

(1) Matt. 2.1-16

(2) Luke 3.23-38

C. The importance of OT Messianic prophecy to understanding the OT witness to Christ

1. Understanding Jesus as the fulfillment of OT Messianic prophecy is the way that Jesus and the apostles used the OT.

2. Prophecies about Messiah can illumine our understanding of the meaning of *Jesus' interpretation* of Scripture.

3. Augustine's adage of the OT being revealed in the NT, and the NT being concealed in the OT is clearly illustrated in Messianic prophecy.

4. Nothing unifies our treatment of Scripture more than seeing the obvious connections which exist between *Jesus of Nazareth* and *the expected Messiah*.

II. OT Messianic Prophecies Which Give Witness to Christ and His Kingdom: an Outline

Messiah Is Both Son of God and Servant of the Lord

Although Jesus has come as God's promised, Spirit-anointed, royal Son to herald and inaugurate the kingdom, Mark writes to correct those who would look to the glory of the final consummation of the kingdom instead of its vulnerable beginnings. The kingdom is here in hidden fashion, and Jesus the Messiah (see Christ), Son of God (1.1), must be understood in terms of suffering and the cross (8.31–33; 9.30–32; 10.32–34; see Predictions of Jesus' Death and Resurrection). The pivotal pronouncement of servanthood in Mark 10.45 (see Ransom Saying) declares the essence of Jesus' ministry. By comprehending this, the disciples will comprehend the essence of discipleship as servanthood, including their motivation, position, ambition, expectations and example (note the crucial placement of the servanthood passages at 9.33–37 and 10.35–45, within the larger discipleship section of 8.27–10.45).

~ Michael Wilkins. "Discipleship." **The Dictionary of Jesus and the Gospels.** J. B. Green, ed. (electronic ed.) Downers Grove, IL: InterVarsity Press, 1997. p. 184.

A. Prophecies concerning the *birth* of Jesus Christ

4

1. The ministry of Christ's forerunner, Mal. 4.5-6

2. His birthplace at Bethlehem, Mic. 5.2

3. The human and divine aspect of his birth, Isa. 7.14 (cf. Gen. 3.15)

B. Prophecies concerning the *person and life* of Jesus Christ

1. The introduction by a coming "voice in the wilderness", Isa. 40.3-5 (cf. Mal. 3.1)

2. His eternal existence and exalted person, Isa. 9.6-7

3. His anointing by the Spirit as the Servant of Yahweh, Isa. 61.2

4. His anticipated kingship and reign, Isa. 9.6-7

    a. Ps. 2

    b. Gen. 49.10

    c. Num. 24.17

    d. 2 Sam. 7.12-16

    e. Ps. 110.1-2

    f. Jer. 23.5-6

5. He whose life would serve as *cornerstone* and *foundation*

    a. Isa. 28.14-18

    b. Zech. 4.7

    c. Ps. 118.22

6. His life would be a light for the Gentiles, Isa. 49.6.

7. His role as prophet, priest, and king

    a. Prophet, Deut. 18.15

    b. Priest, Ps. 110.4

    c. King, Ps. 2

8. The King would enter the city with dignity, glory, and triumph, Zech. 9.9.

C. Prophecies concerning the death of Jesus Christ

While many clear prophecies exist regarding the Messiah's coming, the two principal texts in the OT are Isaiah 53 and Psalm 22, supported by many others which refer to Christ's suffering and death.

1. Isaiah 53: the gory details of Messiah's death

    a. He will be brutally beaten, Isa. 52.14.

    b. He will be wounded for our transgressions and bruised for our iniquities, Isa. 53.5.

    c. Silent before his persecutors, Isa. 53.7

    d. His soul will be an offering for sin, Isa. 53.10.

    e. He will die with the wicked, but be buried with those who are rich, Isa. 53.9.

    f. His death is for others, not his own sin, Isa. 53.9.

2. Psalm 22: Christ's quotation of this Psalm on the cross

    a. He will be forsaken of the Lord, Ps. 22.1.

    b. He will experience derision, ridicule, scorn, Ps. 22.6-8.

    c. He will suffer great agony, Ps. 22.14-16.

    d. His bones will be pulled out of joint, Ps. 22.14.

e. He would suffer unbearable thirst, Ps. 22.15.

f. His hands and feet would be pierced, Ps. 22.16.

g. His garments would be gambled over, Ps. 22.18.

h. He would experience death, Ps. 22.15.

3. Abundant references throughout the OT to Messiah's death

a. Betrayed by a friend, Ps. 41.9

b. Falsely accused for wrongdoing, Ps. 35.11

c. Spit upon in his suffering, Isa. 50.6

d. None of his bones would be broken, Ps. 34.20.

D. Prophecies concerning the *resurrection* of Jesus Christ

1. Many passages anticipate it; few are specific.

2. Critical texts applied specifically to the resurrection of Jesus: Ps. 16.8-11

a. Peter at Pentecost, Acts 2.25-31

b. Paul at Antioch, Acts 13.34-37

3. Texts that strongly imply the resurrection of Messiah

   a. Ps. 22.22

   b. Ps. 118.22-24

   c. Isa. 53.10

4. NT predictions of the resurrection of Christ

   a. John 2.19-21

   b. Matt. 12.38-40

   c. Mark 8.31

   d. Luke 18.33

E. Prophecies concerning the *coming glory* of Jesus Christ

1. The difficulty of the OT prophets to link Messiah's *sufferings* with his coming *glory*, 1 Pet. 1.10-11

2. Psalm 24: the King of glory shall come into the city.

3. Psalm 72: the glorious reign of the Messianic King, Ps. 72.11-13

4. The branch of Yahweh will be beautiful and glorious, Isa. 4.2.

5. The Messiah's dominion shall be universal and everlasting, Dan. 7.14.

6. The NT confirmation of the glorious Messiah

   a. His glorious present session in heaven

      (1) Mark 16.19

      (2) Luke 24.51

      (3) Heb. 4.14

      (4) 1 Pet. 3.22

   b. His return for his people

      (1) John 14.1-3

      (2) 1 Cor. 15.51-52

      (3) 1 Thess. 4.13-18

   c. His glorious return to judge the world

      (1) Matt. 26.64

      (2) Luke 21.27

      (3) Acts 1.11

d. His committing of the Kingdom to God the Father, that he might be all in all, 1 Cor. 15.24-28

Conclusion

» The nature and scope of OT Messianic prophecy as it relates to giving us a clear OT witness to Christ and his Kingdom is both comprehensive and compelling.

» The OT gives numerous and clear prophecies regarding the entire outline of Messiah's life and ministry, from his birth in Bethlehem to the coming glory of his Kingdom.

Segue 1

Student Questions and Response

Please take as much time as you have available to answer these and other questions that the video brought out. In this section we explored the notion of Messiah and its relationship to OT predictions about his coming birth, death, resurrection, and glory. The OT Messianic prophecy includes a handful of basic characteristics which essentially provide insight and connection to the NT through the person of Jesus of Nazareth. They trace his lineage from the seed of the woman in Genesis to the person of Jesus of Nazareth. Your ability to understand and identify the major contours and concepts associated with OT Messianic prophecy will be critical to your grasping the ways in which the OT bears witness to Christ. Explore these prophetic themes through your answers to the questions below.

1. What does the term *Messiah* mean, and what are its renders in the Greek and Aramaic form of the Hebrew? How is the Greek term *Christos* related to it, and what does it mean?

2. What are central characteristics of the OT Messianic prophecy, and how do they directly link the Old and New Testaments in the person of Jesus of Nazareth? Explain.

3. Trace the Messianic *family lineage* through the OT Messianic prophecies from the seed of the woman in Genesis to the person of Jesus. How do these prophetic predictions provide us with *a broad historical perspective* on the Messianic concept in the Bible?

4. In what ways do OT Messianic prophecies offer us the "key to understanding the OT witness to Christ?" Why is this valid, especially since this is the way that Jesus and the apostles applied the OT to his life?

5. Sketch out the main points included in the OT Messianic prophecies covering his birth. What is the overall significance of these predictions as they bear witness to Christ?

6. List the main OT Messianic prophetic predictions about the person and ministry of the Messiah. How does this collection of prophecies and their fulfillment in the person of Jesus help us understand the way in which the OT functions and relates to the NT?

7. What are the major elements of OT prophecy concerning the *passion* of Christ, and how are these fulfilled in the suffering of Jesus upon the cross?

8. What are the central OT texts which deal with the resurrection of Messiah? What is the critical OT text quoted by Peter and Paul that relates specifically to the resurrection of Jesus? What texts strongly imply the resurrection of Messiah? How do NT predictions of Messiah's resurrection relate to the OT themes?

9. Why was it difficult for the OT prophets to link Messiah's sufferings with his coming glory? What are some of the key OT Messianic texts which predict the nature and character of the coming glory of Messiah? How do these enhance our understanding of the OT's witness to Christ?

10. Read Lindars Barnabas' insights below on the NT use of the OT. Do you agree with his statement that the "resurrection, interpreted in light of Messianic texts, is the starting point of Christology (i.e., the theology of the Son of God)?"

4

The Church Believed that Jesus Was the Messiah Because of the Fulfillment of Messianic Prophecy

From the first, the church proclaimed Jesus, risen and exalted, to be the Messiah in fulfillment of Scripture, and this was proved from Messianic texts. The basic exaltation text is Psalm 110.1, which is quoted in the Gospels, Acts, the Pauline Letters, and Hebrews. Resurrection on the third day may have been supported from Hosea 6.2, which is applied to the resurrection of the dead in Jewish sources, but is not actually quoted in the NT. Jonah's three days' sojourn in the belly of the fish (Jon. 1.17; Matt. 2.1), also used of the resurrection of the dead in Jewish sources, is applied to Jesus in Matthew 12.40. Jesus' resurrection as Messiah fulfills Psalm 2.7, quoted in Acts 13.33; Hebrews 1.5; and 5.5 and alluded to in a probably pre-Pauline formula in Romans 1.4. The same text may lie behind the divine words at the baptism of Jesus in Mark 1.11, though they mainly reflect Isaiah 42.1.

Thus, the divine declaration of the Messiahship of Jesus is pushed back from the resurrection to the baptism. Passages from the Messianic Psalm 118 are also applied to the Christological significance of the resurrection in Acts 4.11 and 1 Peter 2.7, and also in Matthew 21.42; Mark 12.10-11; and Luke 20.17, and the application is made to Jesus' entry into Jerusalem in Matt. 21.9; Mark 11.9; and John 12.13. Jesus' future function as the exalted Messiah is expressed in terms of the 'one like a son of man' (Dan. 7.13) in Matthew 24.30; Mark 13.26; and Luke 21.27, and the text from Daniel is alluded to frequently in Matthew. In Matthew 26.64; Mark 14.62; and Luke 22.69, Daniel 7.13 is conflated (combined) with Psalm 110.1; in Revelation 1.7, it is conflated with Zechariah 12.10. ***It is not too much to say that the resurrection, interpreted in the light of Messianic texts, is the starting point of Christology*** *[emphasis mine].*

~ Lindars Barnabas. "Old Testament Quotations in the New Testament." **Harper's Bible Dictionary**. 1st ed. Paul J. Achtemeier, ed. San Francisco: Harper & Row, 1985. p. 725.

4

The Promise Universalized

Segment 2: Gentile Inclusion in Old Testament Messianic Prophecy

Rev. Dr. Don L. Davis

Summary of Segment 2

A serious study of OT Messianic prophecy reveals that God has extended the promise and blessings of Abraham to the Gentiles, to all who believe in Jesus Christ as Messiah. The three critical movements in the NT's use of OT Messianic prophecy include: 1) Jesus' *explanation* of the OT predictions about himself, 2) the apostles' *commentary* on Jesus' meaning in the NT writings, especially in the preaching of the book of Acts, and 3) the Church's *application* of the apostles' commentary of Jesus' understanding of the OT. God included the salvation of the

Gentiles in the promise to Abraham. Now in this age God has unveiled the mystery that was hidden in past ages and times but now revealed through the prophets and the apostles, namely that Gentiles are fellow heirs of the covenant and heirs of salvation. Clues were given prophetically of this inclusion throughout Scripture, e.g., in the *protoevangelium* and God's promise to bless all the families of the earth in Abraham. The apostolic use of OT Messianic prophecies in their preaching as recorded in Acts and the Epistles reveal their developing understanding of Gentile inclusion in the faith. The OT Messianic prophecies regarding the Gentiles show the plan and purpose of God for the nations; not only has God fulfilled his promise for salvation to Abraham, but it also includes the salvation of the Gentiles in that salvation promise.

Our objective for this segment, *Gentile Inclusion in Old Testament Messianic Prophecy*, is to enable you to see that:

- A serious study of OT Messianic prophecy reveals that God has extended the promise and blessings of Abraham to the Gentiles, to all who believe in Jesus Christ as Messiah.
- The three critical movements in the NT's use of OT Messianic prophecy include: 1) Jesus' *explanation* of the OT predictions about himself, 2) the apostles' *commentary* on Jesus' meaning in the NT writings, especially in the preaching of the book of Acts, and 3) the Church's *application* of the apostles' commentary of Jesus' understanding of the OT.
- The Abrahamic covenant promise was universalized to all nations by the inclusion of Gentile salvation in the Messianic hope. This promise includes the unveiling of the mystery that Gentiles are fellow heirs of the covenant and heirs of salvation. Clues are given prophetically of this inclusion throughout Scripture, including the *protoevangelium*, the promise that all the families of the earth will be blessed in Abraham, and the prediction that Messiah would be a light to all the Gentiles.
- Various strands of OT Messianic prophecy were progressively understood by the apostles to represent God's salvation for all peoples, including predictions such as the promise of the outpouring of the Spirit on all flesh, and full inclusion of Gentiles as fellow heirs of the Abrahamic promise.
- The apostolic use of OT Messianic prophecies in their preaching as recorded in Acts and the Epistles reveal their developing understanding of Gentile inclusion in the faith. They cite, among other things, the

outpouring of the Spirit on all flesh, the rejection of Messiah by the builders (Jewish generation), Jesus as light for the Gentiles, the rebuilding of the tent of David including Gentile salvation, and the Messianic blindness of God's people (the Jews) due to their hardness of heart. Also, they mention the global proclamation of the Gospel, the provoking of the Jews to jealousy, and the blessing of Abraham on the Gentiles.

- The OT Messianic prophecies regarding the Gentiles show the plan and purpose of God for the nations; not only has God fulfilled his promise for salvation to Abraham, but he also includes the salvation of the Gentiles in that salvation promise.

I. Promise and Fulfillment: the Three Movements in NT's Use of OT Messianic Prophecy

Video Segment 2 Outline

The Vast Majority of All Prophecy on the Coming of the Messiah

But the great body of Old Testament prophecy relates directly to the advent of the Messiah, beginning with Genesis 3.15, the first great promise, and extending in ever-increasing fulness and clearness all through to the very close of the canon. The Messianic prophecies are too numerous to be quoted. "To him gave all the prophets witness." (Comp. Mic. 5.2; Hag. 2.6–9; Isa. 7.14; 9.6, 7; 11.1, 2; 53; 60.10, 13; Ps. 16.11; 68.18.) Many predictions also were delivered by Jesus and his Apostles. Those of Christ were very numerous. (Comp. Matt. 10.23,24; 11.23; 19.28; 21.43, 44; 24; 25.31–46; 26.17–35, 46, 64; Mark 9.1; 10.30; 13; 11.1–6, 14; 14.12–31, 42, 62; 16.17, etc.)

~ M. G. Easton. "Prophecy." **Easton's Bible Dictionary**. (electronic ed. of the 1897 version). Oak Harbor, WA: Logos Research Systems, Inc., 1996.

A. First Movement: Jesus' *explanation* of the OT Messianic predictions about himself

1. Jesus explained to his apostles after his resurrection the things concerning himself in the OT.

4

2. This confirmed his understanding of himself as the fulfillment of OT Messianic prophecy, the Levitical priesthood, the moral teachings, and the salvation promises of God concerning the Kingdom of God.

B. Second Movement: the apostles' *commentary* on Jesus' meaning in the NT writings, especially the book of Acts

1. They understood what Jesus said and provided us *commentary* on the meaning of Jesus' explanation in their teaching and preaching.

2. The Epistles and Acts contain quotations which reveal their commentary on Jesus' explanations.

C. Third Movement: the Church's *application* of the apostles' commentary of Jesus' understanding of the Scriptures

1. We embrace the apostolic tradition and teaching as they enable us as believers to know the relationship of the OT to the NT.

2. One of the most significant truths regarding the promise is the inclusion of Gentiles in the covenant promise of Abraham.

3. We as Christian leaders and ministers must understand precisely and carefully what God's intent is in including Gentiles in this salvation.

4. Gentiles are included within the Messianic prophecies quoted and written by the apostles. These give us a clear understanding in the relationship of Gentiles to the covenant promise of God.

II. The Messianic Promise Universalized: Gentile Inclusion in the Hope of Messiah

According to Paul, God in this era is now making known a mystery which stands at the very center of what he is seeking to reveal to humankind regarding his intention to save a people for himself in Jesus Christ.

A. The mystery now revealed: Gentile participation in the covenant as fellow heirs and citizens

1. The revelation of the mystery disclosed through the prophetic writings [in the apostles' teaching], Rom. 16.25-27

2. The greatness of the riches of this mystery among the Gentiles, Col. 1.24-27

3. Gentiles are fellow heirs and members of the same body, Eph. 3.4-6.

B. Clues of the universal Gospel in the OT's witness to Christ

1. The *seed of the woman* would destroy the serpent, Gen. 3.15.

2. In Abraham, *all the families of the earth* would be blessed, Gen. 12.1-3.

3. Messiah's life and ministry would be *a Light to the Gentiles*, Isa. 49.6.

4. God would be sought by a *nation not called by his name.*

Gentiles, the Wild Tree, Grafted Into the People of God by Faith

In Romans 11.17–24 the Gentiles are identified with the wild olive tree in contrast to the good olive tree. The olive tree was one of the most extensively cultivated fruit trees in the Mediterranean region and an important source of revenue (1 Sam. 8.14; 2 Kings 5.26). Israel is pictured as an olive tree in the OT: "The Lord called you a thriving olive tree with fruit beautiful in form" (Jer. 11.16 NIV; see also Hos. 14.6). It signifies their spiritual blessing, prosperity and beauty (cf. Ps. 52.8; 128.3). For Paul, in contrast, the wild olive tree, which by nature bears small and worthless fruit, is emblematic of the unfruitfulness of the Gentiles. The Gentile Christians, however, are now engrafted into the cultivated olive tree, the (believing) Jews.

~ Leland Ryken. *Dictionary of Biblical Imagery*. (electronic ed.) Downers Grove, IL: InterVarsity Press, 2000, pp. 324-325.

4

a. Isa. 65.1

b. Isa. 55.5

5. *All the ends of the earth* would remember and turn to the Lord, Ps. 22.27.

6. *All the nations* would flow in the latter days into the house of the Lord, Isa. 2.2-3.

7. In that day [the day of God's vindication and glory] *Messiah would be a Signal for the peoples of the world*, Isa. 11.10.

Jesus Is the Hinge between the Salvation of Israel and Hope of the Nations

The Gentile mission of the early church is another important clue to an understanding of the aims of Jesus. Scholars who have researched the question we started with in this chapter, 'What were Jesus' aims and intentions?,' point out that at least part of the answer is found by noticing what immediately preceded and what very quickly followed his ministry. John the Baptist came first. And all the New Testament traditions stress that Jesus began his ministry from John. We have already seen how that indicates that Jesus shared John's vision that the expected restoration of Israel was being accomplished. And very soon after his death, we find that the little group Jesus left behind had become a dynamic movement committed to taking the good news to the Gentile nations, willing to face all the problems that it caused–practical, geographical, cultural and theological. Jesus was launched by a revival movement for the restoration of Israel. He launched a movement for the blessing of the nations. He himself, therefore, was the hinge, the vital link between the two great movements. He was the climax and fulfillment of the hope of Israel and the beginning of the hope of the nations.

~ Christopher J. H. Wright. **Knowing Jesus Through the Old Testament.** Downers Grove, IL: InterVarsity Press, 1992. p. 166.

4

C. Implications of this strand of prophecy concerning Gentiles and the promise

1. Though clues were present, the promise of Messiah was interpreted as a Jewish hope (with Gentile inclusion by proselytization).

2. Even the apostles were hesitant to include Gentiles in their proclamation of the Good News and welcome into the people of God (e.g., Peter and Cornelius, Acts 10-11).

3. The time of Jesus and the apostles was a *kyros* moment (i.e., a time of critical importance).

   a. The display of the Messiah in fulfillment of the promise, Gal. 4.4-5 (cf. Mark 1.15)

   b. The outpouring of the Holy Spirit on those who believed

      (1) Acts 2.17-21

      (2) Joel 2.28-32

   c. The full explanation of the Gentiles as fellow heirs and citizens in the salvation promise given to Abraham, cf. Eph. 3.4-6

Israel and the Church

Unlike some interpreters today, Paul does not regard God's promises to ethnic Israel as cancelled—only deferred (cf. Deut. 4.25–31); God still had a covenant with the fathers (Deut. 7.8). Most readers today subscribe to one of two systems: Israel and the church are separate and irreconcilable entities, and Israel will be restored; or Christians become the true Israel and ethnic Israel has no more purpose in God's plan. Paul would have rejected both extremes, believing that ethnic Israel as a whole would return to the covenant in the end time, joining the Gentiles and Jewish remnant that already participate in it.
~ Craig S. Keener. *The IVP Bible Background Commentary: New Testament* (Rom. 11.28). (electronic ed.). Downers Grove, IL: IVP, 1993.

III. The Apostolic Testimony of the Promise Universalized: OT Messianic Predictions in Acts and the Epistles

A. Gentile inclusion in OT Messianic prophecy in Acts

1. The outpouring of the Holy Spirit upon all flesh, Joel 2.28-32

a. The day of Pentecost, Acts 2.17-21

b. Cornelius and his party, Acts 10.44-45

2. The rejection of Messiah from the "builders," (Jewish leaders)

a. Jesus as the *rejected cornerstone*

(1) Ps. 118.22

(2) Acts 4.11

b. The *royal rejection* of Messiah, Ps. 2.1-2, Acts 4.24-26

3. Jesus as *a Light for the Gentiles*

a. Isa. 49.6

b. Acts 13.47

4

4. The rebuilding of the *tent of David* will include *Gentile salvation.*

    a. Amos 9.11-12

    b. Acts 15.14-18

5. The *Messianic blindness* of God's people (the Jews) due to their hardness of heart

    a. Isa. 6.9-10

    b. Acts 28.25-29

B. Gentile inclusion in OT Messianic prophecy in the Epistles (Romans and Galatians)

1. Global proclamation of the Gospel

    a. Rom. 10. 15

    b. Isa. 52.7

    c. Nah. 1.15

2. Provoking the Jews to jealousy

   a. Deut. 32.21

   b. Rom. 10.19

3. Israel being disobedient and blind to the Messianic truth

   a. Disobedient

      (1) Isa. 65.1-2

      (2) Rom. 10.20-21

   b. Blind

      (1) Ps. 69.22-23

      (2) Rom. 11.8-10

4. Salvation of the Gentiles

   a. Ps. 18.49

   b. Deut. 32.43

   c. Ps. 117.1

   d. Isa. 11.10

e. Isa. 52.15

f. Rom. 15.9-12

5. Blessing of Abraham on the Gentiles

a. Gen. 12.3

b. Gal. 3.8

C. Implications of the theme of Gentile inclusion in OT Messianic prophecy in Acts and the Epistles

1. The approach of Jesus' *explanation* of OT Messianic predictions concerning himself and the apostles' *commentary* on what Jesus meant is elaborated throughout the Scriptures.

2. The OT witness to Christ and his Kingdom includes Gentile salvation and blessing.

3. The fullness of this meaning has now been made clear since the time of the apostles, that Gentiles are fellow heirs of the promise of Abraham by faith in the shed blood of Christ.

4. The OT Messianic prediction *universalizes the promise of God*, broadening the hope of Messiah from the particular history of Israel to include all nations and peoples who will call on the name of the Lord.

The Nations Will All Come to Know the Lord

Jer. 16.19-21
O Lord, my strength and my stronghold, my refuge in the day of trouble, to you shall the nations come from the ends of the earth and say: "Our fathers have inherited nothing but lies, worthless things in which there is no profit. [20] Can man make for himself gods? Such are not gods!" [21] "Therefore, behold, I will make them know, this once I will make them know my power and my might, and they shall know that my name is the Lord."

5. *Jesus of Nazareth* is this Messiah spoken of in Scripture.

   John 1.45-46 - Philip found Nathanael and said to him, "We have found him of whom Moses in the Law and also the prophets wrote, Jesus of Nazareth, the son of Joseph." [46] Nathanael said to him, "Can anything good come out of Nazareth?" Philip said to him, "Come and see."

Conclusion

» The OT provides a solid, clear, and compelling witness to Jesus Christ.

» Through his covenant promise, God extended the blessings of Abraham to the Gentiles, to all who believe in Jesus Christ as Messiah.

» The Word of God, in both the Old and New Testaments, makes plain that it is God's intention to save from among all humankind, both Jews and Gentiles, a people that will belong to him forever.

» Now, in light of this great salvation, we have been given the privilege and solemn duty to make disciples of Jesus among all people groups, so every people and nation can hear of our God's promise to save, and his fulfillment of that promise in Jesus Christ.

May God give us the grace, vision, and energy to be true to this call and take the Good News of the promise of salvation to the very ends of the earth. To him be all glory and honor, amen, and amen!

Christ Shall Have Dominion

Christ shall have dominion over land and sea
Earth's remotest regions shall His empire be;
They that wilds inhabit shall their worship bring
Kings shall render tribute, nations serve our King.

When the needy seek Him He will mercy show;
Yea, the weak and helpless shall His pity know;
He will surely save them from oppression's might
For their lives are precious in His holy sight.

Ever and forever shall His name endure
Long as suns continue it shall stand secure;
And in Him forever all men shall be blest,
And all nations hail Him King of Kings confessed.

Unto God Almighty joyful Zion sings;
He alone is glorious, doing wondrous things,
Evermore ye people, bless His glorious name;
His eternal glory through the earth proclaim.

~ John Gross, 1871

Segue 2

Student Questions and Response

The following questions were designed to help you review the material in the second video segment. We saw in this section that the Messianic prophecies of the OT disclose God's extension of the promise and blessings of Abraham *to the Gentiles*, to all who believe in Jesus Christ as Messiah. We saw how the NT uses OT Messianic prophecy in three interrelated ways, in Jesus' *explanation* of the OT predictions about himself, in the apostles' *commentary* on Jesus' meaning in the NT writings, especially in the preaching of the book of Acts, and later through the Church's *application* of the apostles' commentary of Jesus' understanding of the OT. The mystery that was hidden in past ages and times is now revealed through the prophets and the apostles: Gentiles are *fellow heirs* of the covenant and heirs of salvation. Making the Good News universal for all peoples is one of the great theological foundations of salvation, missions, and ministry. Therefore, you must understand and be able to articulate these truths in every phase and portion of your ministry. Carefully review the key points covered in the last section by answering the questions below.

1. To begin with, what should we expect to find if we engage in a serious, exegetical study of OT Messianic prophecy about the relationship of God's promise to Abraham and his desire to save the Gentiles? Explain.

2. What are the three critical movements in the NT's use of OT Messianic prophecy? How do these help us understand the primacy of Jesus' views regarding the meaning and application of the OT to himself? Explain.

3. Explain carefully how the Abrahamic covenant promise was universalized to all nations, how it was brought out in the apostolic citations of the "mystery" that has been unveiled in this age through the apostles and prophets (cf. Rom. 16.25-27; Eph. 3.1-10; Col. 1.25-27). What clues of this mystery are given in the actual prophecies about the coming Messiah and his work?

4. What are some of the various strands of OT Messianic prophecy that the apostles referred to and understood to represent that God's salvation is meant *for all peoples*, and not merely for the physical descendants of Abraham?

5. How do the apostles' preaching of OT Messianic prophecies in Acts and their instruction about them in the Epistles reveal their developing understanding of Gentile inclusion in the faith? What were some of the more important citations they referred to on this theme?

6. In what ways did the apostles believe that Gentile inclusion was not meant to cast off Israel from salvation, but rather to provoke them to jealousy to come to Messiah Jesus, even as the Gentiles were doing?

7. Explain *in only one sentence* how the OT Messianic prophecies regarding the Gentiles show the plan and purpose of God for the nations, not just for the Jews but for the Gentiles as well.

CONNECTION

Summary of Key Concepts

This lesson focuses upon the role that OT Messianic prophecy plays in giving prophetic and predictive truth about the Messiah, and also about God's plan to include the Gentiles in his covenant of salvation blessing to Abraham. In a real sense, OT Messianic prophecy provides some of the clearest and strongest linkage of the Old to the New Testament, both in terms of the nature and character of the Messianic person and work of Christ and in the unveiling of God's purpose to draw out for himself a people from all the nations, not just from the physical descendants of Abraham. Review these important insights on the role and scope of OT Messianic prophecy below.

- The term for Messiah in the Greek is *messias*, the Aramaic form of the Hebrew *mashiach*, which means "to anoint"; *Christos* is the equivalent NT terminology meaning "anointed one."

- The OT Messianic prophecy includes a handful of basic characteristics, including its focus on the deliverance of God's people, its strong use of figurative language, its predictions in the "prophetic perfect" tense (as if they were already accomplished), and their lack of easy-to-understand timetables as to their precise fulfilment. The main characteristic is its linkage of the testaments to Jesus Christ as the fulfillment of its prophetic descriptions.

- The key to tracing the Messiah's *family lineage* is following the clues from the beginning of Messianic prophecy, which includes the seed of the woman in Genesis, the promise of God's dwelling in the tents of Seth, the seed of Abraham, the lineage of Isaac through the house of Jacob, of the tribe and clan of Judah, through Boaz, Obed, Jesse and David, down to the person of Jesus of Nazareth.

- In many ways, tracing the themes in OT Messianic prophecy is key to understanding the OT witness to Christ. It is the way that Jesus and the apostles applied the OT to his life—these prophecies illumine our understanding of the way Jesus used the OT, they directly connect the testaments (in the way Augustine suggested, that the OT is revealed in the NT), and finally, they show that Jesus of Nazareth fulfills the prophetic predictions of the expected Messiah.

- The main points included in the OT Messianic prophecies covering his birth include prophecies about the prophetic forerunner, his birthplace at Bethlehem, and his identity as both the human-divine son Immanuel.

- The main OT Messianic prophetic predictions were about his person and life, i.e., his introduction by the coming "voice in the wilderness," his divine status as Wonderful, Counselor, Mighty God, Everlasting Father, and Prince of peace, his anointing as the Servant of Yahweh, and his anticipated kingship and reign. Prophecies of Messiah's life also include his role as the cornerstone of God's salvific work, his role as light for the Gentiles, and his role as prophet, priest, and king.

- OT Messianic prophecies also address the *passion* of Christ, his suffering and death, and among them mention is made of his betrayal, his false trial and verdict, his brutal treatment and death, his vicarious (substitutionary) wounding and bruising for the sins of the world, his crucifixion, his great agony on the cross, his death, and his burial.

- The major OT texts quoted in the NT concerning Messiah's resurrection are usually included in the Gospel accounts and their predictions of it, as well in the apostolic preaching in Acts, especially in Peter's sermon at Pentecost and Paul's preaching at Antioch.

- A general outline of some of the key OT Messianic texts should include predictions of the coming glory of Messiah, his exaltation and vindication as Yahweh's King of glory, his terrifying judgment upon God's enemies, his return for and regathering of his people, the majesty, beauty, and glory of creation's transformation that will occur under his reign, and the everlasting and universal dominion that will be given to him.

- A serious study of OT Messianic prophecy reveals that God has extended the promise and blessings of Abraham to the Gentiles, to all who believe in Jesus Christ as Messiah.

- The three critical movements in the NT's use of OT Messianic prophecy include 1) Jesus' *explanation* of the OT predictions about himself, 2) the apostles' *commentary* on Jesus' meaning in the NT writings, especially in the preaching of the book of Acts, and 3) the Church's *application* of the apostles' commentary of Jesus' understanding of the OT.

- The Abrahamic covenant promise was universalized to all nations by the inclusion of Gentile salvation in the Messianic hope. This promise includes the unveiling of the mystery that Gentiles are fellow heirs of the covenant and heirs of salvation. Clues are given prophetically of this inclusion throughout Scripture, including the *protoevangelium*, the promise that all the families of the earth will be blessed in Abraham, and the prediction that Messiah would be a light to all the Gentiles.

- Various strands of OT Messianic prophecy were progressively understood by the apostles to represent God's salvation for all peoples, including predictions such as the promise of the outpouring of the Spirit on all flesh and full inclusion of Gentiles as fellow heirs of the Abrahamic promise.

- The apostolic use of OT Messianic prophecies in their preaching as recorded in Acts and the Epistles reveal their developing understanding of Gentile inclusion in the faith. They cite, among other things, the outpouring of the Spirit on all flesh, the rejection of Messiah by the builders (Jewish generation), Jesus as light for the Gentiles, the rebuilding of the tent of David including Gentile salvation, and the Messianic blindness of God's people (the Jews) due to their hardness of heart. Also, they mention the global proclamation of the Gospel, the provoking of the Jews to jealousy, and the blessing of Abraham on the Gentiles.

- The OT Messianic prophecies regarding the Gentiles show the plan and purpose of God for the nations; not only has God fulfilled his promise for salvation to Abraham, but he also includes the salvation of the Gentiles in that salvation promise.

4

Student Application and Implications

Now is the time for you to discuss with your fellow students your questions about the role and power of OT Messianic prophecy to illumine our understanding of the Messiah's person and work, and God's intention to provide salvation for the nations through the promise of Abraham. Again, more than any other section in our lesson, this section will be determined by the kinds of questions, concerns, and issues that emerged as a result of your meditation and discussion. What is sought here is your *application* of these truths to your life. The significance of these issues cannot be wasted just in discussions about abstract truth; God intends for us to be transformed by insights. Use the questions below to explore your own specific and personal concerns brought out in the lesson.

* How often do you refer to Jesus as the *Messiah*, the one anointed of God to both save and judge the world? Does referring to him as *Messiah* make any difference at all in how you think of him (Messiah, remember, is the *Hebraic reference* to Jesus)?

* Have you ever done a comprehensive study of OT Messianic prophecy? Where and with whom? When was the last time you spent serious time studying and thinking critically about the relationship of OT prophecy to the person of Jesus?

* What is your attitude regarding the prophetic *genre* (type) of Scripture? Have you ever been involved in the kinds of study that put a premium on trying to identify the general dates and timetables associated with them? Have you ever been confused by these discussions, and how did they end up?

* Do you study prophecy with the intent *first of all* to find the way they link the teaching of the OT with what we know about Messiah in the person of Jesus of Nazareth, as revealed in the NT? Could you reproduce and trace the Messianic *family lineage* by referring to the various prophecies in the OT, beginning with the seed of the woman in Genesis 3.15, and ending with the birth of Messiah, Jesus of Nazareth in the NT?

* What is your opinion about the importance of the themes in OT Messianic prophecy as they relate to the OT's witness to Christ? In other words, how important are they, and why?

* What difference does it make to you that Jesus and the apostles applied the OT prophecies directly to his life, and how might this give you confidence that seeking to use this method may help your understanding of the OT's witness to Christ?

* How many prophecies can you reproduce about the OT Messianic prophecies covering his birth, life and ministry, death, resurrection, and coming glory? (Take out a piece of paper and list all the ones you *know* from

memory; don't be concerned about the "address" of the verse; *focus on what the prophecy states about Messiah*). How would you grade yourself here?

* Do you see any dangers at all in focusing on the OT Messianic prophecies *without studying them alongside their NT fulfillment*? Explain.

* Why do you think so many who have been part of cults, sects, and fringe groups have been attracted to prophecy? What does this say to you (if anything) about being careful and responsible in all your study and exegesis of the Bible?

* Is it possible to read the OT properly (i.e., either devotionally, doctrinally, or for ministry) and ignore the major OT texts about the Messiah? Explain your answer *carefully*.

* Read the following NT texts regarding the prophetic word, and after reading them, summarize your view on the role of OT prophecy *through the lens of the apostolic witness to it.*

 2 Pet. 1.19-21 - And we have something more sure, the prophetic word, to which you will do well to pay attention as to a lamp shining in a dark place, until the day dawns and the morning star rises in your hearts, [20] knowing this first of all, that no prophecy of Scripture comes from someone's own interpretation. [21] For no prophecy was ever produced by the will of man, but men spoke from God as they were carried along by the Holy Spirit.

 Luke 16.29-31 - But Abraham said, "They have Moses and the Prophets; let them hear them." [30] And he said, "No, father Abraham, but if someone goes to them from the dead, they will repent." [31] He said to him, "If they do not hear Moses and the Prophets, neither will they be convinced if someone should rise from the dead."

* Finish the following statement: "If I am to better master the OT Messianic prophetic witness to Christ, *the one thing I am going to have to learn is how to . . .*"

CASE STUDIES

Great Expectations Gone Wrong

Although every informed Christian would recognize the significance of Messianic prophecy in the ongoing theology, worship, and ministry of the Church, many have serious reservations on how much this ought to be emphasized as the core of Christian belief. For instance, a number of cults today rely heavily on prophetic visions and texts to make their claims about their own peculiar brand of Christian faith. The "Heaven's Gate" cult of not too many years ago was essentially an eschatological (i.e., oriented around the end times) cult, with a full and steady diet of prophetic material which was twisted by their leaders to produce strange and tragic consequences to those who followed it. Likewise, the cult of Jim Jones and the People's Church ultimately destroyed itself rooted in Rev. Jones's bizarre interpretation of the prophetic texts, as did David Koresh and the Branch Davidian group. In many cases of weird, strange, and unbiblical community, one can trace its founding and flourishing to false, misleading interpretations of prophetic Scripture. What is the role of Messianic prophetic Scripture in the worship and preaching of the Church, and how do we avoid these weird and false interpretations as shown through the tragic cases above?

Focusing on the Future Can Dull Your Passion for Justice

(Based on a true story). In a discussion about social justice with a progressive urban ministry and its leaders, one of the key leaders made several critical points on the nature of the motive of urban ministry. She asked the question, "Of all the various motives that underlie genuine justice and peace seeking in the city, what virtue or mindset is most helpful and important to possess?" Those in attendance gave a number of different answers: love, compassion, faith, and resolve. After a brief discussion of these, the Director suggested in her calm and clear voice: "Although the various emotions and motivations that you listed are important and contribute to justice seeking, no motivation is as critical as anger. A true hatred of oppression and evil can provide you with all of the necessary courage and energy to wrestle with the forces that will seek to undermine your efforts and sustain its cruel abuse of others." In further discussion someone in the forum suggested that the prophetic Word and its vision of the Messianic Kingdom to come could also fuel such justice work without the unintended consequences of anger. Upon hearing this, the Director responded, "Unfortunately, focusing on theological visions of the future can undermine the kind of focus you need to deal with issues before you here and now. Candidly, I have found that overmuch dwelling on the future can actually dull your passion for seeking justice right here and right now." What do you think about the Director's opinion of the role of prophetic vision, especially the Messianic prophetic vision to in some cases undermine efforts toward justice seeking?

Including the Unlovely and Hard-to-Fit-Ins

3

An aggressive outreach among punk rock culture has been bearing fruit in a downtown church. Through a series of aggressive outreaches to youth in the downtown area of a major American city, a number of street kids have come to the Lord. These are striking people: they are in their early and late twenties, heavily tattooed and pierced, and certainly not conservative in culture or background. Yet, it is clear that they have made authentic commitments to Christ as Lord, and truly desire to learn what it means to be a 21st century disciple of Jesus. One of the things that has been instrumental to so many of them coming to the church and its evangelistic outreaches is the emphasis on freedom. The leaders of the efforts have preached fervently and brilliantly God's intention to include Gentiles in his mercy, ordinary people from any place, non-religious, even the most unlovely and alienated can have a place in the Kingdom of God. The Lord used this message to attract these young people to the church, which has only begun to wrestle with what it will mean to bring them into full fellowship. The church, while open to all people, is largely a middle-class black church, and the vast majority of these kids are white, in love with rock music, and yet feel at home in the church. How would you advise the church to proceed in their own particular form of Gentile inclusion in their fellowship?

4

That's Over and Done With - We're Not Under the Law

4

Convicted by the total disregard in his preaching and teaching over the years on the "Judeo" side of the "Judeo-Christian heritage" of his faith, an urban pastor has determined to preach a series entitled "Jewish Roots: the Ground We Came From." His intent is to expose his congregation in his sermons, special services, and the next retreat to the specifically Jewish-informed practices of the early Church, enabling the people to see as clearly as possible the connection of the Christian faith to its Jewish foundations. After about three months into the preaching and teaching, the Pastor has invited all to the church fellowship hall for a "Passover Celebration." His intent is to walk the people through a Passover service, to explain all the dimensions of it, and show its connections to our Lord's Supper. In a recent Board meeting he shared his idea about the Passover, and one of the elders responded with a concerned look. "Pastor, I know that you want us to understand the Jewish Roots of our faith, and all. But, honestly, some of us are not seeing the point of all of this. We're not under the Law anymore; we've had 21 centuries of Christian faith and practice, and it has not been Jewish in most cases. I just don't see what you're getting at. Isn't that whole thing over and done with, I mean, the Jewish focus of the faith?" If you were the pastor, how would you answer the elder's honest question about the place of Jewish roots and Gentile salvation today?

Restatement of the Lesson's Thesis

A serious study of OT Messianic prophecy reveals that God has extended the promise and blessings of Abraham to the Gentiles, to all who believe in Jesus Christ as Messiah. The three critical movements in the NT's use of OT Messianic prophecy include 1) Jesus' *explanation* of the OT predictions about himself, 2) the apostles' *commentary* on Jesus' meaning in the NT writings, especially in the preaching of the book of Acts, and 3) the Church's *application* of the apostles' commentary of Jesus' understanding of the OT. God included the salvation of the Gentiles in the promise to Abraham. Now in this age God has unveiled the mystery that was hidden in past ages and times but now revealed through the prophets and the apostles, namely that Gentiles are fellow heirs of the covenant and heirs of salvation. Clues were given prophetically of this inclusion throughout Scripture, e.g., in the *protoevangelium* and God's promise to bless all the families of the earth in Abraham. The apostolic use of OT Messianic prophecies in their preaching as recorded in Acts and the Epistles reveal their developing understanding of Gentile inclusion in the faith. The OT Messianic prophecies regarding the Gentiles show the plan and purpose of God for the nations; not only has God fulfilled his promise for salvation to Abraham, but he also includes the salvation of the Gentiles in that salvation promise.

4

The term for Messiah in the Greek is *messias*, the Aramaic form of the Hebrew *mashiach*, which means "to anoint"; *Christos* is the equivalent NT terminology meaning "anointed one." The OT Messianic prophecy includes a handful of basic characteristics, including its focus on the deliverance of God's people, its strong use of figurative language, its predictions in the "prophetic perfect" tense (as if they were already accomplished), and their lack of easy-to-understand timetables as to their precise fulfilment. The main characteristic is its linkage of the testaments to Jesus Christ as the fulfillment of its prophetic descriptions. The key to tracing the Messiah's *family lineage* is following the clues from the beginning of Messianic prophecy, which includes the seed of the woman in Genesis, the promise of God's dwelling in the tents of Seth, the seed of Abraham, the lineage of Isaac through the house of Jacob, of the tribe and clan of Judah, through Boaz, Obed, Jesse and David, down to the person of Jesus of Nazareth. In many ways, tracing the themes in OT Messianic prophecy is key to understanding the OT witness to Christ. It is the way that Jesus and the apostles applied the OT to his life—these prophecies illumine our understanding of the way Jesus used the OT, they directly connect the testaments (in the way Augustine suggested, that the OT is revealed in the NT), and finally, they show that Jesus of Nazareth fulfills the prophetic predictions of the expected Messiah. The main points included in the OT Messianic prophecies cover his birth, his suffering and death, his resurrection, and his coming glory. In every way, the clear testimony of OT Messianic prophecy is that Jesus of Nazareth is the Messiah, providing a solid witness about his life, ministry, and coming Kingdom.

Resources and Bibliographies

If you are interested in pursuing some of the ideas of *The Promise Universalized*, you might want to give these books a try:

Brueggemann, Walter. *The Prophetic Imagination.* (rev. and updated ed.) Minneapolis, MN: Augsburg Fortress Publishers, 2001.

------. *Hopeful Imagination: Prophetic Voices in Exile.* Minneapolis, MN: Augsburg Fortress Publishers, 1986.

Clowney, Edmund P. *Preaching Christ in All Scripture.* Wheaton, IL: Crossway Books, 2003.

------. *The Unfolding Mystery: Discovering Christ in the Old Testament.* Phillipsburg, NJ: P & R Publishing, 1991.

Greidanus, Sidney. *Preaching Christ from the Old Testament: A Contemporary Hermeneutical Method.* Grand Rapids: Wm. B. Eerdmans Publishing Company, 1999.

Spurgeon, Charles H. *Christ in the Old Testament: Sermons on the Foreshadowings of Our Lord in Old Testament History, Ceremony, and Prophecy.* (Pulpit Legend Collection). Chattanooga, TN: AMG Publishers, 2001.

Ministry Connections

What is your motive for ministry–why do you do what you do? This lesson, as much as any in our Capstone module set, provides excellent reasons for ministry. Jesus of Nazareth in fact is the Messiah, and his saving message of life and forgiveness is available even to Gentiles who repent and believe. The certainty of the promise, the truth undergirding our life and work, the soon prospect of actually seeing the one for whom we have spent our lives in service ought to be motivation enough to master and apply the OT's Messianic prophetic vision to our lives.

Gerald Hawthorne speaks of this motivation of *ministry* to *prophetic vision* in reference to Paul:

> *Paul's motivation was multifaceted. He was essentially driven by a realization of the love of Christ for himself personally and for all humanity (2 Cor. 5.14–15; Gal. 2.20). Alongside this was his sense of obligation to carry out the apostolic commission which had been given to him (Rom. 1.14–15; 1 Cor. 9.16–17), and a realization that he must give an account of his life and work to God (1 Cor. 4.1–5; 2 Cor. 5.9–10). The apostle was motivated by a strong desire to see fellow Jews brought to a saving knowledge of Christ (Rom. 9.1–3; 10.1), and he hoped that his ministry among the Gentiles would make them jealous and so save some of them (Rom. 11.13–14). Paul developed a strong affection for his converts, and this made him want to share with them, not only the gospel but his own self also (1 Thess. 2.8). This affection made him want to visit them and pray for them (1 Thess. 2.17–20; 3.9–10), and to spend both his resources and himself for them (2 Cor. 12.15).*
>
> ~ Gerald F. Hawthorne. **Dictionary of Paul and His Letters.** (electronic ed.). Logos Library Systems. Downers Grove, IL: InterVarsity Press, 1997. p. 607.

The power of the OT Messianic prophecy to not simply be a kind of intriguing theological idea but (as it was for the apostles) a life changing radical truth, all comes down to your ability to understand the significance of it. If Jesus *is* Lord, and the OT prophecies of the Messiah *have come to pass in him, then all things are different in the world.* And frankly, should be different in your ministry.

Now, as this module of study winds down, you will be responsible to apply the insights of your module in a practicum that you and your mentor agree to. To share the truths you have gleaned from the rich variety of material covered in this lesson and module can have significant impact if presented clearly and boldly first in your own walk, and then in a clear and coherent manner to others. Thank God that the Spirit will oftentimes provide us with opportunities to apply the Word of God in numerous contexts: our walk with him, our prayers, our relationships at our church, on our jobs, or wherever he may lead.

The project will be your opportunity to share your insights with others, to correlate what you have learned into your life, work, and ministry. The ministry project is designed for this, and in the next days you will have the opportunity to share these insights in real-life, actual ministry environments. Pray that God will give you insight into his ways as you share your insights in your projects.

Counseling and Prayer

Ask God to transform your *heart* as well as your *thoughts* in dealing with this material. It is staggering that we now know *who the Messiah is*, and that *we have the eternal Word's guarantee that Jesus of Nazareth is the one!* If we truly believed this, wouldn't it transform our lives, our relationships, our worlds?! During our prayers let us plead with God to avoid the error of a heartless, empty kind of preaching and teaching that we all can become susceptible to:

> *We believe that one of the serious and most popular errors of the modern pulpit is the putting of more thought than prayer, of more head than of heart in its sermons. Big hearts make big preachers; good hearts make good preachers. A theological school to enlarge and cultivate the heart is the golden desideratum of the gospel. The pastor binds his people to him and rules his people by his heart. They may admire his gifts, they may be proud of his ability, they may be affected for the time by his sermons; but the stronghold of his power is his heart. His scepter is love. The throne of his power is his heart. The good shepherd gives his life for the sheep. Heads never make martyrs. It is the heart which surrenders the life to love and fidelity. It takes great courage to be a faithful pastor, but the heart alone can supply this courage. Gifts and genius may be brave, but it is the gifts and genius of the heart and not of the head. It is easier to fill the head than it is to prepare the heart.*
>
> ~ E. M. Bounds. **Power Through Prayer**.
> Oak Harbor, WA: Logos Research Systems, Inc., 1999.

Ask God not just to fill your heart, but to prepare your heart, to make you his minister who can declare with boldness and joy the remarkable truth about the coming of the Messiah into the world!

Scripture Memory

No assignment due.

Reading Assignment

No assignment due.

Other Assignments

Your ministry project and your exegetical project should now be outlined, determined, and accepted by your instructor. Make sure that you plan ahead, so you will not be late in turning in your assignments.

Final Exam Notice

The final will be a take home exam, and will include questions taken from the first three quizzes, new questions on material drawn from this lesson, and essay questions which will ask for your short answer responses to key integrating questions. Also, you should plan on reciting or writing out the verses memorized for the course on the exam. When you have completed your exam, please notify your mentor and make certain that they get your copy.

Please note: Your module grade cannot be determined if you do not take the final exam and turn in all outstanding assignments to your mentor (ministry project, exegetical project, and final exam).

The Last Word about this Module

4

Throughout this lesson, as in fact through this entire module, we have sought the rich character and universal scope of the OT's witness to Jesus Christ. In every phase of our study we have seen how the OT confirms that Jesus of Nazareth is the true Messiah and Lord of all. He and he alone fulfills, completes, and reveals the rich and diverse witnesses of the OT to Christ and his Kingdom. We have seen how the OT gives numerous and clear prophecies regarding the entire outline of Messiah's life and ministry, from his birth in Bethlehem to the coming glory of his Kingdom. We have seen God's resolve to save from among all humankind, both Jews and Gentiles, a people that will belong to him forever. We have learned of our solemn duty to make disciples of Jesus among all people groups, so every people and nation can hear of our God's promise to save, and his fulfillment of that promise in Jesus Christ.

In all the diverse ways the literature of the OT speaks–in its moral laws of righteousness, in its Tabernacle system with its priests, sacrifices, and festivals, in its numerous character and historical types, in its direct prophecies, and through the history of God's people–one, integrated, and compelling witness is made. Jesus Christ has fulfilled in every particular God's open revelation of whom the Messiah is, what he would do in redeeming his people, and what he will complete at his Second Coming. Jesus is correct: to search the Scriptures is to find *him*, for *truly and indeed*, they (the OT Scriptures) *testify* of him (John 5.39).

May God give to you and all of us the grace, vision, and energy to proclaim the message of both testaments, the truth of his Spirit-breathed Scripture, that Jesus Christ is Lord of all, to the Father's glory, till he come.

To him be the glory! Amen.

Appendices

APPENDIX 1

The Nicene Creed

Memory Verses ⇩

Rev. 4.11 (ESV) *Worthy are you, our Lord and God, to receive glory and honor and power, for you created all things, and by your will they existed and were created.*

John 1.1 (ESV) *In the beginning was the Word, and the Word was with God, and the Word was God.*

1 Cor.15.3-5 (ESV) *For what I received I passed on to you as of first importance: that Christ died for our sins according to the Scriptures, that he was buried, that he was raised on the third day according to the Scriptures, and that he appeared to Peter, and then to the Twelve.*

Rom. 8.11 (ESV) *If the Spirit of him who raised Jesus from the dead dwells in you, he who raised Christ Jesus from the dead will also give life to your mortal bodies through his Spirit who dwells in you.*

1 Pet. 2.9 (ESV) *But you are a chosen race, a royal priesthood, a holy nation, a people for his own possession, that you may proclaim the excellencies of him who called you out of darkness into his marvelous light.*

1 Thess. 4.16-17 (ESV) *For the Lord himself will descend from heaven with a cry of command, with the voice of an archangel, and with the sound of the trumpet of God. And the dead in Christ will rise first. Then we who are alive, who are left, will be caught up together with them in the clouds to meet the Lord in the air, and so we will always be with the Lord.*

We believe in one God, *(Deut. 6.4-5; Mark 12.29; 1 Cor. 8.6)*
the Father Almighty, *(Gen. 17.1; Dan. 4.35; Matt. 6.9; Eph. 4.6; Rev. 1.8)*
Maker of heaven and earth *(Gen 1.1; Isa. 40.28; Rev. 10.6)*
and of all things visible and invisible. *(Ps. 148; Rom. 11.36; Rev. 4.11)*

We believe in one Lord Jesus Christ, the only Begotten Son of God,
begotten of the Father before all ages,
God from God, Light from Light, True God from True God,
begotten not created,
of the same essence as the Father, *(John 1.1-2; 3.18; 8.58; 14.9-10; 20.28; Col. 1.15, 17; Heb. 1.3-6)*
through whom all things were made. *(John 1.3; Col. 1.16)*

Who for us men and for our salvation came down from heaven
and was incarnate by the Holy Spirit and the virgin Mary
and became human. *(Matt. 1.20-23; John 1.14; 6.38; Luke 19.10)*
Who for us too, was crucified under Pontius Pilate,
suffered, and was buried. *(Matt. 27.1-2; Mark 15.24-39, 43-47; Acts 13.29; Rom. 5.8; Heb. 2.10; 13.12)*
The third day he rose again
according to the Scriptures, *(Mark 16.5-7; Luke 24.6-8; Acts 1.3; Rom. 6.9; 10.9; 2 Tim. 2.8)*
ascended into heaven,
and is seated at the right hand of the Father. *(Mark 16.19; Eph. 1.19-20)*
He will come again in glory
to judge the living and the dead,
and his Kingdom will have no end.
(Isa. 9.7; Matt. 24.30; John 5.22; Acts 1.11; 17.31; Rom. 14.9; 2 Cor. 5.10; 2 Tim. 4.1)

We believe in the Holy Spirit, the Lord and life-giver,
(Gen. 1.1-2; Job 33.4; Ps. 104.30; 139.7-8; Luke 4.18-19; John 3.5-6; Acts 1.1-2; 1 Cor. 2.11; Rev. 3.22)
who proceeds from the Father and the Son, *(John 14.16-18, 26; 15.26; 20.22)*
who together with the Father and Son
is worshiped and glorified, *(Isa. 6.3; Matt. 28.19; 2 Cor. 13.14; Rev. 4.8)*
who spoke by the prophets. *(Num. 11.29; Mic. 3.8; Acts 2.17-18; 2 Pet. 1.21)*

We believe in one holy, catholic, and apostolic Church.
(Matt. 16.18; Eph. 5.25-28; 1 Cor. 1.2; 10.17; 1 Tim. 3.15; Rev. 7.9)

We acknowledge one baptism for the forgiveness of sin, *(Acts 22.16; 1 Pet. 3.21; Eph. 4.4-5)*
And we look for the resurrection of the dead
And the life of the age to come. *(Isa. 11.6-10; Mic. 4.1-7; Luke 18.29-30; Rev. 21.1-5; 21.22-22.5)*

Amen.

APPENDIX 2

We Believe: Confession of the Nicene Creed (8.7.8.7. meter*)

Rev. Dr. Don L. Davis, 2007. All Rights Reserved.

* This song is adapted from the Nicene Creed, and set to 8.7.8.7. meter, meaning it can be sung to tunes of the same meter, such as: *Joyful, Joyful, We Adore Thee; I Will Sing of My Redeemer; What a Friend We Have in Jesus; Come, Thou Long Expected Jesus*

Father God Almighty rules, the Maker of both earth and heav'n.
All things seen and those unseen, by him were made, by him were giv'n!
We believe in Jesus Christ, the Lord, God's one and only Son,
Begotten, not created, too, he and our Father God are one!

Begotten from the Father, same, in essence, as both God and Light;
Through him by God all things were made, in him all things were giv'n life.
Who for us all, for our salvation, did come down from heav'n to earth,
Incarnate by the Spirit's pow'r, and through the Virgin Mary's birth.

Who for us too, was crucified, by Pontius Pilate's rule and hand,
Suffered, and was buried, yet on the third day, he rose again.
According to the Sacred Scriptures all that happ'ned was meant to be.
Ascended high to God's right hand, in heav'n he sits in glory.

Christ will come again in glory to judge all those alive and dead.
His Kingdom rule shall never end, for he will rule and reign as Head.
We worship God, the Holy Spirit, Lord and the Life-giver known;
With Fath'r and Son is glorified, Who by the prophets ever spoke.

And we believe in one true Church, God's holy people for all time,
Cath'lic in its scope and broadness, built on the Apostles' line!
Acknowledging that one baptism, for forgiv'ness of our sin,
And we look for Resurrection, for the dead shall live again.

Looking for unending days, the life of the bright Age to come,
When Christ's Reign shall come to earth, the will of God shall then be done!
Praise to God, and to Christ Jesus, to the Spirit–triune Lord!
We confess the ancient teachings, clinging to God's holy Word!

APPENDIX 3

The Story of God: Our Sacred Roots

Rev. Dr. Don L. Davis

The Alpha and the Omega	Christus Victor	Come, Holy Spirit	Your Word Is Truth	The Great Confession	His Life in Us	Living in the Way	Reborn to Serve
The LORD God is the source, sustainer, and end of all things in the heavens and earth. All things were formed and exist by his will and for his eternal glory, the triune God, Father, Son, and Holy Spirit, Rom. 11.36.							
THE TRIUNE GOD'S UNFOLDING DRAMA **God's Self-Revelation in Creation, Israel, and Christ**				THE CHURCH'S PARTICIPATION IN GOD'S UNFOLDING DRAMA **Fidelity to the Apostolic Witness to Christ and His Kingdom**			
The Objective Foundation: The Sovereign Love of God ***God's Narration of His Saving Work in Christ***				**The Subjective Practice: Salvation by Grace through Faith** ***The Redeemed's Joyous Response to God's Saving Work in Christ***			
The Author of the Story	*The Champion* of the Story	*The Interpreter* of the Story	*The Testimony* of the Story	*The People* of the Story	*Re-enactment* of the Story	*Embodiment* of the Story	*Continuation* of the Story
The Father as *Director*	Jesus as *Lead Actor*	The Spirit as *Narrator*	Scripture as *Script*	As Saints, *Confessors*	As Worshipers, *Ministers*	As Followers, *Sojourners*	As Servants, *Ambassadors*
Christian *Worldview*	Communal *Identity*	Spiritual *Experience*	Biblical *Authority*	Orthodox *Theology*	Priestly *Worship*	Congregational *Discipleship*	Kingdom *Witness*
Theistic and Trinitarian Vision	Christ-centered Foundation	Spirit-Indwelt and -Filled Community	Canonical and Apostolic Witness	Ancient Creedal Affirmation of Faith	Weekly Gathering in Christian Assembly	Corporate, Ongoing Spiritual Formation	Active Agents of the Reign of God
Sovereign Willing	Messianic Representing	Divine Comforting	Inspired Testifying	Truthful Retelling	Joyful Excelling	Faithful Indwelling	Hopeful Compelling
Creator True Maker of the Cosmos	**Recapitulation** Typos and Fulfillment of the Covenant	**Life-Giver** Regeneration and Adoption	**Divine Inspiration** God-breathed Word	**The Confession of Faith** Union with Christ	**Song and Celebration** Historical Recitation	**Pastoral Oversight** Shepherding the Flock	**Explicit Unity** Love for the Saints
Owner Sovereign Disposer of Creation	**Revealer** Incarnation of the Word	**Teacher** Illuminator of the Truth	**Sacred History** Historical Record	**Baptism into Christ** Communion of Saints	**Homilies and Teachings** Prophetic Proclamation	**Shared Spirituality** Common Journey through the Spiritual Disciplines	**Radical Hospitality** Evidence of God's Kingdom Reign
Ruler Blessed Controller of All Things	**Redeemer** Reconciler of All Things	**Helper** Endowment and the Power	**Biblical Theology** Divine Commentary	**The Rule of Faith** Apostles' Creed and Nicene Creed	**The Lord's Supper** Dramatic Re-enactment	**Embodiment** Anamnesis and Prolepsis through the Church Year	**Extravagant Generosity** Good Works
Covenant Keeper Faithful Promisor	**Restorer** Christ, the Victor over the powers of evil	**Guide** Divine Presence and Shekinah	**Spiritual Food** Sustenance for the Journey	**The Vincentian Canon** Ubiquity, antiquity, universality	**Eschatological Foreshadowing** The Already/Not Yet	**Effective Discipling** Spiritual Formation in the Believing Assembly	**Evangelical Witness** Making Disciples of All People Groups

APPENDIX 4

The Theology of Christus Victor

A Christ-Centered Biblical Motif for Integrating and Renewing the Urban Church

Rev. Dr. Don L. Davis

	The Promised Messiah	The Word Made Flesh	The Son of Man	The Suffering Servant	The Lamb of God	The Victorious Conqueror	The Reigning Lord in Heaven	The Bridegroom and Coming King
Biblical Framework	Israel's hope of Yahweh's anointed who would redeem his people	In the person of Jesus of Nazareth, the Lord has come to the world	As the promised king and divine Son of Man, Jesus reveals the Father's glory and salvation to the world	As Inaugurator of the Kingdom of God, Jesus demonstrates God's reign present through his words, wonders, and works	As both High Priest and Paschal Lamb, Jesus offers himself to God on our behalf as a sacrifice for sin	In his resurrection from the dead and ascension to God's right hand, Jesus is proclaimed as Victor over the power of sin and death	Now reigning at God's right hand till his enemies are made his footstool, Jesus pours out his benefits on his body	Soon the risen and ascended Lord will return to gather his Bride, the Church, and consummate his work
Scripture References	Isa. 9.6-7 Jer. 23.5-6 Isa. 11.1-10	John 1.14-18 Matt. 1.20-23 Phil. 2.6-8	Matt. 2.1-11 Num. 24.17 Luke 1.78-79	Mark 1.14-15 Matt. 12.25-30 Luke 17.20-21	2 Cor. 5.18-21 Isa. 52-53 John 1.29	Eph. 1.16-23 Phil. 2.5-11 Col. 1.15-20	1 Cor. 15.25 Eph. 4.15-16 Acts. 2.32-36	Rom. 14.7-9 Rev. 5.9-13 1 Thess. 4.13-18
Jesus' History	The pre-incarnate, only begotten Son of God in glory	His conception by the Spirit, and birth to Mary	His manifestation to the Magi and to the world	His teaching, exorcisms, miracles, and mighty works among the people	His suffering, crucifixion, death, and burial	His resurrection, with appearances to his witnesses, and his ascension to the Father	The sending of the Holy Spirit and his gifts, and Christ's session in heaven at the Father's right hand	His soon return from heaven to earth as Lord and Christ: the Second Coming
Description	The biblical promise for the seed of Abraham, the prophet like Moses, the son of David	In the Incarnation, God has come to us; Jesus reveals to humankind the Father's glory in fullness	In Jesus, God has shown his salvation to the entire world, including the Gentiles	In Jesus, the promised Kingdom of God has come visibly to earth, demonstrating his binding of Satan and rescinding the Curse	As God's perfect Lamb, Jesus offers himself up to God as a sin offering on behalf of the entire world	In his resurrection and ascension, Jesus destroyed death, disarmed Satan, and rescinded the Curse	Jesus is installed at the Father's right hand as Head of the Church, Firstborn from the dead, and supreme Lord in heaven	As we labor in his harvest field in the world, so we await Christ's return, the fulfillment of his promise
Church Year	**Advent**	**Christmas**	**Season after Epiphany** Baptism and Transfiguration	**Lent**	**Holy Week** Passion	**Eastertide** Easter, Ascension Day, Pentecost	**Season after Pentecost** Trinity Sunday	**Season after Pentecost** All Saints Day, Reign of Christ the King
	The Coming of Christ	*The Birth of Christ*	*The Manifestation of Christ*	*The Ministry of Christ*	*The Suffering and Death of Christ*	*The Resurrection and Ascension of Christ*	*The Heavenly Session of Christ*	*The Reign of Christ*
Spiritual Formation	As we await his Coming, let us proclaim and affirm the hope of Christ	O Word made flesh, let us every heart prepare him room to dwell	Divine Son of Man, show the nations your salvation and glory	In the person of Christ, the power of the reign of God has come to earth and to the Church	May those who share the Lord's death be resurrected with him	Let us participate by faith in the victory of Christ over the power of sin, Satan, and death	Come, indwell us, Holy Spirit, and empower us to advance Christ's Kingdom in the world	We live and work in expectation of his soon return, seeking to please him in all things

APPENDIX 5

Christus Victor

An Integrated Vision for the Christian Life

Rev. Dr. Don L. Davis

For the Church

- The Church is the primary extension of Jesus in the world
- Ransomed treasure of the victorious, risen Christ
- *Laos:* The people of God
- God's new creation: presence of the future
- Locus and agent of the Already/Not Yet Kingdom

For Theology and Doctrine

- The authoritative Word of Christ's victory: the Apostolic Tradition: the Holy Scriptures
- Theology as commentary on the grand narrative of God
- *Christus Victor* as core theological framework for meaning in the world
- The Nicene Creed: the Story of God's triumphant grace

For Spirituality

- The Holy Spirit's presence and power in the midst of God's people
- Sharing in the disciplines of the Spirit
- Gatherings, lectionary, liturgy, and our observances in the Church Year
- Living the life of the risen Christ in the rhythm of our ordinary lives

Christus Victor

Destroyer of Evil and Death
Restorer of Creation
Victor o'er Hades and Sin
Crusher of Satan

For Gifts

- God's gracious endowments and benefits from *Christus Victor*
- Pastoral offices to the Church
- The Holy Spirit's sovereign dispensing of the gifts
- Stewardship: divine, diverse gifts for the common good

For Worship

- People of the Resurrection: unending celebration of the people of God
- Remembering, participating in the Christ event in our worship
- Listen and respond to the Word
- Transformed at the Table, the Lord's Supper
- The presence of the Father through the Son in the Spirit

For Evangelism and Mission

- Evangelism as unashamed declaration and demonstration of *Christus Victor* to the world
- The Gospel as Good News of kingdom pledge
- We proclaim God's Kingdom come in the person of Jesus of Nazareth
- The Great Commission: go to all people groups making disciples of Christ and his Kingdom
- Proclaiming Christ as Lord and Messiah

For Justice and Compassion

- The gracious and generous expressions of Jesus through the Church
- The Church displays the very life of the Kingdom
- The Church demonstrates the very life of the Kingdom of heaven right here and now
- Having freely received, we freely give (no sense of merit or pride)
- Justice as tangible evidence of the Kingdom come

APPENDIX 6

Old Testament Witness to Christ and His Kingdom

Rev. Dr. Don L. Davis

Christ Is Seen in the OT's:	*Covenant Promise and Fulfillment*	*Moral Law*	*Christophanies*	*Typology*	*Tabernacle, Festival, and Levitical Priesthood*	*Messianic Prophecy*	*Salvation Promises*
Passage	Gen. 12.1-3	Matt. 5.17-18	John 1.18	1 Cor. 15.45	Heb. 8.1-6	Mic. 5.2	Isa. 9.6-7
Example	The Promised Seed of the Abrahamic covenant	The Law given on Mount Sinai	Commander of the Lord's army	Jonah and the great fish	Melchizedek, as both High Priest and King	The Lord's Suffering Servant	Righteous Branch of David
Christ As	Seed of the woman	The Prophet of God	God's present Revelation	Antitype of God's drama	Our eternal High Priest	The coming Son of Man	Israel's Redeemer and King
Where Illustrated	Galatians	Matthew	John	Matthew	Hebrews	Luke and Acts	John and Revelation
Exegetical Goal	To see Christ as heart of God's sacred drama	To see Christ as fulfillment of the Law	To see Christ as God's revealer	To see Christ as antitype of divine typos	To see Christ in the Temple *cultus*	To see Christ as true Messiah	To see Christ as coming King
How Seen in the NT	As fulfillment of God's sacred oath	As *telos* of the Law	As full, final, and superior revelation	As substance behind the historical shadows	As reality behind the rules and roles	As the Kingdom made present	As the One who will rule on David's throne
Our Response in Worship	God's veracity and faithfulness	God's perfect righteousness	God's presence among us	God's inspired Scripture	God's ontology: his realm as primary and determinative	God's anointed servant and mediator	God's resolve to restore his kingdom authority
How God Is Vindicated	God does not lie: he's true to his word	Jesus fulfills all righteousness	God's fulness is revealed to us in Jesus of Nazareth	The Spirit spoke by the prophets	The Lord has provided a mediator for humankind	Every jot and tittle written of him will occur	Evil will be put down, creation restored, under his reign

APPENDIX 7

Summary Outline of the Scriptures

Rev. Dr. Don L. Davis

1. GENESIS - Beginnings
   a. Adam
   b. Noah
   c. Abraham
   d. Isaac
   e. Jacob
   f. Joseph

2. EXODUS - Redemption, (out of)
   a. Slavery
   b. Deliverance
   c. Law
   d. Tabernacle

3. LEVITICUS - Worship and Fellowship
   a. Offerings, sacrifices
   b. Priests
   c. Feasts, festivals

4. NUMBERS - Service and Walk
   a. Organized
   b. Wanderings

5. DEUTERONOMY - Obedience
   a. Moses reviews history and law
   b. Civil and social laws
   c. Palestinian Covenant
   d. Moses' blessing and death

6. JOSHUA - Redemption (into)
   a. Conquer the land
   b. Divide up the land
   c. Joshua's farewell

7. JUDGES - God's Deliverance
   a. Disobedience and judgment
   b. Israel's twelve judges
   c. Lawless conditions

8. RUTH - Love
   a. Ruth chooses
   b. Ruth works
   c. Ruth waits
   d. Ruth rewarded

9. 1 SAMUEL - Kings, Priestly Perspective
   a. Eli
   b. Samuel
   c. Saul
   d. David

10. 2 SAMUEL - David
   a. King of Judah (9 years - Hebron)
   b. King of all Israel (33 years - Jerusalem)

11. 1 KINGS - Solomon's Glory, Kingdom's Decline
   a. Solomon's glory
   b. Kingdom's decline
   c. Elijah the prophet

12. 2 KINGS- Divided Kingdom
   a. Elisha
   b. Israel (N. Kingdom falls)
   c. Judah (S. Kingdom falls)

13. 1 CHRONICLES - David's Temple Arrangements
   a. Genealogies
   b. End of Saul's reign
   c. Reign of David
   d. Temple preparations

14. 2 CHRONICLES - Temple and Worship Abandoned
   a. Solomon
   b. Kings of Judah

15. EZRA - The Minority (Remnant)
   a. First return from exile - Zerubbabel
   b. Second return from exile - Ezra (priest)

16. NEHEMIAH - Rebuilding by Faith
   a. Rebuild walls
   b. Revival
   c. Religious reform

17. ESTHER - Female Savior
   a. Esther
   b. Haman
   c. Mordecai
   d. Deliverance: Feast of Purim

18. JOB - Why the Righteous Suffer
   a. Godly Job
   b. Satan's attack
   c. Four philosophical friends
   d. God lives

19. PSALMS - Prayer and Praise
   a. Prayers of David
   b. Godly suffer; deliverance
   c. God deals with Israel
   d. Suffering of God's people - end with the Lord's reign
   e. The Word of God (Messiah's suffering and glorious return)

20. PROVERBS - Wisdom
   a. Wisdom versus folly
   b. Solomon
   c. Solomon - Hezekiah
   d. Agur
   e. Lemuel

21. ECCLESIASTES - Vanity
   a. Experimentation
   b. Observation
   c. Consideration

22. SONG OF SOLOMON - Love Story

23. ISAIAH - The Justice (Judgment) and Grace (Comfort) of God
   a. Prophecies of punishment
   b. History
   c. Prophecies of blessing

24. JEREMIAH - Judah's Sin Leads to Babylonian Captivity
   a. Jeremiah's call; empowered
   b. Judah condemned; predicted Babylonian captivity
   c. Restoration promised
   d. Prophesied judgment inflicted
   e. Prophesies against Gentiles
   f. Summary of Judah's captivity

25. LAMENTATIONS - Lament over Jerusalem
   a. Affliction of Jerusalem
   b. Destroyed because of sin
   c. The prophet's suffering
   d. Present desolation versus past splendor
   e. Appeal to God for mercy

26. EZEKIEL - Israel's Captivity and Restoration
   a. Judgment on Judah and Jerusalem
   b. Judgment on Gentile nations
   c. Israel restored; Jerusalem's future glory

27. DANIEL - The Time of the Gentiles
   a. History; Nebuchadnezzar, Belshazzar, Daniel
   b. Prophecy

28. HOSEA - Unfaithfulness
   a. Unfaithfulness
   b. Punishment
   c. Restoration

29. JOEL - The Day of the Lord
   a. Locust plague
   b. Events of the future day of the Lord
   c. Order of the future day of the Lord

30. AMOS - God Judges Sin
   a. Neighbors judged
   b. Israel judged
   c. Visions of future judgment
   d. Israel's past judgment blessings

31. OBADIAH - Edom's Destruction
   a. Destruction prophesied
   b. Reasons for destruction
   c. Israel's future blessing

32. JONAH - Gentile Salvation
   a. Jonah disobeys
   b. Other suffer
   c. Jonah punished
   d. Jonah obeys; thousands saved
   e. Jonah displeased, no love for souls

33. MICAH - Israel's Sins, Judgment, and Restoration
   a. Sin and judgment
   b. Grace and future restoration
   c. Appeal and petition

34. NAHUM - Nineveh Condemned
   a. God hates sin
   b. Nineveh's doom prophesied
   c. Reasons for doom

35. HABAKKUK - The Just Shall Live by Faith
   a. Complaint of Judah's unjudged sin
   b. Chaldeans will punish
   c. Complaint of Chaldeans' wickedness
   d. Punishment promised
   e. Prayer for revival; faith in God

36. ZEPHANIAH - Babylonian Invasion Prefigures the Day of the Lord
   a. Judgment on Judah foreshadows the Great Day of the Lord
   b. Judgment on Jerusalem and neighbors foreshadows final judgment of all nations
   c. Israel restored after judgments

37. HAGGAI - Rebuild the Temple
   a. Negligence
   b. Courage
   c. Separation
   d. Judgment

38. ZECHARIAH - Two Comings of Christ
   a. Zechariah's vision
   b. Bethel's question; Jehovah's answer
   c. Nation's downfall and salvation

39. MALACHI - Neglect
   a. The priest's sins
   b. The people's sins
   c. The faithful few

Summary Outline of the Scriptures (continued)

1. MATTHEW - Jesus the King
   a. The Person of the King
   b. The Preparation of the King
   c. The Propaganda of the King
   d. The Program of the King
   e. The Passion of the King
   f. The Power of the King

2. MARK - Jesus the Servant
   a. John introduces the Servant
   b. God the Father identifies the Servant
   c. The temptation initiates the Servant
   d. Work and word of the Servant
   e. Death, burial, resurrection

3. LUKE - Jesus Christ the Perfect Man
   a. Birth and family of the Perfect Man
   b. Testing of the Perfect Man; hometown
   c. Ministry of the Perfect Man
   d. Betrayal, trial, and death of the Perfect Man
   e. Resurrection of the Perfect Man

4. JOHN - Jesus Christ is God
   a. Prologue - the Incarnation
   b. Introduction
   c. Witness of Jesus to his Apostles
   d. Passion - witness to the world
   e. Epilogue

5. ACTS - The Holy Spirit Working in the Church
   a. The Lord Jesus at work by the Holy Spirit through the Apostles at Jerusalem
   b. In Judea and Samaria
   c. To the uttermost parts of the Earth

6. ROMANS - The Righteousness of God
   a. Salutation
   b. Sin and salvation
   c. Sanctification
   d. Struggle
   e. Spirit-filled living
   f. Security of salvation
   g. Segregation
   h. Sacrifice and service
   i. Separation and salutation

7. 1 CORINTHIANS - The Lordship of Christ
   a. Salutation and thanksgiving
   b. Conditions in the Corinthian body
   c. Concerning the Gospel
   d. Concerning collections

8. 2 CORINTHIANS - The Ministry in the Church
   a. The comfort of God
   b. Collection for the poor
   c. Calling of the Apostle Paul

9. GALATIANS - Justification by Faith
   a. Introduction
   b. Personal - Authority of the Apostle and glory of the Gospel
   c. Doctrinal - Justification by faith
   d. Practical - Sanctification by the Holy Spirit
   e. Autographed conclusion and exhortation

10. EPHESIANS - The Church of Jesus Christ
    a. Doctrinal - the heavenly calling of the Church
       A Body
       A Temple
       A Mystery
    b. Practical - The earthly conduct of the Church
       A New Man
       A Bride
       An Army

11. PHILIPPIANS - Joy in the Christian Life
    a. Philosophy for Christian living
    b. Pattern for Christian living
    c. Prize for Christian living
    d. Power for Christian living

12. COLOSSIANS - Christ the Fullness of God
    a. Doctrinal - In Christ believers are made full
    b. Practical - Christ's life poured out in believers, and through them

13. 1 THESSALONIANS - The Second Coming of Christ:
    a. Is an inspiring hope
    b. Is a working hope
    c. Is a purifying hope
    d. Is a comforting hope
    e. Is a rousing, stimulating hope

14. 2 THESSALONIANS - The Second Coming of Christ
    a. Persecution of believers now; judgment of unbelievers hereafter (at coming of Christ)
    b. Program of the world in connection with the coming of Christ
    c. Practical issues associated with the coming of Christ

15. 1 TIMOTHY - Government and Order in the Local Church
    a. The faith of the Church
    b. Public prayer and women's place in the Church
    c. Officers in the Church
    d. Apostasy in the Church
    e. Duties of the officer of the Church

16. 2 TIMOTHY - Loyalty in the Days of Apostasy
    a. Afflictions of the Gospel
    b. Active in service
    c. Apostasy coming; authority of the Scriptures
    d. Allegiance to the Lord

17. TITUS - The Ideal New Testament Church
    a. The Church is an organization
    b. The Church is to teach and preach the Word of God
    c. The Church is to perform good works

18. PHILEMON - Reveal Christ's Love and Teach Brotherly Love
    a. Genial greeting to Philemon and family
    b. Good reputation of Philemon
    c. Gracious plea for Onesimus
    d. Guiltless illustration of Imputation
    e. General and personal requests

19. HEBREWS - The Superiority of Christ
    a. Doctrinal - Christ is better than the Old Testament economy
    b. Practical - Christ brings better benefits and duties

20. JAMES - Ethics of Christianity
    a. Faith tested
    b. Difficulty of controlling the tongue
    c. Warning against worldliness
    d. Admonitions in view of the Lord's coming

21. 1 PETER - Christian Hope in the Time of Persecution and Trial
    a. Suffering and security of believers
    b. Suffering and the Scriptures
    c. Suffering and the sufferings of Christ
    d. Suffering and the Second Coming of Christ

22. 2 PETER - Warning Against False Teachers
    a. Addition of Christian graces gives assurance
    b. Authority of the Scriptures
    c. Apostasy brought in by false testimony
    d. Attitude toward Return of Christ: test for apostasy
    e. Agenda of God in the world
    f. Admonition to believers

23. 1 JOHN - The Family of God
    a. God is Light
    b. God is Love
    c. God is Life

24. 2 JOHN - Warning against Receiving Deceivers
    a. Walk in truth
    b. Love one another
    c. Receive not deceivers
    d. Find joy in fellowship

25. 3 JOHN - Admonition to Receive True Believers
    a. Gaius, brother in the Church
    b. Diotrephes
    c. Demetrius

26. JUDE - Contending for the Faith
    a. Occasion of the epistle
    b. Occurrences of apostasy
    c. Occupation of believers in the days of apostasy

27. REVELATION - The Unveiling of Christ Glorified
    a. The person of Christ in glory
    b. The possession of Jesus Christ - the Church in the World
    c. The program of Jesus Christ - the scene in Heaven
    d. The seven seals
    e. The seven trumpets
    f. Important persons in the last days
    g. The seven vials
    h. The fall of Babylon
    i. The eternal state

APPENDIX 8

From Before to Beyond Time:

The Plan of God and Human History

Adapted from: Suzanne de Dietrich. ***God's Unfolding Purpose****. Philadelphia: Westminster Press, 1976.*

I. Before Time (Eternity Past) 1 Cor. 2.7

A. The Eternal Triune God
B. God's Eternal Purpose
C. The Mystery of Iniquity
D. The Principalities and Powers

II. Beginning of Time (Creation and Fall) Gen. 1.1

A. Creative Word
B. Humanity
C. Fall
D. Reign of Death and First Signs of Grace

III. Unfolding of Time (God's Plan Revealed Through Israel) Gal. 3.8

A. Promise (Patriarchs)
B. Exodus and Covenant at Sinai
C. Promised Land
D. The City, the Temple, and the Throne (Prophet, Priest, and King)
E. Exile
F. Remnant

IV. Fullness of Time (Incarnation of the Messiah) Gal. 4.4-5

A. The King Comes to His Kingdom
B. The Present Reality of His Reign
C. The Secret of the Kingdom: the Already and the Not Yet
D. The Crucified King
E. The Risen Lord

V. The Last Times (The Descent of the Holy Spirit) Acts 2.16-18

A. Between the Times: the Church as Foretaste of the Kingdom
B. The Church as Agent of the Kingdom
C. The Conflict Between the Kingdoms of Darkness and Light

VI. The Fulfillment of Time (The Second Coming) Matt. 13.40-43

A. The Return of Christ
B. Judgment
C. The Consummation of His Kingdom

VII. Beyond Time (Eternity Future) 1 Cor. 15.24-28

A. Kingdom Handed Over to God the Father
B. God as All in All

From Before to Beyond Time

Scriptures for Major Outline Points

I. Before Time (Eternity Past)

1 Cor. 2.7 (ESV) - But we impart a secret and hidden wisdom of God, *which God decreed before the ages* for our glory (cf. Titus 1.2).

II. Beginning of Time (Creation and Fall)

Gen. 1.1 (ESV) - *In the beginning*, God created the heavens and the earth.

III. Unfolding of Time (God's Plan Revealed Through Israel)

Gal. 3.8 (ESV) - And the Scripture, foreseeing that God would justify the Gentiles by faith, *preached the Gospel beforehand to Abraham*, saying, "In you shall all the nations be blessed" (cf. Rom. 9.4-5).

IV. Fullness of Time (The Incarnation of the Messiah)

Gal. 4.4-5 (ESV) - *But when the fullness of time had come*, God sent forth his Son, born of woman, born under the law, to redeem those who were under the law, so that we might receive adoption as sons.

V. The Last Times (The Descent of the Holy Spirit)

Acts 2.16-18 (ESV) - But this is what was uttered through the prophet Joel: "'*And in the last days it shall be*,' God declares, 'that I will pour out my Spirit on all flesh, and your sons and your daughters shall prophesy, and your young men shall see visions, and your old men shall dream dreams; even on my male servants and female servants in those days I will pour out my Spirit, and they shall prophesy.'"

VI. The Fulfillment of Time (The Second Coming)

Matt. 13.40-43 (ESV) - Just as the weeds are gathered and burned with fire, *so will it be at the close of the age*. The Son of Man will send his angels, and they will gather out of his kingdom all causes of sin and all lawbreakers, and throw them into the fiery furnace. In that place there will be weeping and gnashing of teeth. Then the righteous will shine like the sun in the Kingdom of their Father. He who has ears, let him hear.

VII. Beyond Time (Eternity Future)

1 Cor. 15.24-28 (ESV) - Then comes the end, when he delivers the Kingdom to God the Father after destroying every rule and every authority and power. For he must reign until he has put all his enemies under his feet. The last enemy to be destroyed is death. For "God has put all things in subjection under his feet." But when it says, "all things are put in subjection," it is plain that he is excepted who put all things in subjection under him. When all things are subjected to him, then the Son himself will also be subjected to him who put all things in subjection under him, that God may be all in all.

APPENDIX 9

"There Is a River"

Identifying the Streams of a Revitalized Authentic Christian Community in the City[1]

Rev. Dr. Don L. Davis • Psalm 46.4 (ESV) - There is a river whose streams make glad the city of God, the holy habitation of the Most High.

Tributaries of Authentic Historic Biblical Faith			
Recognized Biblical Identity	*Revived Urban Spirituality*	*Reaffirmed Historical Connectivity*	*Refocused Kingdom Authority*
The Church Is **One**	*The Church Is* **Holy**	*The Church Is* **Catholic**	*The Church Is* **Apostolic**
A Call to Biblical Fidelity *Recognizing the Scriptures as the anchor and foundation of the Christian faith and practice*	A Call to the Freedom, Power, and Fullness of the Holy Spirit *Walking in the holiness, power, gifting, and liberty of the Holy Spirit in the body of Christ*	A Call to Historic Roots and Continuity *Confessing the common historical identity and continuity of authentic Christian faith*	A Call to the Apostolic Faith *Affirming the apostolic tradition as the authoritative ground of the Christian hope*
A Call to Messianic Kingdom Identity *Rediscovering the story of the promised Messiah and his Kingdom in Jesus of Nazareth*	A Call to Live as Sojourners and Aliens as the People of God *Defining authentic Christian discipleship as faithful membership among God's people*	A Call to Affirm and Express the Global Communion of Saints *Expressing cooperation and collaboration with all other believers, both local and global*	A Call to Representative Authority *Submitting joyfully to God's gifted servants in the Church as undershepherds of true faith*
A Call to Creedal Affinity *Embracing the Nicene Creed as the shared rule of faith of historic orthodoxy*	A Call to Liturgical, Sacramental, and Catechetical Vitality *Experiencing God's presence in the context of the Word, sacrament, and instruction*	A Call to Radical Hospitality and Good Works *Expressing kingdom love to all, and especially to those of the household of faith*	A Call to Prophetic and Holistic Witness *Proclaiming Christ and his Kingdom in word and deed to our neighbors and all peoples*

[1] *This schema is an adaptation and is based on the insights of the* **Chicago Call** *statement of May 1977, where various leading evangelical scholars and practitioners met to discuss the relationship of modern evangelicalism to the historic Christian faith.*

APPENDIX 10

A Schematic for a Theology of the Kingdom and the Church

The Urban Ministry Institute

The Reign of the One, True, Sovereign, and Triune God, the LORD God, Yahweh, God the Father, Son, and Holy Spirit		
The Father Love - 1 John 4.8 Maker of heaven and earth and of all things visible and invisible	**The Son** Faith - Heb. 12.2 Prophet, Priest, and King	**The Spirit** Hope - Rom. 15.13 Lord of the Church
Creation All that exists through the creative action of God.	**Kingdom** The Reign of God expressed in the rule of his Son Jesus the Messiah.	**Church** The one, holy, apostolic community which functions as a witness to (Acts 28.31) and a foretaste of (Col. 1.12; James 1.18; 1 Pet. 2.9; Rev. 1.6) the Kingdom of God.
Rom. 8.18-21 → The eternal God, sovereign in power, infinite in wisdom, perfect in holiness, and steadfast in love, is the source and goal of all things.	**Freedom** (Slavery) Jesus answered them, "Truly, truly, I say to you, everyone who commits sin is a slave to sin. The slave does not remain in the house forever; the son remains forever. So if the Son sets you free, you will be free indeed." - John 8.34-36 (ESV)	*The Church is an Apostolic Community Where the Word is Rightly Preached, Therefore it is a Community of:* **Calling** - For freedom Christ has set us free; stand firm therefore, and do not submit again to a yoke of slavery. - Gal. 5.1 (ESV) (cf. Rom. 8.28-30; 1 Cor. 1.26-31; Eph. 1.18; 2 Thess. 2.13-14; Jude 1.1) **Faith** - ". . . for unless you believe that I am he you will die in your sins". . . . So Jesus said to the Jews who had believed in him, "If you abide in my word, you are truly my disciples, and you will know the truth, and the truth will set you free." - John 8.24b, 31-32 (ESV) (cf. Ps. 119.45; Rom. 1.17; 5.1-2; Eph. 2.8-9; 2 Tim. 1.13-14; Heb. 2.14-15; James 1.25) **Witness** - The Spirit of the Lord is upon me, because he has anointed me to proclaim good news to the poor. He has sent me to proclaim liberty to the captives and recovering of sight to the blind, to set at liberty those who are oppressed, to proclaim the year of the Lord's favor. - Luke 4.18-19 (ESV) (cf. Lev. 25.10; Prov. 31.8; Matt. 4.17; 28.18-20; Mark 13.10; Acts 1.8; 8.4, 12; 13.1-3; 25.20; 28.30-31)
Rev. 21.1-5 → O, the depth of the riches and wisdom and knowledge of God! How unsearchable are his judgments, and how inscrutable his ways! For who has known the mind of the Lord, or who has been his counselor? Or who has ever given a gift to him, that he might be repaid?" For from him and through him and to him are all things. To him be glory forever! Amen! - Rom. 11.33-36 (ESV) (cf. 1 Cor. 15.23-28; Rev.)	**Wholeness** (Sickness) But he was wounded for our transgressions; he was crushed for our iniquities; upon him was the chastisement that brought us peace, and with his stripes we are healed. - Isa. 53.5 (ESV)	*The Church is One Community Where the Sacraments are Rightly Administered, Therefore it is a Community of:* **Worship** - You shall serve the Lord your God, and he will bless your bread and your water, and I will take sickness away from among you. - Exod. 23.25 (ESV) (cf. Ps. 147.1-3; Heb. 12.28; Col. 3.16; Rev. 15.3-4; 19.5) **Covenant** - And the Holy Spirit also bears witness to us; for after the saying, "This is the covenant that I will make with them after those days, declares the Lord: I will put my laws on their hearts, and write them on their minds," then he adds, "I will remember their sins and their lawless deeds no more." - Heb. 10.15-17 (ESV) (cf. Isa. 54.10-17; Ezek. 34.25-31; 37.26-27; Mal. 2.4-5; Luke 22.20; 2 Cor. 3.6; Col. 3.15; Heb. 8.7-13; 12.22-24; 13.20-21) **Presence** - In him you also are being built together into a dwelling place for God by his Spirit. - Eph. 2.22 (ESV) (cf. Exod. 40.34-38; Ezek. 48.35; Matt. 18.18-20)
Isa. 11.6-9 →	**Justice** (Selfishness) Behold, my servant whom I have chosen, my beloved with whom my soul is well pleased. I will put my Spirit upon him, and he will proclaim justice to the Gentiles. He will not quarrel or cry aloud, nor will anyone hear his voice in the streets; a bruised reed he will not break, and a smoldering wick he will not quench, until he brings justice to victory. - Matt. 12.18-20 (ESV)	*The Church is a Holy Community Where Discipline is Rightly Ordered, Therefore it is a Community of:* **Reconciliation** - For he himself is our peace, who has made us both one and has broken down in his flesh the dividing wall of hostility by abolishing the law of commandments and ordinances, that he might create in himself one new man in place of the two, so making peace, and might reconcile us both to God in one body through the cross, thereby killing the hostility. And he came and preached peace to you who were far off and peace to those who were near. For through him we both have access in one Spirit to the Father. - Eph. 2.14-18 (ESV) (cf. Exod. 23.4-9; Lev. 19.34; Deut. 10.18-19; Ezek. 22.29; Mic. 6.8; 2 Cor. 5.16-21) **Suffering** - Since therefore Christ suffered in the flesh, arm yourselves with the same way of thinking, for whoever has suffered in the flesh has ceased from sin, so as to live for the rest of the time in the flesh no longer for human passions but for the will of God. - 1 Pet. 4.1-2 (ESV) (cf. Luke 6.22; 10.3; Rom. 8.17; 2 Tim. 2.3; 3.12; 1 Pet. 2.20-24; Heb. 5.8; 13.11-14) **Service** - But Jesus called them to him and said, "You know that the rulers of the Gentiles lord it over them, and their great ones exercise authority over them. It shall not be so among you. But whoever would be great among you must be your servant, and whoever would be first among you must be your slave even as the Son of Man came not to be served but to serve, and to give his life as a ransom for many." - Matt. 20.25-28 (ESV) (cf. 1 John 4.16-18; Gal. 2.10)

APPENDIX 11

Living in the Already and the Not Yet Kingdom

Rev. Dr. Don L. Davis

The Spirit: The pledge of the inheritance ***(arrabon)***

The Church: The foretaste ***(aparche)*** of the Kingdom

"In Christ": The rich life ***(en Christos)*** we share as citizens of the Kingdom

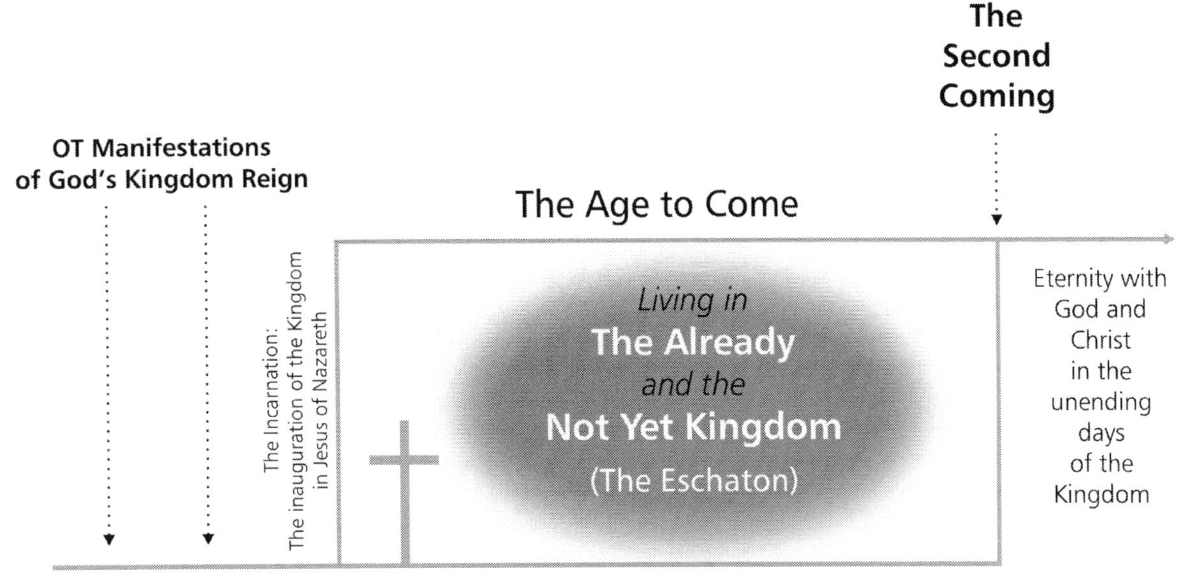

Internal enemy: The flesh (*sarx*) and the sin nature

External enemy: The world (*kosmos*) the systems of greed, lust, and pride

Infernal enemy: The devil (*kakos*) the animating spirit of falsehood and fear

Jewish View of Time

This Present Age — The Age to Come

The Coming of Messiah

The restoration of Israel

The end of Gentile oppression

The return of the earth to Edenic glory

Universal knowledge of the Lord

APPENDIX 12

Jesus of Nazareth: The Presence of the Future

Rev. Dr. Don L. Davis

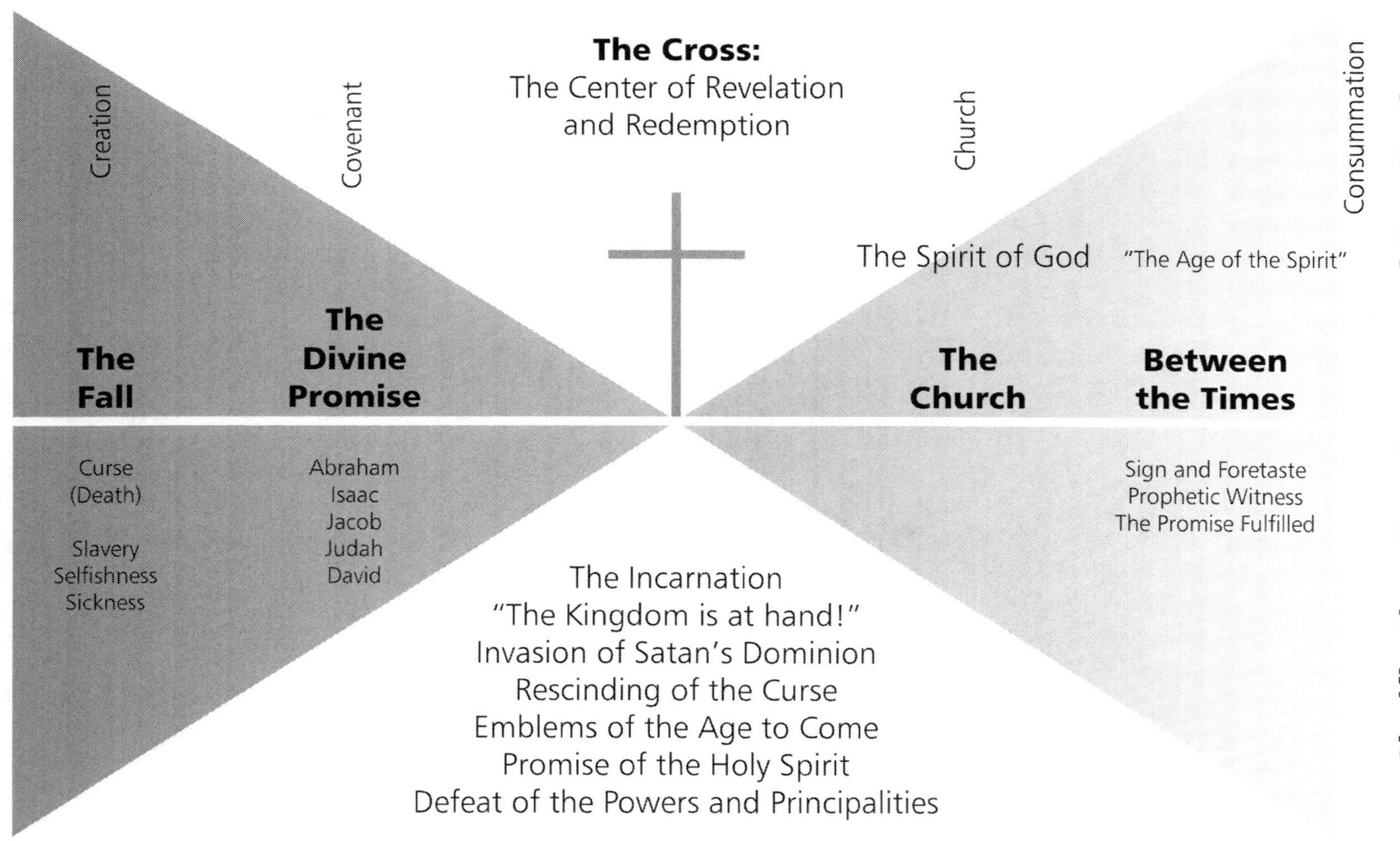

APPENDIX 13

Traditions

(Paradosis)

Dr. Don L. Davis and Rev. Terry G. Cornett

Strong's Definition

Paradosis. Transmission, i.e. (concretely) a precept; specifically, the Jewish traditionary law

Vine's Explanation

denotes "a tradition," and hence, by metonymy, (a) "the teachings of the rabbis," . . . (b) "apostolic teaching," . . . of instructions concerning the gatherings of believers, of Christian doctrine in general . . . of instructions concerning everyday conduct.

1. The concept of tradition in Scripture is essentially positive.

Jer. 6.16 (ESV) - Thus says the Lord: "Stand by the roads, and look, and ask for the ancient paths, where the good way is; and walk in it, and find rest for your souls. But they said, 'We will not walk in it'" (cf. Exod. 3.15; Judg. 2.17; 1 Kings 8.57-58; Ps. 78.1-6).

2 Chron. 35.25 (ESV) - Jeremiah also uttered a lament for Josiah; and all the singing men and singing women have spoken of Josiah in their laments to this day. They made these a rule in Israel; behold, they are written in the Laments (cf. Gen. 32.32; Judg. 11.38-40).

Jer. 35.14-19 (ESV) - The command that Jonadab the son of Rechab gave to his sons, to drink no wine, has been kept, and they drink none to this day, for they have obeyed their father's command. I have spoken to you persistently, but you have not listened to me. I have sent to you all my servants the prophets, sending them persistently, saying, 'Turn now every one of you from his evil way, and amend your deeds, and do not go after other gods to serve them, and then you shall dwell in the land that I gave to you and your fathers.' But you did not incline your ear or listen to me. The sons of Jonadab the son of Rechab have kept the command that their father gave them, but this people has not obeyed me. Therefore, thus says the

Traditions (continued)

Lord, the God of hosts, the God of Israel: Behold, I am bringing upon Judah and all the inhabitants of Jerusalem all the disaster that I have pronounced against them, because I have spoken to them and they have not listened, I have called to them and they have not answered." But to the house of the Rechabites Jeremiah said, "Thus says the Lord of hosts, the God of Israel: Because you have obeyed the command of Jonadab your father and kept all his precepts and done all that he commanded you, therefore thus says the Lord of hosts, the God of Israel: Jonadab the son of Rechab shall never lack a man to stand before me."

2. Godly tradition is a wonderful thing, but not all tradition is godly.

Any individual tradition must be judged by its faithfulness to the Word of God and its usefulness in helping people maintain obedience to Christ's example and teaching.[1] In the Gospels, Jesus frequently rebukes the Pharisees for establishing traditions that nullify rather than uphold God's commands.

Mark 7.8 (ESV) - You leave the commandment of God and hold to the tradition of men" (cf. Matt. 15.2-6; Mark 7.13).

Col. 2.8 (ESV) - See to it that no one takes you captive by philosophy and empty deceit, according to human tradition, according to the elemental spirits of the world, and not according to Christ.

3. Without the fullness of the Holy Spirit, and the constant edification provided to us by the Word of God, tradition will inevitably lead to dead formalism.

Those who are spiritual are filled with the Holy Spirit, whose power and leading alone provides individuals and congregations a sense of freedom and vitality in all they practice and believe. However, when the practices and teachings of any given tradition are no longer infused by the power of the Holy Spirit and the Word of God, tradition loses its effectiveness, and may actually become counterproductive to our discipleship in Jesus Christ.

Eph. 5.18 (ESV) - And do not get drunk with wine, for that is debauchery, but be filled with the Spirit.

[1] "All Protestants insist that these traditions must ever be tested against Scripture and can never possess an independent apostolic authority over or alongside of Scripture." (J. Van Engen, "Tradition," ***Evangelical Dictionary of Theology****, Walter Elwell, Gen. ed.) We would add that Scripture is itself the "authoritative tradition" by which all other traditions are judged. See "Appendix A, The Founders of Tradition: Three Levels of Christian Authority," p. 4.*

Traditions (continued)

Gal. 5.22-25 (ESV) - But the fruit of the Spirit is love, joy, peace, patience, kindness, goodness, faithfulness, gentleness, self-control; against such things there is no law. And those who belong to Christ Jesus have crucified the flesh with its passions and desires. If we live by the Spirit, let us also walk by the Spirit.

2 Cor. 3.5-6 (ESV) - Not that we are sufficient in ourselves to claim anything as coming from us, but our sufficiency is from God, who has made us competent to be ministers of a new covenant, not of the letter but of the Spirit. For the letter kills, but the Spirit gives life.

4. Fidelity to the Apostolic Tradition (teaching and modeling) is the essence of Christian maturity.

2 Tim. 2.2 (ESV) - and what you have heard from me in the presence of many witnesses entrust to faithful men who will be able to teach others also.

1 Cor. 11.1-2 (ESV) - Be imitators of me, as I am of Christ. Now I commend you because you remember me in everything and maintain the traditions even as I delivered them to you (cf.1 Cor. 4.16-17, 2 Tim. 1.13-14, 2 Thess. 3.7-9, Phil. 4.9).

1 Cor. 15.3-8 (ESV) - For I delivered to you as of first importance what I also received: that Christ died for our sins in accordance with the Scriptures, that he was buried, that he was raised on the third day in accordance with the Scriptures, and that he appeared to Cephas, then to the twelve. Then he appeared to more than five hundred brothers at one time, most of whom are still alive, though some have fallen asleep. Then he appeared to James, then to all the apostles. Last of all, as to one untimely born, he appeared also to me.

5. The Apostle Paul often includes an appeal to the tradition for support in doctrinal practices.

1 Cor. 11.16 (ESV) - If anyone is inclined to be contentious, we have no such practice, nor do the churches of God (cf. 1 Cor. 1.2, 7.17, 15.3).

Traditions (continued)

1 Cor. 14.33-34 (ESV) - For God is not a God of confusion but of peace. As in all the churches of the saints, the women should keep silent in the churches. For they are not permitted to speak, but should be in submission, as the Law also says.

6. When a congregation uses received tradition to remain faithful to the "Word of God," they are commended by the apostles.

1 Cor. 11.2 (ESV) - Now I commend you because you remember me in everything and maintain the traditions even as I delivered them to you.

2 Thess. 2.15 (ESV) - So then, brothers, stand firm and hold to the traditions that you were taught by us, either by our spoken word or by our letter.

2 Thess. 3.6 (ESV) - Now we command you, brothers, in the name of our Lord Jesus Christ, that you keep away from any brother who is walking in idleness and not in accord with the tradition that you received from us.

Appendix A

The Founders of Tradition: Three Levels of Christian Authority

Exod. 3.15 (ESV) - God also said to Moses, "Say this to the people of Israel, 'The Lord, the God of your fathers, the God of Abraham, the God of Isaac, and the God of Jacob, has sent me to you.' This is my name forever, and thus I am to be remembered throughout all generations."

1. The Authoritative Tradition: the Apostles and the Prophets (The Holy Scriptures)

Eph. 2.19-21 (ESV) - So then you are no longer strangers and aliens, but you are fellow citizens with the saints and members of the household of God, built on the foundation of the apostles and prophets, Christ Jesus himself being the cornerstone, in whom the whole structure, being joined together, grows into a holy temple in the Lord.

~ The Apostle Paul

Traditions (continued)

Those who gave eyewitness testimony to the revelation and saving acts of Yahweh, first in Israel, and ultimately in Jesus Christ the Messiah. This testimony is binding for all people, at all times, and in all places. It is the authoritative tradition by which all subsequent tradition is judged.

2. The Great Tradition: the Ecumenical Councils and their Creeds[2]

What has been believed everywhere, always, and by all.

~ Vincent of Lerins

The Great Tradition is the core dogma (doctrine) of the Church. It represents the teaching of the Church as it has understood the Authoritative Tradition (the Holy Scriptures), and summarizes those essential truths that Christians of all ages have confessed and believed. To these doctrinal statements the whole Church, (Catholic, Orthodox, and Protestant)[3] gives its assent. The worship and theology of the Church reflects this core dogma, which finds its summation and fulfillment in the person and work of Jesus Christ. From earliest times, Christians have expressed their devotion to God in its Church calendar, a yearly pattern of worship which summarizes and reenacts the events of Christ's life.

3. Specific Church Traditions: the Founders of Denominations and Orders

The Presbyterian Church (U.S.A.) has approximately 2.5 million members, 11,200 congregations and 21,000 ordained ministers. Presbyterians trace their history to the 16th century and the Protestant Reformation. Our heritage, and much of what we believe, began with the French lawyer John Calvin (1509-1564), whose writings crystallized much of the Reformed thinking that came before him.

~ The Presbyterian Church, U.S.A.

Christians have expressed their faith in Jesus Christ in various ways through specific movements and traditions which embrace and express the Authoritative Tradition and the Great Tradition in unique ways. For instance,

[2] See Appendix B, "Defining the Great Tradition."

[3] Even the more radical wing of the Protestant reformation (Anabaptists) who were the most reluctant to embrace the creeds as dogmatic instruments of faith, did not disagree with the essential content found in them. "They assumed the Apostolic Creed–they called it 'The Faith,' ***Der Glaube****, as did most people." See John Howard Yoder,* ***Preface to Theology: Christology and Theological Method.*** *Grand Rapids: Brazos Press, 2002. pp. 222-223.*

Traditions (continued)

Catholic movements have arisen around people like Benedict, Francis, or Dominic, and among Protestants people like Martin Luther, John Calvin, Ulrich Zwingli, and John Wesley. Women have founded vital movements of Christian faith (e.g., Aimee Semple McPherson of the Foursquare Church), as well as minorities (e.g., Richard Allen of the African Methodist Episcopal Church or Charles H. Mason of the Church of God in Christ, who also helped to spawn the Assemblies of God), all which attempted to express the Authoritative Tradition and the Great Tradition in a specific way consistent with their time and expression.

The emergence of vital, dynamic movements of the faith at different times and among different peoples reveal the fresh working of the Holy Spirit throughout history. Thus, inside Catholicism, new communities have arisen such as the Benedictines, Franciscans, and Dominicans; and outside Catholicism, new denominations have emerged (Lutherans, Presbyterians, Methodists, Church of God in Christ, etc.). Each of these specific traditions have "founders," key leaders whose energy and vision helped to establish a unique expression of Christian faith and practice. Of course, to be legitimate, these movements must adhere to and faithfully express both the Authoritative Tradition and the Great Tradition. Members of these specific traditions embrace their own unique practices and patterns of spirituality, but these unique features are not necessarily binding on the Church at large. They represent the unique expressions of that community's understanding of and faithfulness to the Authoritative and Great Traditions.

Specific traditions seek to express and live out this faithfulness to the Authoritative and Great Traditions through their worship, teaching, and service. They seek to make the Gospel clear within new cultures or sub-cultures, speaking and modeling the hope of Christ into new situations shaped by their own set of questions posed in light of their own unique circumstances. These movements, therefore, seek to contextualize the Authoritative tradition in a way that faithfully and effectively leads new groups of people to faith in Jesus Christ, and incorporates those who believe into the community of faith that obeys his teachings and gives witness of him to others.

Traditions (continued)

Appendix B

Defining the "Great Tradition"

The Great Tradition (sometimes called the "classical Christian tradition") is defined by Robert E. Webber as follows:

> *[It is] the broad outline of Christian belief and practice developed from the Scriptures between the time of Christ and the middle of the fifth century*
>
> ~ Webber. **The Majestic Tapestry.**
> Nashville: Thomas Nelson Publishers, 1986. p. 10.

This tradition is widely affirmed by Protestant theologians both ancient and modern.

> *Thus those ancient Councils of Nicea, Constantinople, the first of Ephesus, Chalcedon, and the like, which were held for refuting errors, we willingly embrace, and reverence as sacred, in so far as relates to doctrines of faith, for they contain nothing but the pure and genuine interpretation of Scripture, which the holy Fathers with spiritual prudence adopted to crush the enemies of religion who had then arisen.*
>
> ~ John Calvin. **Institutes.** IV, ix. 8.

> *. . . most of what is enduringly valuable in contemporary biblical exegesis was discovered by the fifth century.*
>
> ~ Thomas C. Oden. **The Word of Life.**
> San Francisco: HarperSanFrancisco, 1989. p. xi

> *The first four Councils are by far the most important, as they settled the orthodox faith on the Trinity and the Incarnation.*
>
> ~ Philip Schaff. **The Creeds of Christendom.** Vol. 1.
> Grand Rapids: Baker Book House, 1996. p. 44.

Our reference to the Ecumenical Councils and Creeds is, therefore, focused on those Councils which retain a widespread agreement in the Church among Catholics, Orthodox, and Protestants. While Catholic and Orthodox share common agreement on the first seven councils, Protestants tend to affirm and use primarily the first four. Therefore, those councils which continue to be shared by the whole Church are completed with the Council of Chalcedon in 451.

Traditions (continued)

It is worth noting that each of these four Ecumenical Councils took place in a pre-European cultural context and that none of them were held in Europe. They were councils of the whole Church and they reflected a time in which Christianity was primarily an eastern religion in it's geographic core. By modern reckoning, their participants were African, Asian, and European. The councils reflected a church that "... has roots in cultures far distant from Europe and preceded the development of modern European identity, and [of which] some of its greatest minds have been African" (Oden, *The Living God*, San Francisco: HarperSanFrancisco, 1987, p. 9).

Perhaps the most important achievement of the Councils was the creation of what is now commonly called the Nicene Creed. It serves as a summary statement of the Christian faith that can be agreed on by Catholic, Orthodox, and Protestant Christians.

The first four Ecumenical Councils are summarized in the following chart:

Name/Date/Location	Purpose
First Ecumenical Council *325 A.D.* *Nicea, Asia Minor*	Defending against: *Arianism* Question answered: *Was Jesus God?* Action: *Developed the initial form of the Nicene Creed to serve as a summary of the Christian faith*
Second Ecumenical Council *381 A.D.* *Constantinople, Asia Minor*	Defending against: *Macedonianism* Question answered: *Is the Holy Spirit a personal and equal part of the Godhead?* Action: *Completed the Nicene Creed by expanding the article dealing with the Holy Spirit*
Third Ecumenical Council *431 A.D.* *Ephesus, Asia Minor*	Defending against: *Nestorianism* Question answered: *Is Jesus Christ both God and man in one person?* Action: *Defined Christ as the Incarnate Word of God and affirmed his mother Mary as* **theotokos** *(God-bearer)*
Fourth Ecumenical Council *451 A.D.* *Chalcedon, Asia Minor*	Defending against: *Monophysitism* Question answered: *How can Jesus be both God and man?* Action: *Explained the relationship between Jesus' two natures (human and Divine)*

APPENDIX 14

Readings on Christ

Rev. Dr. Don L. Davis

What Is Christianity without Christ?

Christianity without Christ is a chest without its treasure, a frame without a portrait, a corpse without breath.

~ John Stott. **Focus on Christ.**
Cleveland: William Collins Publishers, Inc., 1979.

What Is the Bible all About?

What is the Bible all about? How can I understand its meaning? Why are there sixty-six books in the Bible? How do I know it is the Word of God?

All of these questions can be answered in one word - Christ.

Jesus Christ is the key to both the inspiration and the interpretation of the Bible. Further, it is Christ who confirmed the collection of books as both complete and authoritative.

~ Norman Geisler. **A Popular Survey of the Old Testament.**
Grand Rapids: Baker Book House, 1977. p. 11.

The End of the Line

[Matthew] is being deliberately schematic [i.e., providing us with a big picture], with a theological intention. He is pointing out that Old Testament history falls into three approximately equal spans of time between the critical events:

- from the foundational covenant with Abraham to the establishing of the monarchy under David;
- from David to the destruction and loss of the monarchy in the Babylonian exile;
- and from the exile to the coming of the Messiah himself who alone could occupy the throne of David.

Jesus is thus 'the end of the line,' as far as the Old Testament story goes. It has run its completed course in preparation for him, and now its goal and climax has been reached.

~ Christopher J. H. Wright. **Knowing Jesus through the Old Testament.**
Downers Grove: InterVarsity Press, 1992. pp. 6-7.

Readings on Christ (continued)

The Cosmic and All-Sufficient Center

Jesus of Nazareth continues to enjoy an extraordinary boom. People are fascinated by him, even in spite of themselves. Many who never reach the point of confessing him as God and Savior yet regard him with profound admiration. True, there are others who resent and reject him. But the one thing people seem unable to do is to ignore him and leave him alone.

Even in other religions and ideologies Jesus is held in high honor. . . . As T.R. Glover wrote in *The Jesus of History*: "Jesus remains the very heart and soul of the Christian movement, still controlling men, still capturing men. . . . In fine, there is no figure in human history that signifies more. Men may love him or hate him, but they do it intensely."

. . . Jesus Christ is the center of Christianity, and therefore both the Christian faith and the Christian life, if they are to be authentic, must be focused on Christ. In his work *Christian Faith and Other Faiths*, the late Bishop Stephen Neill wrote: "The old saying 'Christianity is Christ' is almost exactly true. The historical figure of Jesus of Nazareth is the criterion by which every Christian affirmation has to be judged, and in the light of which it stands or falls."

~ John Stott. **Life in Christ.**
Grand Rapids: Baker Books, 1991. p. 7.

The Magnetism of Jesus' Teaching: Where Did it Come From?

Why was Jesus such a fascinating teacher? What caused these large crowds to follow him? In reply one might say that it was what Jesus said that drew the crowds. With Jesus the voice of prophecy had once again returned to Israel after 400 years. In the ministry of Jesus, the Spirit of God was once again active in Israel (cf. Matt. 12.28; Luke 4.16-21). God was once again visiting his people and proclaiming his will. One reason people came to hear Jesus was that many were convinced that God was speaking through Jesus of Nazareth and that what he was saying was indeed the Word of God (Luke 5.1; 11.28; Mark 4.14-20). . . .

No doubt an additional factor that enters the picture involves the personality of Jesus, for the personality of Jesus gave life and vitality to his message. It was the Word made flesh (John 1.14) which was the medium through which and by which the Word of God came. People loved to listen to Jesus because of the kind of person

Readings on Christ (continued)

he was. Publicans, sinners, children, the crowds–all found in Jesus one whom they enjoyed being near. It was therefore not only *what* he taught but also *who* he was that attracted people to hear him. . . . The *what* of his message and the *who*, i.e., the "personality" and "authority" of the messenger, all played a part in making Jesus an exciting teacher.

~ Robert H. Stein. **The Method and Message of Jesus' Teachings.** Philadelphia: The Westminster Press, 1978. pp.7-8.

The Challenge of the Biblical Stories

John Dominic Crossan

John Dominic Crossan is an original member and former co-chair of the Jesus Seminar as well as chairman of the Historical Jesus Section of the Society of Biblical Literature. He earned a doctorate in divinity from Maynooth College, Ireland. His postdoctoral studies have been in biblical research at the Pontifical Biblical Institute, Rome, and in archeological research at the Ecole Biblique, Jerusalem. Crossan has taught at several seminaries in the Chicago area and was professor of religious studies at DePaul University for twenty-six years. He has written over a dozen books on the historical Jesus.

The Gospels are normative, I think for us as Christians not just in their production, in what they have created, but in the way they are written. A Gospel goes back, as it were, to the twenties. It writes Jesus from the 20s into the 70s, the 80s, the 90s. A Gospel always takes the historical Jesus and laminates him together with the Christ we believe in–the two of them together. John rewrites the 20s as Mark had done before him. The historical Jesus remains crucial for Christianity because we must in each generation of the Church redo our historical work and redo our theological work. We can't skip it. . . .

When I look a Buddhist friend in the face, I cannot say with integrity: "Our story about Jesus' virginal birth is true and factual. Your story that when the Buddha came out of his mother's womb, he was walking, talking, teaching, and preaching (which I must admit is even better than our story)–that's a myth. We have the truth; you have a lie."

I don't think that can be said any longer, for our insistence that our faith is fact and that others' faith is a lie is, I think, a cancer that eats at the heart of Christianity.

~ William F. Buckley, Jr. **Will the Real Jesus Please Stand Up?** Paul Copan, ed. Grand Rapids: Baker Books, 1998. p. 39.

Readings on Christ (continued)

Christus Victor: The Warrior Who Is Messiah

Ps. 68.10 - You ascended on high, leading a host of captives in your train and receiving gifts among men, even among the rebellious, that the Lord God may dwell there.

Ps. 110.1-2 - The Lord says to my Lord: "Sit at my right hand, until I make your enemies your footstool." The Lord sends forth from Zion your mighty scepter. Rule in the midst of your enemies!

[*Christus Victor's*] central theme is the idea of the Atonement as a Divine conflict and victory; Christ–*Christus Victor*–fights against and triumphs over the evil powers of the world, the 'tyrant' under which mankind is in bondage and suffering, and in him God reconciles the world to himself . . . . The background of the idea is dualistic; God is pictured as in Christ carrying through a victorious conflict against powers of evil which are hostile to his will. This constitutes Atonement, because the drama is a cosmic drama, and the victory over the powers bring to pass a new relation, a relation of reconciliation, between God and the world; and, still more, because in a measure the hostile powers are regarded as in the service of the will of God the Judge of all, and the executants of his judgment. Seen from this side, the triumph over the opposing powers is regarded as a reconciling of God himself; he is reconciled by the very act in which he reconciles the world to himself.

~ Gustaf Aulen, **Christus Victor**.
New York: MacMillan Publishers, 1969. pp. 20-21.

The Risen Messiah Himself Is Our Life

Col. 3.1-4 - If then you have been raised with Christ, seek the things that are above, where Christ is, seated at the right hand of God. Set your minds on things that are above, not on things that are on earth. For you have died, and your life is hidden with Christ in God. When Christ who is your life appears, then you also will appear with him in glory.

Let us keep in mind that instead of giving us one object after another, God gives his Son to us. Because of this, we can always lift up our hearts and look to the Lord, saying, "Lord, You are my way; Lord, You are my truth; Lord, You are my life. It is you, Lord, who is related to me, not your things." May we ask God to give us grace that we may see Christ in all spiritual things. Day by day we are convinced that aside

Readings on Christ (continued)

from Christ there is no way, nor truth, nor life. How easily we make things as way, truth, and life. Or, we call hot atmosphere as life, we label clear thought as life. We consider strong emotion or outward conduct as life. In reality, though, these are not life. We ought to realize that only the Lord is life, Christ is our life. And it is the Lord who lives out this life in us. Let us ask him to deliver us from the many external and fragmentary affairs that we may touch only him. May we see the Lord in all things –way, truth, and life are all found in knowing him. May we really meet the Son of God and let him live in us. Amen.

~ Watchman Nee. **Christ, the Sum of All Spiritual Things.** New York: Christian Fellowship Publishers, 1973. p. 20.

APPENDIX 15

Faithfully Re-presenting Jesus of Nazareth

Don L. Davis

Eph. 4.17-19 (ESV) - Now this I say and testify in the Lord, that you must no longer walk as the Gentiles do, in the futility of their minds. [18] They are darkened in their understanding, alienated from the life of God because of the ignorance that is in them, due to their hardness of heart. [19] They have become callous and have given themselves up to sensuality, greedy to practice every kind of impurity.

Eph. 4.20-23 (ESV) - But that is not the way you learned Christ! - [21] assuming that you have heard about him and were taught in him, as the truth is in Jesus, [22] to put off your old self, which belongs to your former manner of life and is corrupt through deceitful desires, [23] and to be renewed in the spirit of your minds.

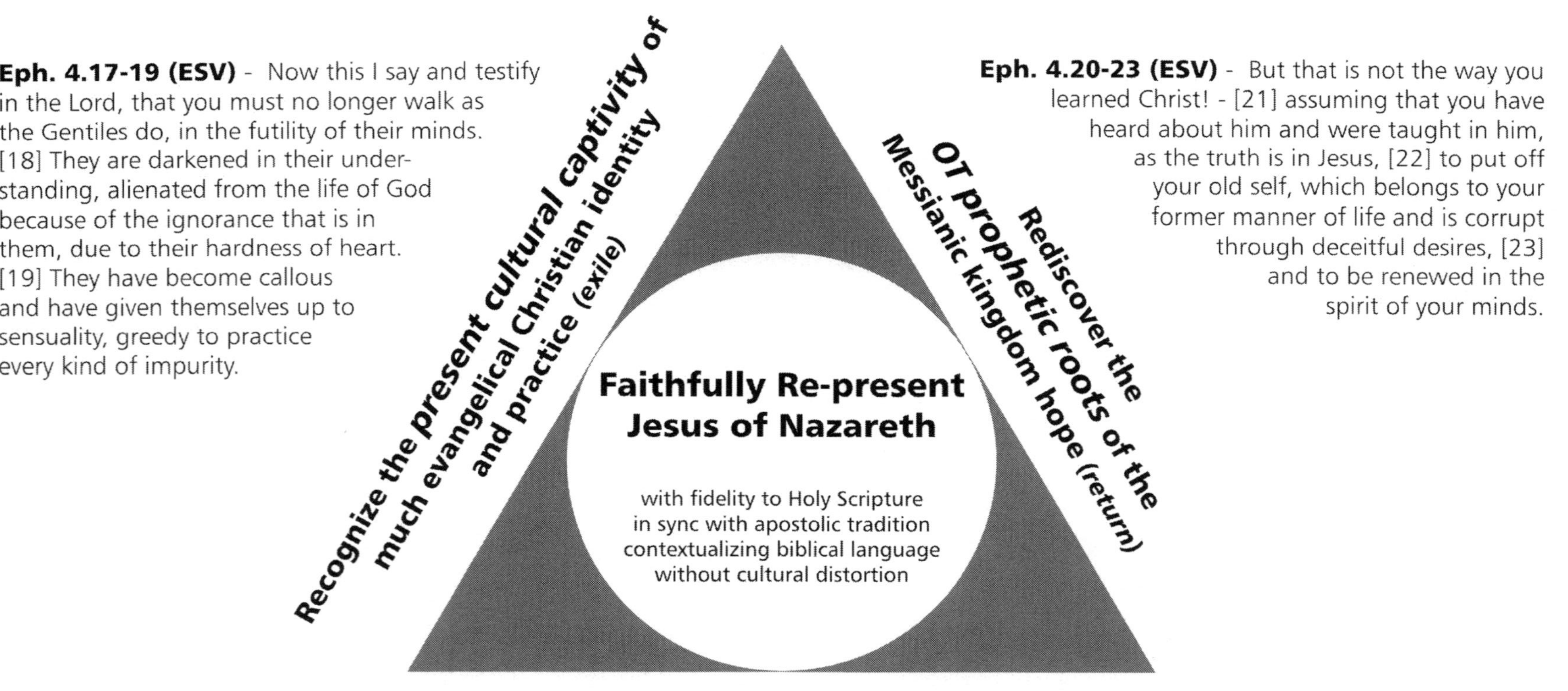

Eph. 4.24-25 (ESV) - and to put on the new self, created after the likeness of God in true righteousness and holiness. [25] Therefore, having put away falsehood, let each one of you speak the truth with his neighbor, for we are members one of another.

APPENDIX 16

Messianic Prophecies Cited in the New Testament

Rev. Dr. Don L. Davis

	NT Citation	OT Reference	Indication of the Fulfillment of the Messianic Prophecy
1	Matt. 1.23	Isa. 7.14	The virgin birth of Jesus of Nazareth
2	Matt. 2.6	Mic. 5.2	The birth of Messiah in Bethlehem
3	Matt. 2.15	Hos. 11.1	That Yahweh would call Messiah out of Egypt, the second Israel
4	Matt. 2.18	Jer. 31.15	Rachel weeping over infants slain by Herod seeking to destroy Messianic seed
5	Matt. 3.3	Isa. 40.3	John the Baptist's preaching fulfills the Messianic forerunner of Isaiah
6	Matt. 4.15-16	Isa. 9.1-2	Galilean ministry of Jesus fulfills Isaiah's prophecy of Messiah's light to the Gentiles
7	Matt. 8.17	Isa. 53.4	Healing ministry of Jesus fulfills Isaiah prophecy regarding Messiah's power to exorcize and heal
8	Matt. 11.14-15	Isa. 35.5-6; 61.1	Jesus' healing ministry confirms his identity as Yahweh's anointed Messiah
9	Matt. 11.10	Mal. 3.1	Jesus confirms John the Baptist's identity as the messenger of Yahweh in Malachi
10	Matt. 12.18-21	Isa. 42.1-4	Jesus' healing ministry fulfills Isaiah's prophecy of Messiah's compassion for the weak
11	Matt. 12.40	Jon. 1.17	As Jonah was three days and nights in the belly of the sea monster, so Jesus would be in the earth
12	Matt. 13.14-15	Isa. 6.9-10	The spiritual dullness of Jesus' audience
13	Matt. 13.35	Ps. 78.2	Messiah would teach in parables to the people
14	Matt. 15.8-9	Isa. 29.13	Hypocritical nature of the audience of Jesus
15	Matt. 21.5	Zech. 9.9	Triumphal entry of Messiah the King into Jerusalem upon the foal of a donkey
16	Matt. 21.9	Ps. 118.26-27	Hosannas to the King of Jerusalem
17	Matt. 21.16	Ps. 8.2	Out of the mouth of babes Yahweh declares salvation
18	Matt. 21.42	Ps. 118.22	The Stone which the builders rejected has become the Capstone
19	Matt. 23.39	Ps. 110.1	The enthronement of Yahweh's Lord

Messianic Prophecies Cited in the New Testament (continued)

	NT Citation	OT Reference	Indication of the Fulfillment of the Messianic Prophecy
20	Matt. 24.30	Dan. 7.13	The Son of Man to come, of Daniel's prophecy, is none other than Jesus of Nazareth
21	Matt. 26.31	Zech. 13.7	The Shepherd smitten by Yahweh and the sheep scattered
22	Matt. 26.64	Ps. 110.1	Jesus of Nazareth is the fulfillment of Daniel's Messianic Son of Man
23	Matt. 26.64	Dan. 7.3	Jesus will come in the clouds of heaven as Daniel's exalted ruler
24	Matt. 27.9-10	Zech. 11.12-13	Messiah is betrayed for thirty pieces of silver
25	Matt. 27.34-35	Ps. 69.21	God's anointed is given wine mingled with gall
26	Matt. 27.35	Ps. 22.18	The soldiers cast lots for the garments of the Messiah
27	Matt. 27.43	Ps. 22.8	Messiah receives mockery and derision upon the cross
28	Matt. 27.46	Ps. 22.1	Messiah forsaken by God for the sake of others
29	Mark 1.2	Mal. 3.1	John the Baptist is the fulfillment of the prophecy regarding the Lord's messenger
30	Mark 1.3	Isa. 40.3	John the Baptist is the voice calling in the wilderness to prepare the Lord's way
31	Mark 4.12	Isa. 6.9	The spiritual dullness of the audience in regards to Messiah's message
32	Mark 7.6	Isa. 29.13	Hypocrisy of the audience in their response to Messiah
33	Mark 11.9	Ps. 118.25	Hosanna's given to Messiah's entry as King into Jerusalem
34	Mark 12.10-11	Ps. 118.25	The stone which the builders rejected has become the chief cornerstone
35	Mark 12.36	Ps. 110.1	The Lord enthrones the Lord of David upon his throne in Zion
36	Mark 13.26	Dan. 7.13	Jesus is the prophesied Son of Man who will return in glory in the clouds
37	Mark 14.27	Zech 13.7	Jesus will be forsaken by his own, for the shepherd will be smitten and the sheep scattered
38	Mark 14.62	Dan. 7.13	Jesus is the Messiah, the Son of Man of Daniel's vision
39	Mark 14.62	Ps. 110.1	The Son of Man, who is Jesus, will come from the right hand of Yahweh
40	Mark 15.24	Ps. 22.18	Lots are cast for the garments of Messiah during his passion
41	Mark 15.34	Ps. 22.1	Messiah is forsaken by God for the redemption of the world

Messianic Prophecies Cited in the New Testament (continued)

	NT Citation	OT Reference	Indication of the Fulfillment of the Messianic Prophecy
42	Luke 1.17	Mal. 4.6	John the Baptist will come in the power and the spirit of Elijah
43	Luke 1.76	Mal. 3.1	John goes before the Lord to prepare the way
44	Luke 1.79	Isa. 9.1-2	Messiah will give light to those who dwell in darkness
45	Luke 2.32	Isa. 42.6; 49.6	Messiah will be a light to the Gentiles
46	Luke 3.4-5	Isa. 40.3	John is Isaiah's voice that cries in the wilderness to prepare the Lord's way
47	Luke 4.18-19	Isa. 61.1-2	Jesus is Yahweh's servant, anointed by his Spirit to bring the good news of the Kingdom
48	Luke 7.27	Mal. 3.1	Jesus confirms John's identity as the preparer of the Lord's way
49	Luke 8.10	Isa. 6.9	The dullness of the audience to Messiah Jesus
50	Luke 19.38	Ps. 118.26	Jesus fulfills in his entry into Jerusalem the Messianic prophecy of the King of Israel
51	Luke 20.17	Ps. 118.26	Jesus is Yahweh's stone which the builders rejected, which has become the Capstone
52	Luke 20.42-43	Ps. 110.1	David calls his lord the Messiah and Lord, who is enthroned in Zion by Yahweh
53	Luke 22.37	Isa. 53.12	Messiah is classed among criminals
54	Luke 22.69	Ps. 110.1	Jesus will return from the right hand of God, from where he has been enthroned
55	Luke 23.34	Ps. 22.18	Lots are cast for the garments of Messiah
56	John 1.23	Isa. 40.3	John's preaching is the fulfillment of Isaiah's prophecy about the forerunner of the Messiah
57	John 2.17	Ps. 69.17	Zeal for the house of the Lord will consume the Messiah
58	John 6.45	Isa. 54.13	All those whom God teaches will come to Messiah
59	John 7.42	Ps. 89.4; Mic. 5.2	Messiah, the seed of David, will be from Bethlehem
60	John 12.13	Ps. 118.25-26	Hosannas are given to Israel's triumphant Messiah King
61	John 12.15	Zech. 9.9	The King of Israel enters Jerusalem upon the foal of a donkey
62	John 12.38	Isa. 53.1	As Isaiah prophesied, few believed the report of Yahweh about his anointed one
63	John 12.40	Isa. 6.10	Isaiah saw the glory of Messiah and spoke of the dullness of his audience to him

Messianic Prophecies Cited in the New Testament (continued)

	NT Citation	OT Reference	Indication of the Fulfillment of the Messianic Prophecy
64	John 13.18; cf. 17.12	Ps. 41.9	Betrayal of Messiah by one of his intimate followers
65	John 15.25	Pss. 35.19; 69.4	Messiah will be hated without cause
66	John 19.24	Ps. 22.18	The garments of Messiah will be divided
67	John 19.28	Ps. 69.21	Messiah will be offered wine upon the cross
68	John 19.36	Exod. 12.46; Num. 9.12; Ps. 34.20	Not one bone of the Messiah will be broken
69	John 19.37	Zech. 12.10	The repentant nation of Israel will look upon him whom they have pierced
70	Acts 1.20	Pss. 69.25; 109.8	Judas is to be replaced with another
71	Acts 2.16-21	Joel 2.28-32	The Spirit is to be poured out in the last days upon all flesh
72	Acts 2.25-28	Ps. 16.8-11	Messiah could not undergo decay or corruption in Sheol
73	Acts 2.34-35	Ps. 110.1	Messiah is enthroned at Yahweh's right hand until his enemies are defeated
74	Acts 3.22-23	Deut. 18.15, 19	God would raise up for the people a prophet like Moses
75	Acts 3.25	Gen. 22.18	All nations of the earth would be blessed in the seed of Abraham
76	Acts 4.11	Ps. 118.22	Messiah Jesus is the rejected stone whom God has made the cornerstone
77	Acts 4.25	Ps. 2.1	Yahweh will laugh at the opposition given by the nations to him and his anointed
78	Acts 7.37	Deut. 18.15	Yahweh will give to Israel a prophet like Moses
79	Acts 8.32-33	Isa. 53.7-9	Messiah Jesus is the Suffering Servant of Yahweh
80	Acts 13.33	Ps. 2.7	God has fulfilled the promise to Israel in Jesus by raising him from the dead
81	Acts 13.34	Isa. 53.3	Messiah Jesus is the fulfillment of the sure mercies of David
82	Acts 13.35	Ps. 16.10	Messiah would not undergo corruption in the grave
83	Acts 13.47	Isa. 49.6	Through Paul, the message of Messiah becomes a light to the nations
84	Acts 15.16-18	Amos 9.11-12	The dynasty of David is restored in Jesus, and Gentiles are welcomed into the Kingdom
85	Rom. 9.25-26	Hos. 2.23; 1.10	Gentiles are to become the people of God

Messianic Prophecies Cited in the New Testament (continued)

	NT Citation	OT Reference	Indication of the Fulfillment of the Messianic Prophecy
86	Rom. 9.33; 10.11	Isa. 28.16	Messiah becomes a stone of stumbling to those who reject God's salvation
87	Rom. 10.13	Joel 2.32	Anyone calling on the name of the Lord will be saved
88	Rom. 11.8	Isa. 29.10	Israel through unbelief has been hardened to Messiah
89	Rom. 11.9-10	Ps. 69.22-23	Judgment has hardened upon Israel
90	Rom. 11.26	Isa. 59.20-21	A deliverer will come from Zion
91	Rom. 11.27	Isa. 27.9	Forgiveness of sins will be given through a new covenant
92	Rom. 14.11	Isa. 45.23	All will be finally judged by Yahweh
93	Rom. 15.9	Ps. 18.49	Gentiles praise God through faith in Messiah
94	Rom. 15.10	Deut. 32.43	God receives praise from the nations
95	Rom. 15.11	Ps. 117.1	The peoples of the earth give God glory
96	Rom. 15.12	Isa. 11.10	Gentiles will hope in the root of Jesse
97	Rom. 15.21	Isa. 52.15	The Good News will be preached to those without understanding
98	1 Cor. 15.27	Ps. 8.7	All things are under the feet of God's representative head
99	1 Cor. 15.54	Isa. 25.8	Death will be swallowed up in victory
100	1 Cor. 15.55	Hos. 13.14	Death will one day lose its sting altogether
101	2 Cor. 6.2	Isa. 49.8	Now is the day of salvation through faith in Messiah Jesus
102	2 Cor. 6.16	Ezek. 37.27	God will dwell with his people
103	2 Cor. 6.18	Hos. 1.10; Isa 43.6	Believers in Messiah Jesus are the sons and daughters of God
104	Gal. 3.8, 16	Gen. 12.3; 13.15; 17.8	The Scriptures, foreseeing Gentile justification by faith, preached the Gospel beforehand through the promise to Abraham, that all nations would be blessed in his seed
105	Gal. 4.27	Isa. 54.1	Jerusalem is the mother of us all
106	Eph. 2.17	Isa. 57.19	Peace of Messiah Jesus is preached both to the Jew and the Gentile
107	Eph. 4.8	Ps. 68.18	Messiah in his ascension has conquered and given gifts to us all by his grace
108	Eph. 5.14	Isa. 26.19; 51.17; 52.1; 60.1	The regeneration of the Lord has occurred; his light has shined on us

Messianic Prophecies Cited in the New Testament (continued)

	NT Citation	OT Reference	Indication of the Fulfillment of the Messianic Prophecy
109	Heb. 1.5	Ps. 2.7	Messiah is God's Son
110	Heb. 1.5	2 Sam. 7.14	Messiah Jesus is the anointed Son of God
111	Heb. 1.6	Deut. 32.43	Angels worshiped Messiah when he entered the world
112	Heb. 1.8-9	Ps. 45.6-7	Messiah Jesus is referred to as God by Yahweh in direct address
113	Heb. 1.10-12	Ps. 102.25-27	The Son is the agent of God's creation and is eternal
114	Heb. 1.13	Ps. 110.1	Messiah Jesus is enthroned at the Father's right hand
115	Heb. 2.6-8	Ps. 8.4-6	All things have been made subject to the Son's authority
116	Heb. 2.12	Ps. 22.22	Messiah Jesus is a brother to all of the redeemed
117	Heb. 2.13	Isa. 8.17-18	Messiah puts his trust in Yahweh God
118	Heb. 5.5	Ps. 2.7	Messiah is God's Son
119	Heb. 5.6	Ps. 110.4	Messiah is an eternal priest after the order of Melchizedek
120	Heb. 7.17, 21	Ps. 110.4	Messiah Jesus is an eternal High Priest
121	Heb. 8.8-12	Jer. 31.31-34	A new covenant has been made in the blood of Jesus
122	Heb. 10.5-9	Ps. 40.6	The death of Messiah Jesus replaces the atoning system of Temple sacrifice
123	Heb. 10.13	Ps. 110.1	Yahweh has enthroned Messiah Jesus as Lord
124	Heb. 10.16-17	Jer. 31.33-34	The Holy Spirit bears witness of the sufficiency of the New Covenant
125	Heb. 10.37-38	Hab. 2.3-4	He who will come will do so, in a little while
126	Heb. 12.26	Hag. 2.6	All heaven and earth will be shaken
127	1 Pet. 2.6	Isa. 28.16	God lays a cornerstone in Zion
128	1 Pet. 2.7	Ps. 118.22	The stone which the builders rejected, God has made the Capstone
129	1 Pet. 2.8	Isa. 8.14	Messiah is a stone of stumbling to those who do not believe
130	1 Pet. 2.10	Hos. 1.10; 2.23	Gentiles through Messiah are now invited to become the people of God
131	1 Pet. 2.22	Isa. 53.9	The sinless Messiah Jesus was sacrificed for us

APPENDIX 17

The Prophetic Vision as Source of Biblical Faith Commitment

Rev. Dr. Don L. Davis

Faith is an essential part of human life. Humans are confessing, believing and trusting creatures. ***And where we place our faith determines the world view which we will adopt. Put another way, our ultimate faith commitment sets the contours of our world view.*** It shapes our vision for a way of life. People who doubt their world view are restless and feel they have no ground to stand on. They are often in the throes of a psychological crisis. ***But the emotional crisis is fundamentally religious because our world view rests on a faith commitment.***

What is a faith commitment? It is the way we answer four basic questions facing everyone:

1) ***Who am I?*** Or, what is the nature, task, and purpose of human beings?
2) ***Where am I?*** Or, what is the nature of the world and universe I live in?
3) ***What's wrong?*** Or, what is the basic problem or obstacle that keeps me from attaining fulfillment? In other words, how do I understand evil?
4) ***What is the remedy?*** Or, how is it possible to overcome this hindrance to my fulfillment? In other words, how do I find salvation?

When we've answered these questions, that is, when our faith is settled, then we begin to see reality in some sensible pattern. ***Out of our faith proceeds a world view, without which human life simply cannot go on.***

~ Brian J. Walsh and J. Richard Middleton. **The Transforming Vision.** Downers Grove: InterVarsity Press, 1984. p. 35.

APPENDIX 18

Preaching and Teaching Jesus of Nazareth as Messiah and Lord Is the Heart of All Biblical Ministry

Don L. Davis

Phil. 3.8 (ESV) - Indeed, I count everything as loss because of the surpassing worth of *knowing Christ [Messiah] Jesus my Lord*. For his sake I have suffered the loss of all things and count them as rubbish, in order *that I may gain Christ [Messiah].*

Acts 5.42 (ESV) - And every day, in the temple and from house to house, they *did not cease teaching and preaching Jesus as the Christ [Messiah].*

1 Cor. 1.23 (ESV) - but we preach *Christ [Messiah] crucified*, a stumbling block to Jews and folly to Gentiles.

2 Cor. 4.5 (ESV) - For what we proclaim is not ourselves, but *Jesus Christ [Messiah] as Lord*, with ourselves as your servants for Jesus' sake.

1 Cor. 2.2 (ESV) - For I decided to know nothing among you except *Jesus Christ [Messiah] and him crucified.*

Eph. 3.8 (ESV) - To me, though I am the very least of all the saints, this grace was given, *to preach to the Gentiles the unsearchable riches of Christ [Messiah].*

Phil. 1.18 (ESV) - What then? Only that in every way, whether in pretense or in truth, *Christ [Messiah] is proclaimed*, and in that I rejoice. Yes, and I will rejoice.

Col. 1.27-29 (ESV) - To them God chose to make known how great among the Gentiles are the riches of the glory of this mystery, which is *Christ [Messiah] in you, the hope of glory*. [28] Him we proclaim, warning everyone and teaching everyone with all wisdom, that we may *present everyone mature in Christ [Messiah]*. [29] *For this I toil, struggling with all his energy* that he powerfully works within me.

APPENDIX 19

Summary of Messianic Interpretations in the Old Testament

Rev. Dr. Don L. Davis, adapted from James Smith, The Promised Messiah

Legend

EJ - Early Jewish Interpretation

NTA - New Testament Allusion

NTE - New Testament Exegesis

CF - Church Fathers

	Bible Reference	Summary of the Messianic Prophecy	EJ	NTA	NTE	CF
1	Gen. 3.15	One from the ranks of the seed of the woman will crush the head of the serpent	X	X		X
2	Gen. 9.25-27	God will come and dwell in the tents of Shem	X	X		X
3	Gen. 12.3; 18.18; 22.18; 26.4; 28.14	All nations of the earth will be blessed through the seed of Abraham, Isaac, and Jacob	X	X	X	X
4	Gen. 49.10-11	The scepter won't depart from Judah until Shiloh comes, and all the nations will be obedient to him	X	X		X
5	Num. 24.16-24	A powerful ruler from Israel will come and crush the enemies of God's people	X	X		X
6	Deut. 18.15-18	A prophet like Moses will come and all the righteous will listen to him		X	X	X
7	Deut. 32.43	The angels of God commanded to rejoice as the Firstborn of God comes into the world		X		
8	1 Sam. 2.10	God will judge the ends of the earth but will give strength to his anointed	X			X
9	1 Sam. 2.35-36	A faithful Priest will come and dispense blessing upon the people				
10	2 Sam. 7.12-16	The Seed of David will sit upon an eternal throne and will build the house of God		X		X
11	Ps. 89	God's covenant to send Messiah through David cannot be revoked	X			
12	Ps. 132	God has chosen David and Zion		X		
13	Ps. 8	The Son of Man is made a little lower than the angels, and is exalted as ruler over all creation		X	X	X
14	Ps. 40	Messiah volunteers to enter the world, to suffer, and is delivered			X	X

Summary of Messianic Interpretations in the Old Testament (continued)

	Bible Reference	Summary of the Messianic Prophecy	EJ	NTA	NTE	CF
15	Ps. 118	Messiah survives the power of death to become the chief Cornerstone, the Capstone of God's building			X	X
16	Ps. 78.1-2	Messiah will speak to the people in parables			X	
17	Ps. 69	Messiah's zeal for the house of God will bring hatred and abuse, but his enemies will receive their just dues			X	X
18	Ps. 109	The one who betrays Messiah will suffer a terrible fate			X	X
19	Ps. 22	After unparalleled suffering, Messiah conquers death and rejoices with his brethren			X	X
20	Ps. 2	Messiah is enthroned in Zion, defeats his opposition, and rules over creation	X		X	X
21	Ps. 16	Yahweh will not allow Messiah to see corruption in Sheol			X	X
22	Ps. 102	Messiah the Creator is eternal, though suffering severe persecution				X
23	Ps. 45	Messiah is God, and has been anointed by God to sit upon an eternal throne; his people are his lovely bride	X			X
24	Ps. 110	Messiah is a priest-king after the order of Melchizedek, and he sits at the right hand of God, ruling over all humankind	X		X	X
25	Ps. 72	Messiah reigns over a universal and righteous kingdom of blessing	X			X
26	Ps. 68	Messiah wins a great victory, then ascends back on high	X		X	X
27	Job 9.33; 16.19-21; 17.3; 33.23-28	A Mediator, Interpreter, Advocate, and Witness will walk in the latter days upon the earth				
28	Job 19.23-27	A Redeemer will stand upon the earth in the latter days and the righteous will see him				X
29	Joel 2.23	A Wonderful Teacher will arise and usher in an age of great abundance	X			X
30	Hos. 1.10-2.1	A Second Moses will lead God's people out of bondage into a glorious new era			X	
31	Hos. 3.5	After the exile, God's people will serve Yahweh their God, and David their king	X			
32	Hos. 11.1	God calls his Son, the Second Israel, out of Egypt			X	

Summary of Messianic Interpretations in the Old Testament (continued)

	Bible Reference	Summary of the Messianic Prophecy	EJ	NTA	NTE	CF
33	Isa. 4.2-6	The beautiful and glorious Shoot of Yahweh will be the pride of the remnant of Israel	X			
34	Isa. 7.14-15	A virgin will conceive and bear a son whose name will be called Immanuel			X	X
35	Isa. 8.17-18	Messiah waits for the time of his coming, and he and his children are signs and wonders in Israel		X	X	
36	Isa. 9.1-7	Messiah will bring light to Galilee and one will sit on the throne of David to usher in the reign of God in righteousness and justice	X	X		X
37	Isa. 11.1-16	A Shoot from the stem of Jesse will be filled with the Spirit of Yahweh, and will usher into the earth a Kingdom of righteousness and peace	X	X	X	X
38	Isa. 16.5	Downtrodden peoples will look to the house of David for justice and lovingkindness				
39	Isa. 28.16	God is going to lay in Zion a tried and tested Stone, a precious Cornerstone	X	X	X	X
40	Isa. 30.19-26	The people of God will see their divine Teacher and will enjoy his abundant blessing as a result of listening to him	X			
41	Isa. 32.1-2	A Leader of the future will be a shelter from the storm, like water in a dry place				
42	Isa. 33.17	The eyes of the people of God will see the King in his beauty				
43	Isa. 42.17	Yahweh's Servant will bring forth justice to the nations, and will be a Covenant to the people, a Light to the nations	X		X	X
44	Isa. 49.1-13	Yahweh's Servant is divinely appointed to teach, to raise up the tribes of Jacob, and to be a Light to the Gentiles	X			X
45	Isa. 50.4-11	Yahweh's Servant is an obedient disciple who endures suffering and indignity				X
46	Isa. 52.13-53.12	God's Servant is rejected, suffers horribly for the sins of others, dies, but then sees his seed and is satisfied	X	X	X	X
47	Isa. 55.3-5	A son of David will be made a Witness, Leader, and Commander for the peoples				X
48	Isa. 59.20-21	A Redeemer will come to penitent Zion	X		X	

Summary of Messianic Interpretations in the Old Testament (continued)

	Bible Reference	Summary of the Messianic Prophecy	EJ	NTA	NTE	CF
49	Isa. 61.1-11	Messiah has been anointed by the Spirit of Yahweh to proclaim the Good News to the poor, and liberty and deliverance to the captives	X		X	X
50	Mic. 2.12-13	The divine Breaker will lead the people of God out of bondage	X			
51	Mic. 5.1-5	A glorious Ruler will arise from Bethlehem to shepherd the people of God and give them victory over their enemies	X	X	X	X
52	Hab. 3.12-15	Yahweh comes forth from the salvation of his Anointed, and will strike through the head of the house of evil				
53	Jer. 23.5-6	God will raise up a Righteous Branch who will act wisely and execute justice and righteousness in the land	X			
54	Jer. 30.9, 21	Upon return from exile, God's people will serve David their King who will serve as Mediator and draw near to God for them	X			
55	Jer. 31.21-22	God will create a new thing in the land	X			X
56	Jer. 33.14-26	Yahweh will raise up his righteous Servant in the land, and will not fail to fulfill his promise to David and to Levi	X			
57	Ezek. 17.22-24	A tender Twig from the house of David will become a stately Cedar with birds of every kind nesting under it	X			X
58	Ezek. 21.25-27	The crown is removed from the last king of Judah until he comes whose right it is				
59	Ezek. 34.23-31	God will set over those who return from Babylon one Shepherd, his servant, David		X		
60	Ezek. 37.21-28	God's people will be united and will have one King, "My Servant David"		X		
61	Ezek. 44.48	A Prince in the future age will be accorded honor, and through him sacrifices will be offered to God	X			
62	Dan. 7.13-14	One like a Son of Man will come before the Ancient of Days to receive an everlasting Kingdom and Dominion	X	X	X	X
63	Dan. 9.24-27	After 69 "weeks" of years, Messiah will appear, he will be cut off, and will cause sacrifice and oblation to cease	X			X
64	Hag. 2.6-9	After the shaking of the nations, the Desire of all Nations will come and fill the Temple of God with glory	X		X	

Summary of Messianic Interpretations in the Old Testament (continued)

	Bible Reference	Summary of the Messianic Prophecy	EJ	NTA	NTE	CF
65	Hag. 2.21-23	Zerubbabel will be made God's signet Ring in the day when the thrones of kingdoms and the Gentiles are overthrown by Yahweh				
66	Zech. 3.8-10	The Servant of Yahweh, his Shoot, is symbolized by Joshua the High Priest and by an engraved stone	X			X
67	Zech. 6.12-13	A man whose name is Shoot shall build the Temple of the Lord, and he will be a Priest and a King	X			X
68	Zech. 9.9-11	The King of Zion comes riding upon the foal of a donkey	X		X	X
69	Zech. 10.3-4	God will send one who is the Cornerstone, the Tent Peg, the Battle Bow, the one who possesses all sovereignty	X			
70	Zech. 11.4-14	Thirty pieces of silver thrown to the potter in the house of God			X	X
71	Zech. 13.7	The sword of divine justice smites the Shepherd and the sheep are scattered			X	X
72	Mal. 3.1	The Lord's messenger will clear the way before him, and the Lord will suddenly come to his Temple	X	X	X	X
73	Mal. 4.2	The Sun of Righteousness will arise with healing in his wings	X	X		

APPENDIX 20

Messiah Yeshua in Every Book of the Bible

*Adapted from Norman L. Geisler, **A Popular Survey of the Old Testament***

Christ in the Books of the Old Testament

1. The Seed of the Woman (Gen. 3.15)
2. The Passover Lamb (Exod. 12.3-4)
3. The Atoning Sacrifice (Lev. 17.11)
4. The Smitten Rock (Num. 20.8, 11)
5. The Faithful Prophet (Deut. 18.18)
6. The Captain of the Lord's Host (Josh. 5.15)
7. The Divine Deliverer (Judg. 2.18)
8. The Kinsman Redeemer (Ruth 3.12)
9. The Anointed One (1 Sam. 2.10)
10. The Son of David (2 Sam. 7.14)
11. The Coming King (1 Kings)
12. The Coming King (2 Kings)
13. The Builder of the Temple (1 Chron. 28.20)
14. The Builder of the Temple (2 Chron.)
15. The Restorer of the Temple (Ezra 6.14, 15)
16. The Restorer of the Nation (Neh. 6.15)
17. The Preserver of the Nation (Esther 4.14)
18. The Living Redeemer (Job 19.25)
19. The Praise of Israel (Ps. 150.6)
20. The Wisdom of God (Prov. 8.22, 23)
21. The Great Teacher (Eccles. 12.11)
22. The Fairest of Ten Thousand (Song of Sol. 5.10)
23. The Suffering Servant (Isa. 53.11)
24. The Maker of the New Covenant (Jer. 31.31)
25. The Man of Sorrows (Lam. 3.28-30)
26. The Glory of God (Ezek. 43.2)
27. The Coming Messiah (Dan. 9.25)
28. The Lover of the Unfaithful (Hos. 3.1)
29. The Hope of Israel (Joel 3.16)
30. The Husbandman (Amos 9.13)
31. The Savior (Obad. 21)
32. The Resurrected One (Jon. 2.10)
33. The Ruler in Israel (Mic. 5.2)
34. The Avenger (Nah. 2.1)
35. The Holy God (Hab. 1.13)
36. The King of Israel (Zeph. 3.15)
37. The Desire of Nations (Hag. 2.7)
38. The Righteous Branch (Zech. 3.8)
39. The Sun of Righteousness (Mal. 4.2)

Messiah Yeshua in Every Book of the Bible (continued)

Christ in the Books of the New Testament

1. The King of the Jews (Matt. 2.2)
2. The Servant of the Lord (Mark 10.45)
3. The Son of Man (Luke 19.10)
4. The Son of God (John 1.1)
5. The Ascended Lord (Acts 1.10)
6. The Believer's Righteousness (Rom. 1.17)
7. Our Sanctification (1 Cor. 1.30)
8. Our Sufficiency (2 Cor. 12.9)
9. Our Liberty (Gal. 2.4)
10. The Exalted Head of the Church (Eph. 1.22)
11. The Christian's Joy (Phil. 1.26)
12. The Fullness of Deity (Col. 2.9)
13. The Believer's Comfort (1 Thess. 4.16, 17)
14. The Believer's Glory (2 Thess. 1.12)
15. The Christian's Preserver (1 Tim. 4.10)
16. The Christian's Rewarder (2 Tim. 4.8)
17. The Blessed Hope (Titus 2.13)
18. Our Substitute (Philem. 17)
19. The Great High Priest (Heb. 4.15)
20. The Giver of Wisdom (James 1.5)
21. The Rock (1 Pet. 2.6)
22. The Precious Promise (2 Pet. 1.4)
23. The Life (1 John)
24. The Truth (2 John)
25. The Way (3 John)
26. The Advocate (Jude)
27. The King of kings and Lord of lords (Rev. 19.16)

APPENDIX 21

Old Testament Names, Titles, and Epithets for the Messiah

*Adapted from Norman L. Geisler, **A Popular Survey of the Old Testament***

1. Advocate, Job 16.19
2. Angel (messenger), Job 33.23
3. Anointed, 1 Sam. 2.19; Ps. 2.2
4. Battle-bow, Zech. 10.4
5. Bethlehem's Ruler, Mic. 5.2
6. Breaker, Mic. 2.13
7. Commander, Isa. 55.4
8. Cornerstone (Capstone), Ps. 118.22; Isa. 28.16
9. Covenant of the People, Isa. 42.6
10. Crusher, Gen. 3.15
11. David, Hos. 3.5; Jer. 30.9
12. Desire of all Nations, Hag. 2.7
13. Eternal One, Ps. 102.25-27
14. Eternal Priest, Ps. 110.4
15. Everlasting Father, Isa. 9.6
16. Faithful Priest, 1 Sam. 2.35
17. Firstborn, Ps. 89.27
18. Forsaken Sufferer, Ps. 22
19. Foundation, Isa. 28.16; Zech. 10.4
20. God, Ps. 45.6-7
21. Head, Hos. 1.11; Mic. 2.13
22. Healer, Isa. 42.7
23. He who Comes, Ps. 118.26
24. Horn of David, Ps. 132.17
25. Immanuel, Isa. 7.14
26. Interpreter, Job 33.23
27. Israel, Hos. 11.1; Isa. 49.3
28. King, Ps. 2.5; Hos. 3.5
29. Lamp for David, Ps. 132.17
30. Last, Job 19.25
31. Launderer, Mal. 3.2
32. Leader, Isa. 55.4
33. Liberator, Isa. 42.7
34. Light, Isa. 9.2
35. Light of the Gentiles, Isa. 42.6; 49.6
36. Lord, Mal. 3.1
37. Man, Zech. 6.12; 13.7
38. Man of Sorrows, Isa. 53.3
39. Mediator, Job 33.23
40. Messenger of the Covenant, Mal. 3.1
41. Messiah-Prince, Dan. 9.25
42. Mighty God, Isa. 9.6
43. Mighty Hero, Ps. 45.3
44. My Equal, Zech. 13.7
45. Nail (peg), Zech. 10.4
46. Our Peace, Mic. 5.5
47. Parable Teller, Ps. 78.1-2
48. Pierced One, Zech. 12.10

Old Testament Names, Titles, and Epithets for the Messiah (continued)

49. Poor and Afflicted, Ps. 69.29
50. Priestly Ruler, Jer. 30.21; Zech. 6.13
51. Prince, Ezek. 37.25; 44-48
52. Prince of Peace, Isa. 9.6
53. Proclaimer of Good Tidings to the Poor, Isa. 61.2
54. Prophet like Moses, Deut. 18.15,18
55. Redeemer, Job 19.25; Isa. 59.20
56. Refiner, Mal. 3.2
57. Refuge, Isa. 32.1
58. Rejected Shepherd, Zech. 11
59. Rejected Stone, Ps. 118.22
60. Righteous Shoot, Jer. 23.5; 33.15
61. Root out of Dry Ground, Isa. 53.2
62. Ruler of all Nature, Ps. 8.5-8
63. Ruler of the Earth, Isa. 16.5
64. Scepter, Num. 24.17
65. Second Moses, Hos. 11.1
66. Seed of Abraham, Gen. 12.3; 18.18
67. Seed of David, 2 Sam. 2.12
68. Seed of the Woman, Gen. 3.15
69. Servant, Isa. 42.1; 49.3, 6
70. Shade, Isa. 32.2
71. Shelter, Isa. 32.1
72. Shepherd, Ezek. 34.23; 37.24
73. Shiloh, Gen. 49.10
74. Shoot, Zech. 3.8; 6.12
75. Shoot from the Stump of Jesse, Isa. 11.1
76. Shoot of Yahweh, Isa. 4.2
77. Sign and Wonder, Isa. 8.18
78. Signet Ring, Hag. 2.23
79. Son of God, 2 Sam. 7.14; Ps. 2.7
80. Son of Man, Ps. 8.4; Dan. 7.13
81. Star, Num. 24.17
82. Stone, Zech. 3.9
83. Substitutionary Sufferer, Isa. 53
84. Sun of Righteousness, Mal. 4.5
85. Teacher, Isa. 30.20
86. Teacher for Righteousness, Joel 2.23
87. Tender Shoot, Isa. 53.2
88. Tender Twig, Ezek. 17.22
89. Temple Builder, Zech. 6.12
90. Tent Dweller, Gen. 9.26-27
91. Tested Stone, Isa. 28.16
92. Trailblazer, Ps. 16.11
93. Victor, Ps. 68.18
94. Volunteer, Ps. 40.7
95. Water of Life, Isa. 32.2
96. Witness, Job 16.19
97. Witness to the Peoples, Isa. 55.4
98. Wonderful Counselor, Isa. 9.6
99. Yahweh, Our Righteousness, Jer. 23.6
100. Zerubbabel, Hag. 2.23

APPENDIX 22

Promise vs. Prediction

The Apostolic Hermeneutic of the Old Testament

Adapted from Christopher J. H. Wright

And So It Was Fulfilled: Five Scenes of Jesus' Early Life				
Incident in Jesus' Life	**Matthew Citation**	**The Old Testament Reference**	**Commentary on the Actual Historical Context of the Old Testament Text**	**Hermeneutic Significance**
Assurance to Joseph concerning the child conceived in Mary	Matt. 1.18-25	Isa. 7.14, the Immanuel sign given to King Ahaz by Isaiah	Immanuel prophecy was given as a sign to King Ahaz in his own historical context, and does not immediately provide any sense of a long range prediction of Messianic relevance	The Holy Spirit provided the Apostles with divine wisdom in making connections with not only the plain Messianic predictions, but also those aspects of the history of Israel which represent in a direct way some aspect of the life and ministry of Jesus.
Jesus' birth in Bethlehem, the city of David	Matt. 2.1-12	Mic. 5.2, prophecy of the Governor and Ruler of Israel to come from Bethlehem	A direct Messianic prediction about the birthplace of the future Governor of Israel and the nations	
The escape to Egypt, and the return from there	Matt. 2.13-15	Hos. 11.1, God's deliverance of his people Israel, his "son," out of Egypt at the Exodus	No prediction present; Hosea reference is a prophetic allusion to the Exodus of the people of God from Egypt	The ability to correlate particular events of Israel to the life and ministry of Messiah Jesus is precisely the nature of the apostolic Spirit-illumined hermeneutic which coincides with divine and Spirit-inspired Scripture.
Herod's murder of the boys in Bethlehem	Matt. 2.16-18	Jer. 31.15, Jeremiah's lament for the Israelite nation who were going into exile, into Babylonian captivity	The OT text is a figurative picture of the mourning of Rachel (Israel) at the time of the Exile in 587 BC after the fall of Jerusalem to the Babylonians. No explicit Messianic prediction is contained in the text.	
Jesus' family settlement in Nazareth of Galilee	Matt. 2.19-23	Several possible allusions in the OT, Judg. 13.5; 1 Sam. 1.11; Amos 2.10-11	Texts have relevance within their setting, but not in an explicit way to fulfill Messianic predictions	We are invited to exegete the Scriptures and make correlations in the same way as the Lord and the Apostles, although our connections should never be considered normative in the same way as theirs.

APPENDIX 23

Messiah Jesus: Fulfillment of the Old Testament Types

*Adapted from Norman Geisler, **To Understand the Bible, Look for Jesus**, pp. 38-41.*

Messiah Jesus Fulfills the Tabernacle Types

Tabernacle Types	Jesus of Nazareth as the Antitype
The One Door	I am the Door John 10.9
The Brazen Altar	Gives his life as a ransom for many Mark 10.45
The Laver	If I do not wash you, you have no part with me John 13.8, 10; 1 John 1.7
The Lampstand	I am the Light of the Word John 8.12
The Shewbread	I am the Bread of Life John 6.48
The Altar of Incense	I am praying for them John 17.9
The Veil	This is my body Matt. 26.26
The Mercy Seat	I lay down my life for the sheep John 10.15

Messiah Jesus: Fulfillment of the Old Testament Types (continued)

Contrast Between Aaron's and Melchizedek's Priesthood

Nature of the Order	The Order of Aaron's Levitical Priesthood	The Order of Messiah Jesus' Priesthood (Melchizedek's Priesthood)
Consecration	Temporal and fading	Eternal priesthood Heb. 7.21-23
Priest	Fallible, vulnerable to sin	Sinless and perfect Heb. 7.26
Priesthood	Changeable	Unchangeable priesthood Heb. 7.24
Ministry	Continual offering of sacrifice	Secured an eternal redemption once for all Heb. 9.12, 26
Mediation	Imperfect representation	Perfect representation between God and humankind Heb. 2.14-18
Sacrifice	Unable and insufficient to take the sin of the offenders away	Offered a single sacrifice for sin for all time Heb. 10.11-12
Intercession	Was interrupted by weakness and death	Always lives to make intercession for us Heb. 7.25

Messiah Jesus: Fulfillment of the Old Testament Types (continued)

Messiah Jesus Fulfills the Levitical Sacrifices and Offerings

The Levitical Offering	How Offering is Fulfilled in Jesus of Nazareth
The Burnt Offering	The perfection of his life Heb. 9.14
The Meal Offering	The dedication and presentation of his life Heb. 5.7; John 4.34
The Peace Offering	He is the peace of our relationships and souls Heb. 4.1-2; Eph. 2.14
The Sin Offering	He bore the penalty for our offense Heb. 10.12; 1 John 2.2
The Trespass Offering	Provision for the offender Heb. 10.20-21; 1 John 1.7

Messiah Jesus: Fulfillment of the Old Testament Types (continued)

Messiah Jesus Fulfills the Levitical Feasts and Festivals

Levitical Feast (Lev. 23)	The Fulfillment in Jesus of Nazareth
The Passover (April)	The death of Jesus Christ 2 Cor. 5.17
Unleavened Bread (April)	Holy and humble walk for Jesus 1 Cor. 5.8
First Fruits (April)	The resurrection of Messiah Jesus 1 Cor. 15.23
The Feast of Pentecost (June)	Outpouring of the Spirit by the Father and the Son Acts 1.5; 2.4
Trumpets (September)	Messiah Jesus' regathering of the Nation Israel Matt. 24.31
The Day of Atonement (September)	Propitiation and cleansing through Jesus Rom. 11.26
Tabernacles (September)	Rest and reunion with Messiah Jesus Zech. 14.16-18

APPENDIX 24

Picking Up on Different Wavelengths

Integrated vs. Fragmented Mindsets and Lifestyles

Dr. Don L. Davis

A Fragmented Mindset and Lifestyle	An Integrated Lifestyle and Mindset
Sees things primarily in relation to one's own needs	Sees all things as one and whole
Sees something other than God as a substitute point of reference and coordination for meaning and truth	Sees God in Christ as the ultimate point of reference and coordination for all meaning and truth
Seeks God's blessing upon one's own personal enhancement	Aligns personal goals with God's ultimate plan and purposes
Understands the purpose of life to experience the greatest level of personal fulfillment and enhancement possible	Understands the purpose of life to make the maximum contribution possible to God's purpose in the world
Only relates to others in connection to their effect upon and place within one's individual personal space	Deeply identifies with all people and things as an integral part of God's great plan for his own glory
Defines theology as seeking to express someone's perspective on some religious idea or concept	Defines theology as seeking to comprehend God's ultimate designs and plans for himself in Jesus Christ
Applications are rooted in seeking right responses to particular issues and situations	Applications are byproducts of understanding what God is doing for himself in the world
Focuses on the style of analysis (to discern the processes and make-up of things)	Focuses on the style of synthesis (to discern the connection and unity of all things)
Seeks to understand biblical revelation primarily from the standpoint of one's private life ("God's plan for my life")	Seeks to understand biblical revelation primarily from the standpoint of God's plan for whole ("God's plan for the ages")
Governed by pressing concerns to ensure one's own security and significance in one's chosen endeavors ("My personal life plan")	Decision making is governed by commitment to participate as co-workers with God in the overall vision ("God's working in the world")
Coordinates itself around personal need as a working paradigm and project	Connects and correlates itself around God's vision and plan as a working paradigm
Sees mission and ministry as the expression of one's personal giftedness and burden, bringing personal satisfaction and security	Sees mission and ministry as the present, practical expression of one's identity vis-a-vis the panoramic vision of God
Relates knowledge, opportunity, and activity to the goals of personal enhancement and fulfillment	Relates knowledge, opportunity, and activity to a single, integrated vision and purpose
All of life is perceived to revolve around the personal identity and needs of the individual	All of life is perceived to revolve around a single theme: the revelation of God in Jesus of Nazareth

Picking Up on Different Wavelengths (continued)

Scriptures on the Validity of Seeing All Things as Unified and Whole

Ps. 27.4 (ESV) - One thing have I asked of the Lord, that will I seek after: that I may dwell in the house of the Lord all the days of my life, to gaze upon the beauty of the Lord and to inquire in his temple.

Luke 10.39-42 (ESV) - And she had a sister called Mary, who sat at the Lord's feet and listened to his teaching. [40] But Martha was distracted with much serving. And she went up to him and said, "Lord, do you not care that my sister has left me to serve alone? Tell her then to help me." [41] But the Lord answered her, "Martha, Martha, you are anxious and troubled about many things, [42] but one thing is necessary. Mary has chosen the good portion, which will not be taken away from her."

Phil. 3.13-14 (ESV) - Brothers, I do not consider that I have made it my own. But one thing I do: forgetting what lies behind and straining forward to what lies ahead [14] I press on toward the goal for the prize of the upward call of God in Christ Jesus.

Ps. 73.25 (ESV) - Whom have I in heaven but you? And there is nothing on earth that I desire besides you.

Mark 8.36 (ESV) - For what does it profit a man to gain the whole world and forfeit his life?

Luke 18.22 (ESV) - When Jesus heard this, he said to him, "One thing you still lack. Sell all that you have and distribute to the poor, and you will have treasure in heaven; and come, follow me."

John 17.3 (ESV) - And this is eternal life, that they know you the only true God, and Jesus Christ whom you have sent.

1 Cor. 13.3 (ESV) - If I give away all I have, and if I deliver up my body to be burned, but have not love, I gain nothing.

Gal. 5.6 (ESV) - For in Christ Jesus neither circumcision nor uncircumcision counts for anything, but only faith working through love.

Picking Up on Different Wavelengths (continued)

Col. 2.8-10 (ESV) - See to it that no one takes you captive by philosophy and empty deceit, according to human tradition, according to the elemental spirits of the world, and not according to Christ. [9] For in him the whole fullness of deity dwells bodily, [10] and you have been filled in him, who is the head of all rule and authority.

1 John 5.11-12 (ESV) - And this is the testimony, that God gave us eternal life, and this life is in his Son. [12] Whoever has the Son has life; whoever does not have the Son of God does not have life.

Ps. 16.5 (ESV) - The Lord is my chosen portion and my cup; you hold my lot.

Ps. 16.11 (ESV) - You make known to me the path of life; in your presence there is fullness of joy; at your right hand are pleasures forevermore.

Ps. 17.15 (ESV) - As for me, I shall behold your face in righteousness; when I awake, I shall be satisfied with your likeness.

Eph. 1.9-10 (ESV) - making known to us the mystery of his will, according to his purpose, which he set forth in Christ [10] as a plan for the fullness of time, to unite all things in him, things in heaven and things on earth.

John 15.5 (ESV) - I am the vine; you are the branches. Whoever abides in me and I in him, he it is that bears much fruit, for apart from me you can do nothing.

Ps. 42.1 (ESV) - As a deer pants for flowing streams, so pants my soul for you, O God.

Hab. 3.17-18 (ESV) - Though the fig tree should not blossom, nor fruit be on the vines, the produce of the olive fail and the fields yield no food, the flock be cut off from the fold and there be no herd in the stalls, [18] yet I will rejoice in the Lord; I will take joy in the God of my salvation.

Matt. 10.37 (ESV) - Whoever loves father or mother more than me is not worthy of me, and whoever loves son or daughter more than me is not worthy of me.

Ps. 37.4 (ESV) - Delight yourself in the Lord, and he will give you the desires of your heart.

Ps. 63.3 (ESV) - Because your steadfast love is better than life, my lips will praise you.

Picking Up on Different Wavelengths (continued)

Ps. 89.6 (ESV) - For who in the skies can be compared to the Lord? Who among the heavenly beings is like the Lord

Phil. 3.8 (ESV) - Indeed, I count everything as loss because of the surpassing worth of knowing Christ Jesus my Lord. For his sake I have suffered the loss of all things and count them as rubbish, in order that I may gain Christ

1 John 3.2 (ESV) - Beloved, we are God's children now, and what we will be has not yet appeared; but we know that when he appears we shall be like him, because we shall see him as he is.

Rev. 21.3 (ESV) - And I heard a loud voice from the throne saying, "Behold, the dwelling place of God is with man. He will dwell with them, and they will be his people, and God himself will be with them as their God.

Rev. 21.22-23 (ESV) - And I saw no temple in the city, for its temple is the Lord God the Almighty and the Lamb. [23] And the city has no need of sun or moon to shine on it, for the glory of God gives it light, and its lamp is the Lamb.

Ps. 115.3 (ESV) - Our God is in the heavens; he does all that he pleases.

Jer. 32.17 (ESV) - Ah, Lord God! It is you who has made the heavens and the earth by your great power and by your outstretched arm! Nothing is too hard for you.

Dan. 4.35 (ESV) - all the inhabitants of the earth are accounted as nothing, and he does according to his will among the host of heaven and among the inhabitants of the earth; and none can stay his hand or say to him, "What have you done?"

Eph. 3.20-21 (ESV) - Now to him who is able to do far more abundantly than all that we ask or think, according to the power at work within us, [21] to him be glory in the Church and in Christ Jesus throughout all generations, forever and ever. Amen.

APPENDIX 25

Principles Behind Prophecy

Dr. Don L. Davis

1. Prophecy provides divinely inspired truth about God, his universe, and his will.
   - Who is God and what is the nature of the "real"?
   - What is the truth, and how can we know it?
   - Where did we come from, why are we here, and how shall we act?

2. Prophecy originates and has its source in the Holy Spirit.
   - It is his gift (Rom. 12.6; 1 Cor. 12.10; Eph. 4.8).
   - Prophet = "person of the Spirit," *pneumatikos* (1 Cor. 14.37 and Hos. 9.7)
   - The hope of Moses (Num. 11.16, 29; cf. Luke 10.1)

3. Diverse and various forms of revelation (Jer. 18.18, Law from the priest, counsel from the wise, and word from the prophet).
   - Lived in communities and guilds, some were attached to the temple, while others were priests (cf. 2 Kings 2.3ff.; Ezek. 1.3; Jer. 1.1).
   - Sages and wisdom teachers were "recipients and mediators" of the divine gift (cf. Gen. 41.38; 2 Sam. 14.20; 16.23; 1 Kings 3.9, etc.).
   - Wisdom teacher and prophet both: Daniel.

4. Prophecy not self-authenticating: it must be judged valid.
   - Conflict existed between prophets within both the Old Testament and New Testament (cf. 1 Kings 22; Jer. 23; 28 and 2 Cor. 11.4, 13; 1 John 4.1-3).
   - Prophetic claims must agree with Moses (Deut. 13.1-5) and Jesus (Matt. 7.15; 24.11; 2 Pet. 2.1).
   - If the word comes to pass, it is from the Lord (Deut. 18.15-22).
   - All prophecy is to be examined for its truth value (1 Thess. 5.19-21).

5. The testimony of Jesus is the spirit of prophecy (Rev. 19.10).
   - Prophecy speaks to Messiah's suffering and glory (Luke 24.25-27; 44).
   - The prophetic Scriptures focus on his person and work (John 5.39-40).
   - Apostolic preaching connected him to their message (Acts 3.12-18; 10.43; 13.27; Rom. 3.21-22; 1 Pet. 1.10-12; 2 Pet. 1.19-21).

APPENDIX 26

A Harmony of the Ministry of Jesus

*Adapted from Walter M. Dunnett, **Exploring the New Testament**, p. 14.*

Gospel	The Period of Preparation	The Period of Public Ministry		The Period of Suffering	The Period of Triumph
		Opening	Closing		
Matthew	1.1-4.16	4.17-16.20	16.21-26.2	26.3-27.66	28.1-20
Mark	1.1-1.13	1.14-8.30	8.31-13.37	14.1-15.47	16.1-20
Luke	1.1-4.13	4.14-9.21	9.22-21.38	22.1-23.56	24.1-53
John	1.1-34	1.35-6.71	7.1-12.50	13.1-19.42	20.1-21.25

APPENDIX 27

Appearances of the Resurrected Messiah

Dr. Don L. Davis

	Appearance	Scripture
1	Appearance to Mary Magdalene	John 20.11-17; Mark 16.9-11
2	Appearance to the women	Matt. 28.9-10
3	Appearance to Peter	Luke 24.34; 1 Cor. 15.5
4	Appearance to the disciples on the road to Emmaus	Mark 16.12-13; Luke 24.13-35
5	Appearance to the ten disciples, referred to as the "Eleven" (with Thomas absent)	Mark 16.14; Luke 24.36-43; John 20.19-24
6	Appearance to the Eleven with Thomas present one week later	John 20.26-29
7	Appearance to seven disciples by the Sea of Galilee	John 21.1-23
8	Appearance to five hundred	1 Cor. 15.6
9	Appearance to James, the Lord's brother	1 Cor. 15.7
10	Appearance to the eleven disciples on the mountain in Galilee*	Matt. 28.16-20
11	Appearance to his disciples at his ascension on the Mount of Olives*	Luke 24.44-53; Acts 1.3-9
12	Appearance to Stephen prior to his death as the Church's first martyr (witness)	Acts 7.55-56
13	Appearance to Paul on the road to Damascus	Acts 9.3-6; cf. 22.6-11; 26.13-18; 1 Cor. 15.8
14	Appearance to Paul in Arabia	Acts 20.24; 26.17; Gal. 1.12,17
15	Appearance to Paul in the Temple	Acts 22.17-21; cf. 9.26-30; Gal. 1.18
16	Appearance to Paul in prison in Caesarea	Acts 23.11
17	Appearance to John during his exile in Patmos	Rev. 1.12-20

* Items 10 and 11 describe the events commonly referred to as "The Great Commission" and "The Ascension," respectively.

APPENDIX 28

Ethics of the New Testament: Living in the Upside-Down Kingdom of God

True Myth and Biblical Fairy Tale

Dr. Don L. Davis

The Principle of Reversal

The Principle Expressed	Scripture
The poor shall become rich, and the rich shall become poor	Luke 6.20-26
The law breaker and the undeserving are saved	Matt. 21.31-32
Those who humble themselves shall be exalted	1 Pet. 5.5-6
Those who exalt themselves shall be brought low	Luke 18.14
The blind shall be given sight	John 9.39
Those claiming to see shall be made blind	John 9.40-41
We become free by being Christ's slave	Rom. 12.1-2
God has chosen what is foolish in the world to shame the wise	1 Cor. 1.27
God has chosen what is weak in the world to shame the strong	1 Cor. 1.27
God has chosen the low and despised to bring to nothing things that are	1 Cor. 1.28
We gain the next world by losing this one	1 Tim. 6.7
Love this life and you'll lose it; hate this life, and you'll keep the next	John 12.25
You become the greatest by being the servant of all	Matt. 10.42-45
Store up treasures here, you forfeit heaven's reward	Matt. 6.19
Store up treasures above, you gain heaven's wealth	Matt. 6.20
Accept your own death to yourself in order to live fully	John 12.24
Release all earthly reputation to gain heaven's favor	Phil. 3.3-7
The first shall be last, and the last shall become first	Mark 9.35
The grace of Jesus is perfected in your weakness, not your strength	2 Cor. 12.9
God's highest sacrifice is contrition and brokenness	Ps. 51.17
It is better to give to others than to receive from them	Acts 20.35
Give away all you have in order to receive God's best	Luke 6.38

APPENDIX 29

From Deep Ignorance to Credible Witness

Rev. Dr. Don L. Davis

Level	Description	Scriptures	Key Text
8	**Witness - Ability to give witness and teach**	*2 Tim. 2.2; Matt. 28.18-20; 1 John 1.1-4; Prov. 20.6; 2 Cor. 5.18-21*	*And the things you have heard me say in the presence of many witnesses entrust to reliable men who will also be qualified to teach others. - 2 Tim. 2.2*
7	**Lifestyle - Consistent appropriation and habitual practice based on beliefs**	*Heb. 5.11-6.2; Eph. 4.11-16; 2 Pet. 3.18; 1 Tim. 4.7-10*	*And Jesus increased in wisdom and in stature, and in favor with God and man. - Luke 2.52*
6	**Demonstration - Expressing conviction in corresponding conduct, speech, and behavior**	*James 2.14-26; 2 Cor. 4.13; 2 Pet. 1.5-9; 1 Thess. 1.3-10*	*Nevertheless, at your word I will let down the net. - Luke 5.5*
5	**Conviction - Committing oneself to think, speak, and act in light of information**	*Heb. 2.3-4; Heb. 11.1, 6; Heb. 3.15-19; Heb. 4.2-6*	*Do you believe this? - John 11.26*
4	**Discernment - Understanding the meaning and implications of information**	*John 16.13; Eph. 1.15-18; Col. 1.9-10; Isa. 6.10; 29.10*	*Do you understand what you are reading? - Acts 8.30*
3	**Knowledge - Ability to recall and recite information**	*2 Tim. 3.16-17; 1 Cor. 2.9-16; 1 John 2.20-27; John 14.26*	*For what does the Scripture say? - Rom. 4.3*
2	**Interest - Responding to ideas or information with both curiosity and openness**	*Ps. 42.1-2; Acts 9.4-5; John 12.21; 1 Sam. 3.4-10*	*We will hear you again on this matter. - Acts 17.32*
1	**Awareness - General exposure to ideas and information**	*Mark 7.6-8; Acts 19.1-7; John 5.39-40; Matt. 7.21-23*	*At that time, Herod the tetrarch heard about the fame of Jesus. - Matt. 14.1*
0	**Ignorance - Unfamiliarity with information due to naivete, indifference, or hardness**	*Eph. 4.17-19; Ps. 2.1-3; Rom. 1.21; 2.19; 1 John 2.11*	*Who is the Lord that I should heed his voice? - Exod. 5.2*

APPENDIX 30

In Christ

Rev. Dr. Don L. Davis

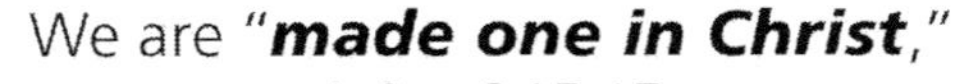

"In Christ"

The Mystery of Our Total Identification with Christ
John 15.4-5

We are "***made one in Christ***,"
1 Cor. 6.15-17

We were ***baptized into him***,
1 Cor. 12.13

We were ***crucified with him***,
Gal. 2.20

We ***died with him***,
Rom. 6.3-4; Col. 3.3

We were ***buried with him***,
Rom. 6.3-4

We were ***raised with him***,
Eph. 2.4-7; Col. 3.1

We ***ascended with him***,
Eph. 2.6

We ***sit with him*** in heavenly places,
Eph. 2.6

We will be ***caught up together with him***,
1 Thess. 4.13-18

We ***suffer with him***,
Rom. 8.17-18

We will be ***resurrected in him***,
1 Cor. 15.48-49

We will be ***glorified with him***,
Rom. 8.17

We will be ***made like him***,
1 John 3.2

We will be ***joint-heirs with him***,
Rom. 8.17

We will ***reign forever with him***,
Rev. 3.21

APPENDIX 31

Substitute Centers to a Christ-Centered Vision

Goods and Effects Which Our Culture Substitutes as the Ultimate Concern

Rev. Dr. Don L. Davis

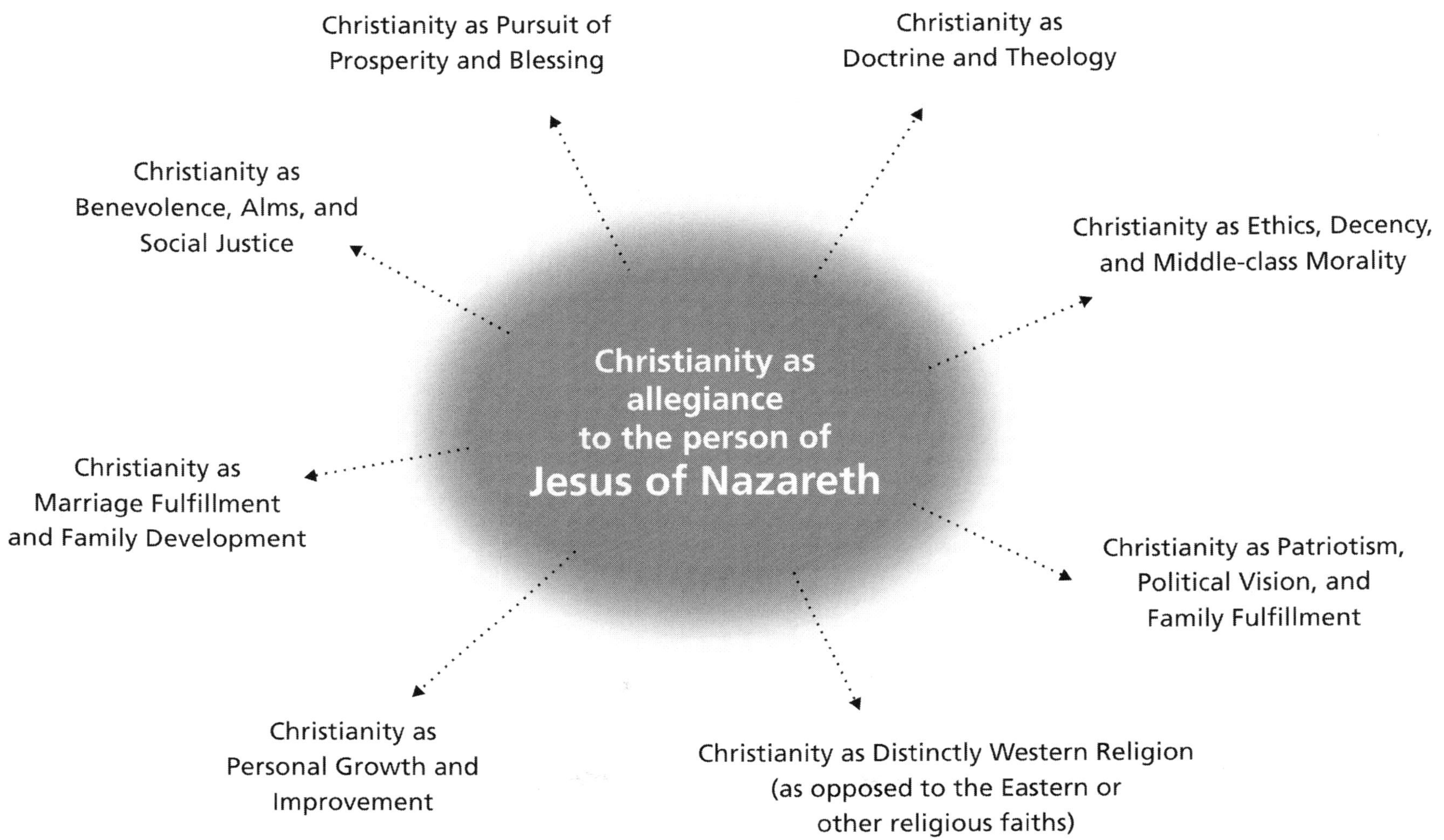

Christianity as allegiance to the person of Jesus of Nazareth

- Christianity as Pursuit of Prosperity and Blessing
- Christianity as Doctrine and Theology
- Christianity as Benevolence, Alms, and Social Justice
- Christianity as Ethics, Decency, and Middle-class Morality
- Christianity as Marriage Fulfillment and Family Development
- Christianity as Patriotism, Political Vision, and Family Fulfillment
- Christianity as Personal Growth and Improvement
- Christianity as Distinctly Western Religion (as opposed to the Eastern or other religious faiths)

APPENDIX 32

The Picture and the Drama

Image and Story in the Recovery of Biblical Myth

Don L. Davis

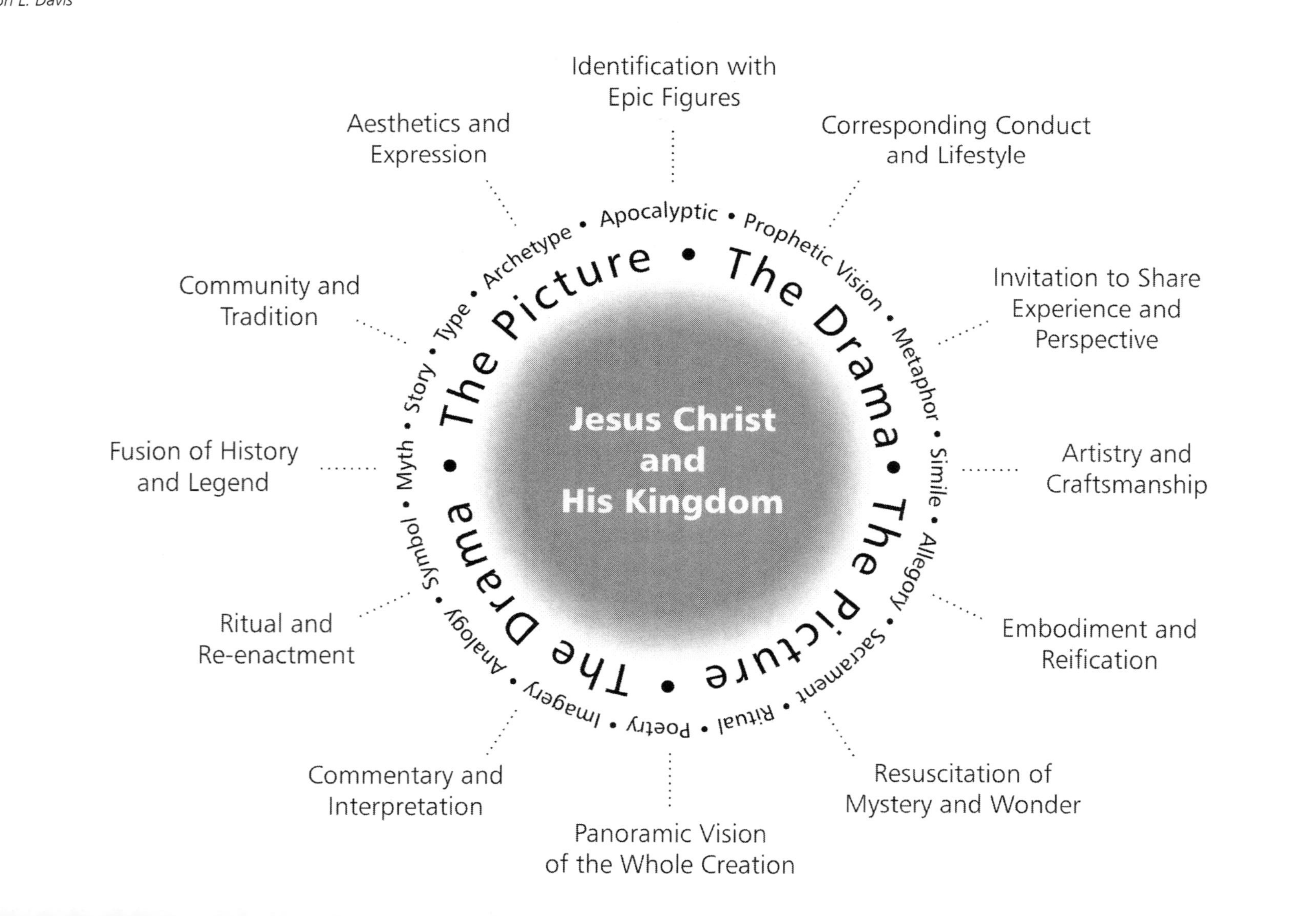

APPENDIX 33

Toward a Hermeneutic of Critical Engagement

Rev. Dr. Don L. Davis

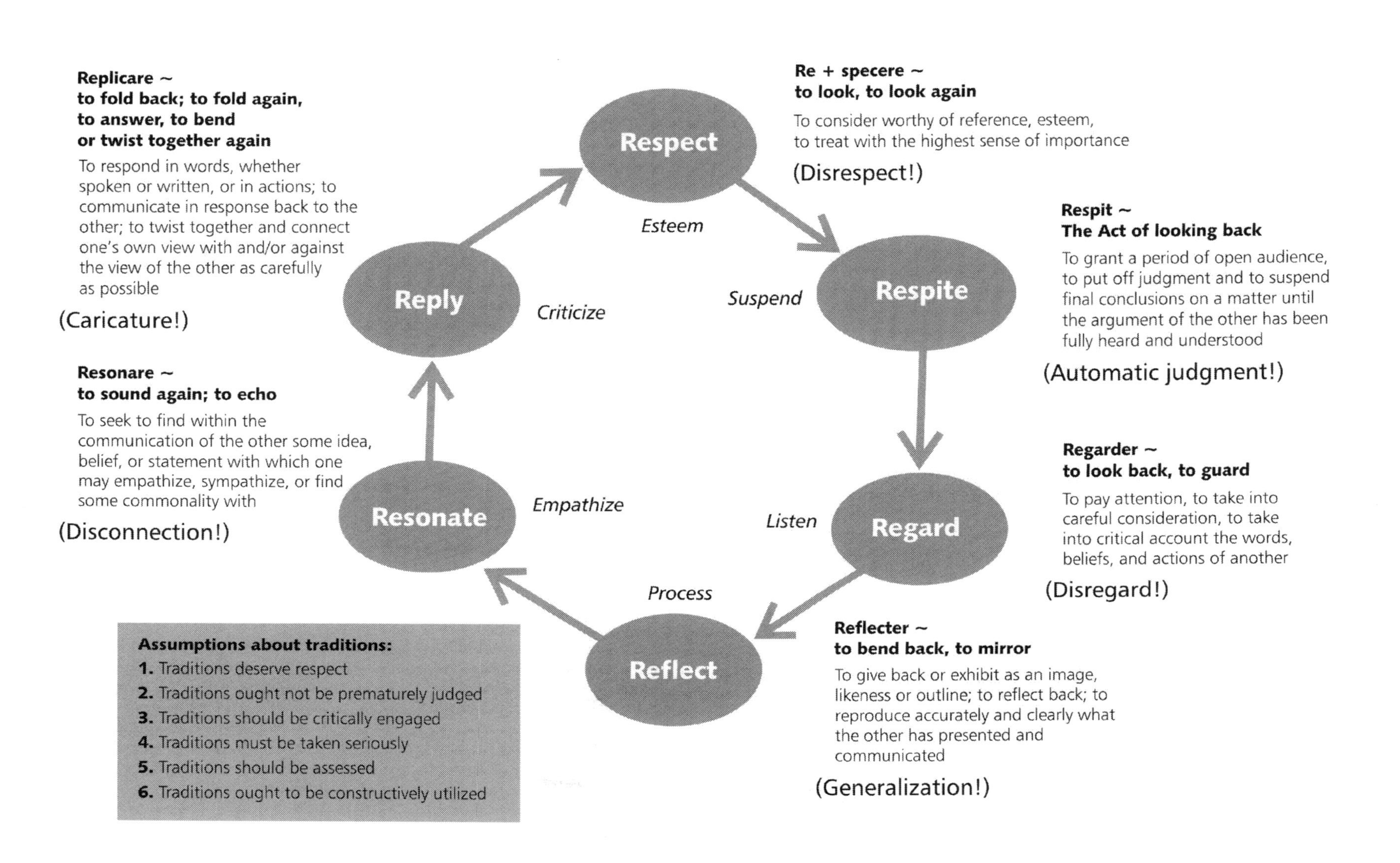

APPENDIX 34

Chart of Biblical Studies

Rev. Dr. Don L. Davis

Type of Criticism	The Task in Bible Study	What is Studied	View of the Bible	Proof Level	Strengths	Weaknesses	Level of Criticism
Form Criticism	Trace the oral traditions and earliest stories associated with the texts	Oral traditions of the people of God, along with the early Church	Product of human tradition	Low	Evolving sense of the Bible's origin	Too speculative	Higher
Source Criticism	Discover the written sources used in the creation of the books	Comparing texts in various books to see similarities and contrasts	Product of human ingenuity	Low	Ability to identify key sources	No way to prove its claims	Higher
Linguistic Criticism	Study the ancient languages, words and grammar	Study of the ancient Hebrew, koine Greek, and Aramaic	Product of human culture	Mid	In-depth meaning of ancient language	Too far removed from the language	Lower
Textual Criticism	Compare the variant manuscripts to find the best reading	Focus on different manuscripts and their families of texts	Product of textual research	High	Multitude of reliable manuscripts available	Far too extensive number	Lower
Literary Criticism	Determine the author, style, recipient, and genre	Different types of literature, background study on the books	Product of literary genius	High	Discovering what types of literature mean	We tend to read too much into it	Higher

Chart of Biblical Studies (continued)

Type of Criticism	The Task in Bible Study	What is Studied	View of the Bible	Proof Level	Strengths	Weaknesses	Level of Criticism
Canonical Criticism	Analyze the Church's acceptance, view and use of the text	History of the Bible in ancient Israel and the early Church (councils, conventions)	Product of religious community	High	Taking the community's view of the Bible seriously	Tends to make the Bible merely a group book	Higher
Redaction Criticism	Focus on the theology of the person who wrote it	Intense study of individual books to understand the meaning of the author's theme and views	Product of creative personality	Mid	Deep analysis of an author's entire collection of writings	Does not correlate the Bible with other books	Higher
Historical Criticism	Investigate the historical setting, culture, and background	Research of the ancient cultures, their customs, and their history	Product of historical forces	Mid	Firmer grasp of historical issues of the text	Too far removed from the history	Higher
Translation Studies	Provide a clear, readable translation based on the best manuscripts	Understanding of the receiving culture's language along with the meanings of the text for the best translation	Product of dynamic interpretation	Mid	Pursuing a version of the Bible in one's own tongue and thought world	Reflects our own opinions about the text's meaning	Lower

APPENDIX 35

The Shadow and the Substance

Understanding the Old Testament as God's Witness to Jesus Christ

Rev. Dr. Don L. Davis

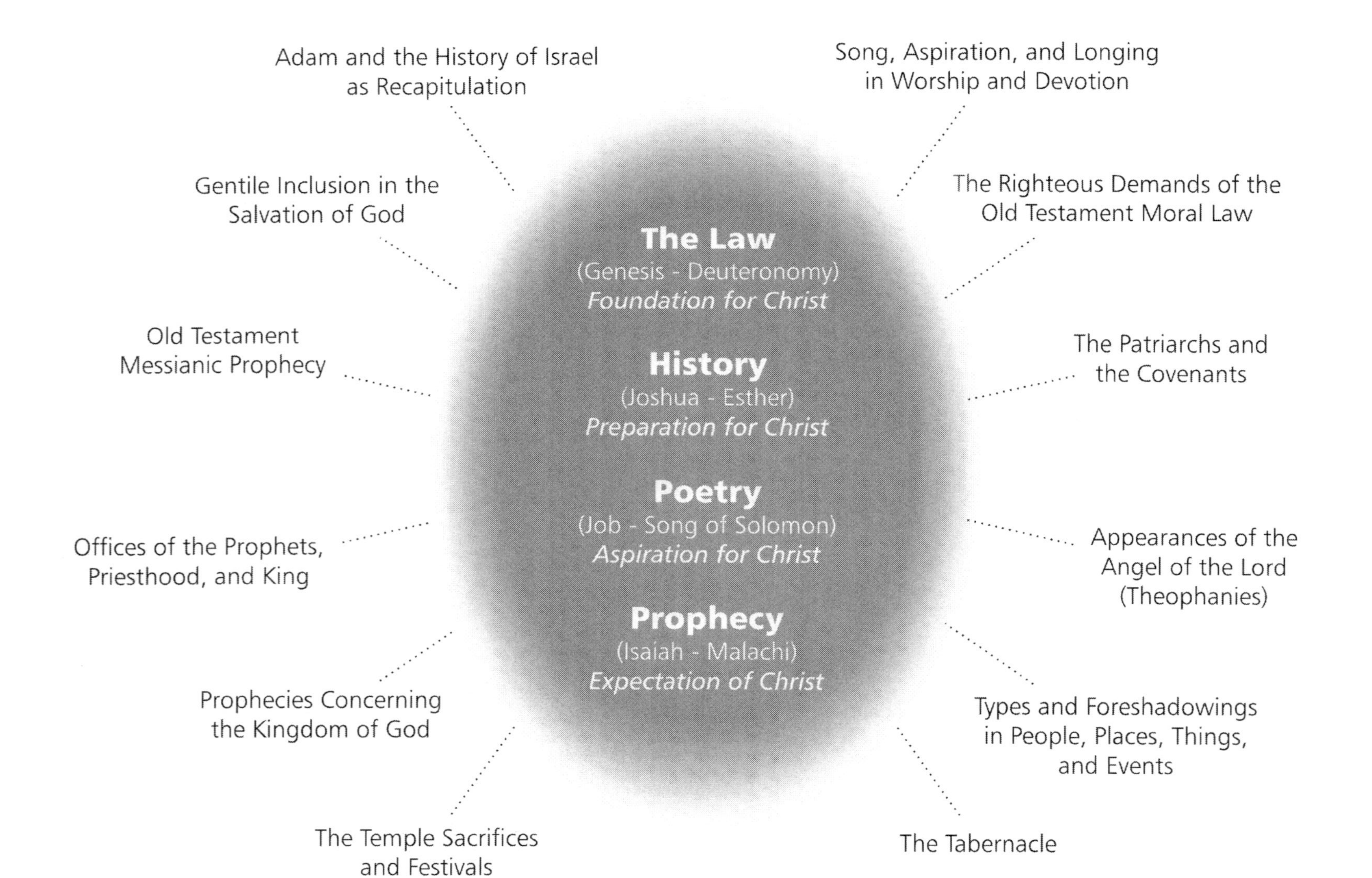

APPENDIX 36

Analytical vs. Christocentric Approach to Old Testament Study

Rev. Dr. Don L. Davis

An Analytical Approach	A Christocentric Approach
Focuses on individual verses, chapters, books, and sections in and of themselves	Focuses on how the content of book points to and gives witness to Messiah Jesus
Breaks Old Testament into many pieces for analysis and exegesis	Looks at Old Testament as single whole which gives single witness to Jesus
Concentrates on studying each book as its own self-contained unit	Concentrates on studying each book as it provides contribution to Christ's coming
Demands linguistic and socio-cultural expertise	Demands spiritual wisdom and discernment
Can only be legitimately done by experts	Can be done by all the saints of God
Difficult to give overview of Old Testament	Uses Christ as key to the interpretation of the Old Testament overview
Focuses on knowledge of content	Focuses on developing relationship to Christ
Hard to disciple others in knowledge of Old Testament and its contents	Designed to help teachers ground believers in the knowledge of Christ through the Old Testament
Can be remarkably boring and dry	Stirs the heart in longing and love for Jesus

APPENDIX 37

Learning to Be a Theo-smith

Adopting a Hebraic Approach to Truth

Rev. Dr. Don L. Davis

Understanding and seeking truth, not from a scientific rationalistic base, but a mythopoetic foundation

S tories and the Story of God

M ystery, dialectic, the unknowable, and the "really real"

I magery, symbol, and metaphor

T ypes, analogies, connections, and inspired associations

H olism, global thinking, concreteness, sacred place, and enactment

S alvific passion for the Kingdom of God

APPENDIX 38

Typology Readings

Rev. Dr. Don L. Davis

The Study of Types Critical to New Testament Mastery

➢ *Ada R. Habershon, **Study of the Types**. Grand Rapids: Kregel Publishing, (1957) 1974. pp. 19, 21*

There are many passages in the New Testament which we cannot understand without having become in some measure familiar with the types. The epistle to the Hebrews is almost entirely made up of references to the Old Testament: as the substance, Christ, is proved to be better than the shadows–better than Moses, than Joshua, than Abraham, than Aaron, than the first Tabernacle, than the Levitical sacrifices, than the whole cloud of witnesses in the picture gallery of faith; and lastly, his blood is proved to be better than the blood of Abel.

We sometimes forget that the writers of the New Testament were *students of the Old Testament*; that it was *their Bible*, and that they would naturally allude again and again to the types and shadows, expecting their readers also to be familiar with them. *If we fail to see these allusions, we lose much of the beauty of the passage, and cannot rightly understand it. . . .*

[The study of types] gives us a sure antidote for the poison of the so-called "higher criticism." If we acknowledge the Divine intention of every detail of the types, even though we may not understand all their teaching, and if we believe there is a lesson in every incident recorded, the attacks of modern criticism will not harm us. We may not be clear enough to understand what the critics say, or to answer their criticisms; but *if our eyes have been opened to see the beauty of the types, the doubts which such writers suggest will not trouble us, and we shall have a more profitable occupation than reading their works.* When so much of this destructive criticism is about, we cannot do better than urge all–even the youngest Christians–to take up the typical study of God's Word; for though *he has hid these things from the wise and prudent, he reveals them unto babes.*

Do We Presently Study the Bible in the Same Way and with the Same Methods as the Lord and the Apostles?

➢ *James DeYoung and Sarah Hurty, **Beyond the Obvious**. Gresham, OR: Vision House Publishing, 1995. p. 24*

After more than twenty years of teaching the grammatical-historical hermeneutic, I can see only one problem with it: it doesn't appear to be the way the biblical writers always did it! When we examine how the biblical writers used previously written Scripture, we see that they seemed to "discover" meaning there that, judged by its

Typology Readings (continued)

original context, can hardly be imagined to have been in the mind of the original author. This problem is especially evident in the way the New Testament authors used Old Testament passages to prove that Jesus Christ fulfilled prophecy (or to make some theological point.)

Can or Should We Reproduce the Exegesis of the New Testament?

To the question whether we can reproduce the exegesis of the New Testament, S. L. Johnson answers: "Unhesitatingly the reply is yes, although we are not allowed to claim for our results the infallibility of the Lord and his Apostles. They are reliable teachers of biblical doctrine and they are reliable teachers of hermeneutics and exegesis. We not only can reproduce their exegetical methodology, we must if we are to be taught their understanding of the Scriptures."

James DeYoung and Sarah Hurty, ***Beyond the Obvious****. p. 265*

What of Typology as a Valid, Important Method of Bible Interpretation?

[Typology] is a genuine approach widely practiced in the New Testament. For example, the furniture of the tabernacle and other matters associated with it and the temple (the altar and sacrifices, the veil, the golden cover of the ark of the covenant) are all types of Christ and of the heavenly realm (see Heb. 9). When we come to typology, we must avoid being too broad or too narrow in our interpretation. We can be too broad if we find typology everywhere. We can be too narrow if we reject typology as an exegetical method on the basis of the claim that it is not consistent with a literal meaning which embraces on meaning, found by means of grammatical-historical study. . . .

Yet we believe that typology is not to be divorced from exegesis, even though it cannot be fully "regulated hermeneutically, but takes place in the freedom of the Holy Spirit." It very much involves a deeper meaning and was readily practiced by the Bible in its exegetical method (see 1 Cor. 10; Rom. 5).

James DeYoung and Sarah Hurty, ***Beyond the Obvious****. p. 74*

Typology Readings (continued)

Diverse Usages of the Term *Typos* in the New Testament

➢ *Patrick Fairbairn, **Typology of Scripture**. Grand Rapids: Kregel Publishing. p. 42*

The language of Scripture being essentially popular, its use of particular terms naturally partakes of the freedom and variety which are wont to appear in the current speech of a people; and it rarely if ever happens that words are employed, in respect to topics requiring theological treatment, with such precision and uniformity as to enable us, from this source alone, to attain to proper accuracy and fullness.

The word type (*typos*) forms no exception to this usage.

- Occurring once, at least, in the natural sense of *mark* or *impress* made by a hard substance on one of softer material (John 20.25)
- It commonly bears the general import of *model*, *pattern*, or *exemplar*, but with such a wide diversity of application as to comprehend a material object of worship, or idol (Acts 7.43)
- An *external framework* constructed for the service of God (Acts 7.44; Heb. 8.5)
- The *form* or *copy* of an epistle (Acts 23.25)
- A *method of doctrinal instruction* delivered by the first heralds and teachers of the Gospel (Rom. 7.17)
- A *representative character*, or, in certain respects, normal example (Rom. 5.14; 1 Cor. 10.11; Phil. 3.17; 1 Thess. 1.7; 1 Pet. 5.3)

Such in the New Testament Scriptures is the diversified use of the word *type* (disguised, however, under other terms in the authorized version).

Extreme Misuse of Typology is Very Possible

➢ *J. Sidlow Baxter, **The Strategic Grasp of the Bible**.*

We marvel with peculiar awe at the ability and agility which some well-meaning brethren display in seeing what is not there; as also we marvel, with a sense of our denseness, at the super-spirituality which they evince in aerifying the most unsuspicious details of Scripture into rare spiritual significances.

The "three white baskets" which Pharaoh's ill-fated baker dreamed were on his head are to ourselves part of a true story; but to see in those same three basket recondite

Typology Readings (continued)

bearings upon the doctrine of the Trinity makes one part of our mind laugh and another part groan. We feel the same sort of reaction when we are assured that the bride's hair in the Song of Solomon is the mass of the nations converted to Christianity.

It is an eye-opener to learn that the "two pence" which the Good Samaritan gave to the innkeeper were covertly Baptism and the Lord's Supper. We cannot but feel sorry for Matthew, Mark, Luke and John, when another ministerial victim of typomania tells us the "four barrels" of water which Elijah commanded to be poured over the altar on Mount Carmel were the four Gospel writers.

As for the clergyman who would persuade us the boat in which our Lord crossed Galilee is the Church of England, while the "other little ships" which accompanied it were the other denominations, we cannot shake off a sly idea that the novel expositor himself, like the boats, must have been all "at sea." We feel just the same about Pope Gregory the Great's exposition of Job, in which Job's verbose "friends" typify heretics; and his seven sons the twelve Apostles; his seven thousand sheep God's faithful people and his three thousand hump-backed camels the depraved Gentiles!"

The Three Errors of Typology to Avoid

There are three dangers, however, which must be avoided:

- Limiting the type, and therefore not using it
- Exaggerating the type, and therefore overusing it
- Imagining the type, and therefore misusing it

*J. Boyd Nicholson from the foreword to **Harvest Festivals**.*

The Case Against the "Older View" of Typology

The case against typology:

- Concerned only with finding "prefigurations" of Christ all over the Old Testament
- God ordained Old Testament events, institutions, and/or persons for the primary purpose of foreshadowing Christ.

*Christopher J. H. Wright, **Knowing Jesus through the Old Testament**.. Downers Grove: InterVarsity Press, 1992. pp. 115-116*

Typology Readings (continued)

Two bad results of this old hermeneutic:

- No need to find much reality and meaning in the events and persons themselves (Old Testament becomes nothing more than a collection of shadows)
- Interpreted every obscure detail of Old Testament "type" as a foreshadowing of Jesus (hermeneutics becomes magic, like pulling a rabbit out of a hat)

Conclusion: typology is not *the* way of interpreting the Old Testament for itself. "But when we go back and read the whole of Psalm 2, Isaiah 42 and Genesis 22, it is equally true that they have enormous depths of truth and meaning for us to explore which are not *directly* related to Jesus himself. Typology is a way of helping us understand Jesus in the light of the Old Testament. It is not the exclusive way to understand the full meaning of the Old Testament itself" (Wright, 116).

Rebutting Wright's Claims

- Jesus used typology (e.g., the brazen serpent, manna in the wilderness, the Temple of his body, the Good Shepherd, etc.)
- The Apostles and early Christian interpreters used typology as their normal way of reading the Old Testament (e.g., Moses' striking the Rock, the wilderness journey of the nation of Israel, Jesus as the second Israel, etc.)
- The Bible refers to itself in this way (e.g., the Book of Hebrews, the Tabernacle, the priesthood, etc.)

The question: Should we use the Old Testament as Jesus and the Apostles did, with some reference to *typology*?

The Christological Hermeneutic: Messiah Jesus Connects the Testaments

➢ *Norman Geisler, To Understand the Bible Look for Jesus. (1979) 2002. p. 68*

Christ at once sums up in himself the *perfection of the Old Testament precepts*, the *substance of Old Testament shadows and types*, and the *fulfillment of Old Testament forecasts.* Those truths about him which bud forth in the Old Testament come into

Typology Readings (continued)

full bloom in the New Testament; the flashlight of prophetic truth turns into the floodlight of divine revelation.

The Old Testament foreshadows find their fulfillment in the New Testament in several ways: (1) The *moral precepts* of the Old Testament become fulfilled or perfected in the life and teachings of Christ. (2) The *ceremonial* and *typical* truths were only shadows of the true substance to be found in Christ. (3) The *Messianic prophecies* foretold in the Old Testament were finally fulfilled in the history of the New Testament. In each of these relationships it can be seen that the Testaments are inseparably connected. The New is not only supplementary to the Old but it is the necessary complement to it.

As the book of Hebrews puts it, "God had foreseen something better for us, that apart from us they [Old Testament believers] should not be made perfect" (Heb. 11.40). For what was contained in the Old Testament is fully explained only in the New Testament.

The Way Paul and the Apostles Read Scripture

Manlo Simonetti, Biblical Interpretation in the Early Church. p. 11-12

As can be clearly seen, the hermeneutical procedure which Paul and the other New Testament authors use to interpret the Law in a spiritual sense is allegorical, in that a meaning other than the literal or immediate sense is perceived from the given text. The usual term which Paul employs to define the relationship between the two levels of meaning is *typos* = form, figure, symbol, or prefiguration (Rom. 5.14; 1 Cor. 10.6, etc.); but in Galatians 4.24, where he presents the sons of Hagar and Sarah as prefigurations of the Jews and Christians, he says 'Now this is an allegory (*allegoroumena*), showing that he regarded 'typos' as synonymous with 'allegory.'

In deference to Paul's terminology, modern scholars call this kind of interpretation - which, as we shall see, enjoyed immense success and became the authentic Christian way of reading the Old Testament - 'typology' or 'typological interpretation.' In antiquity [i.e., in olden times] it was called 'spiritual' or 'mystical.'

It was rooted in the firm conviction that the old Law was consistently directed towards the great Christ-event, and that, as a result, it would give up its true significance only to those who interpreted it in Christological terms.

APPENDIX 39

The Tabernacle of Moses

*Vern Poythress, **The Shadow of Christ in the Law of Moses**, p. 17.*

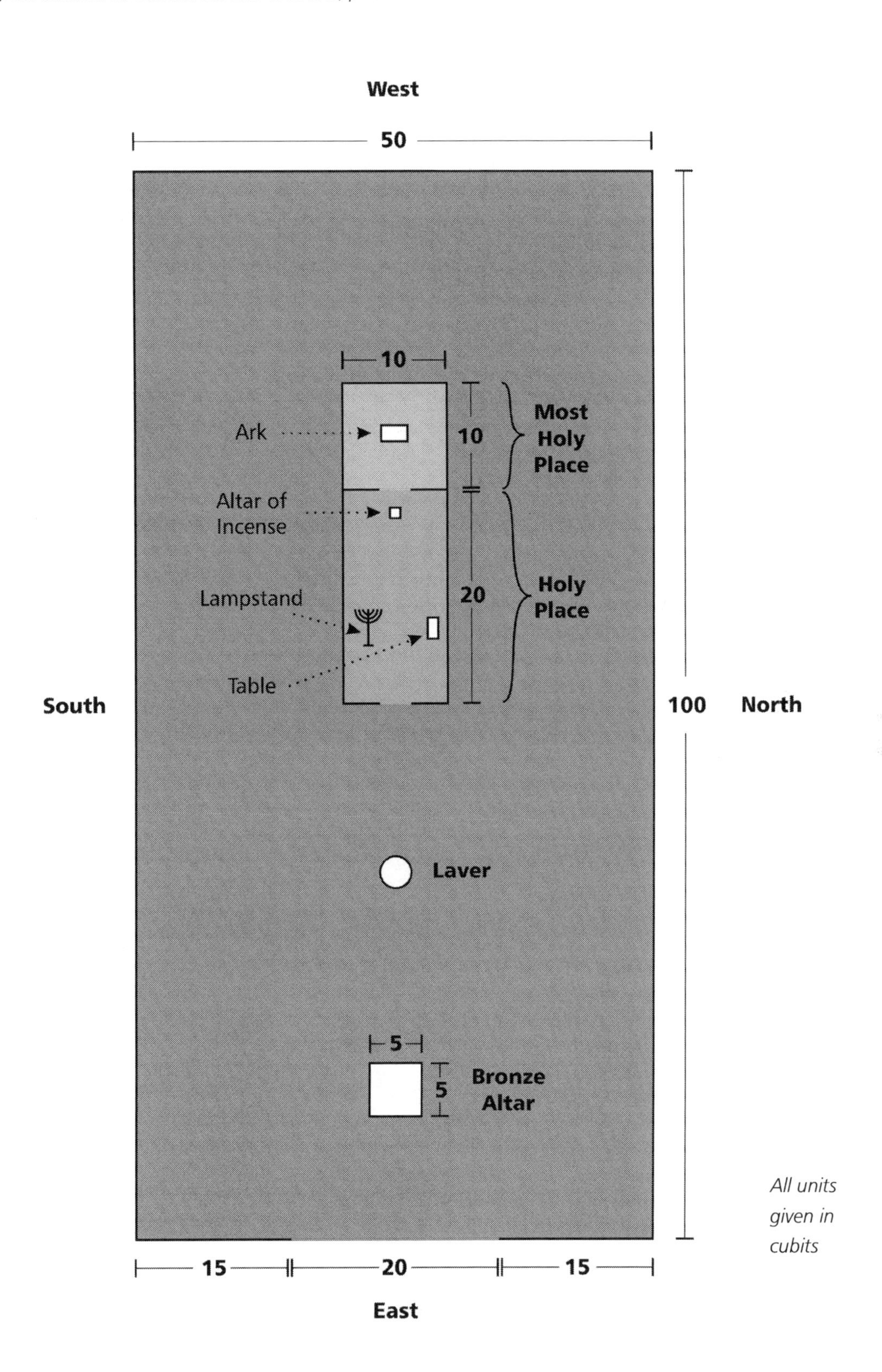

All units given in cubits

APPENDIX 40

Arrangement of the Twelve Tribes around the Tabernacle

*Vern S. Poythress, **The Shadow of Christ in the Law of Moses.***

Tribes Encamped

Manasseh		Dan		Issachar
	Asher		Naphtali	
Ephraim		TABERNACLE		Judah
	Simeon		Gad	
Benjamin		Reuben		Zebulon

Tribes Marching

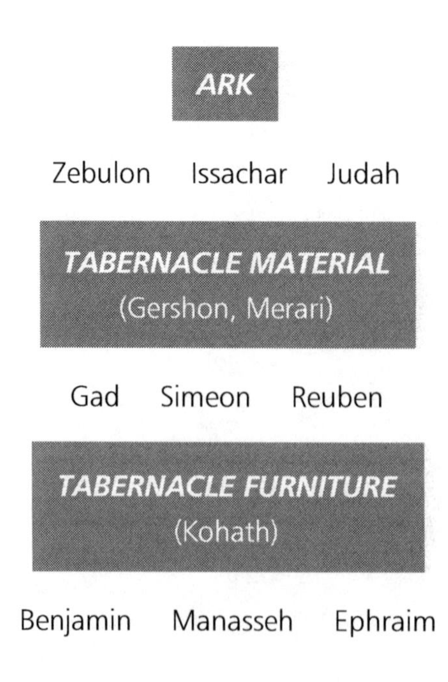

APPENDIX 41

Degrees of Authority Given to Fruit of Christocentric Use of the Old Testament

Rev. Dr. Don L. Davis

The Old Testament correlates with the New Testament, and through the aid of the Holy Spirit and the test of Scripture we may explore these connections between the people, events, and happenings of the Old Testament so as to understand how they testify of and foreshadow the Messiah, Jesus of Nazareth.

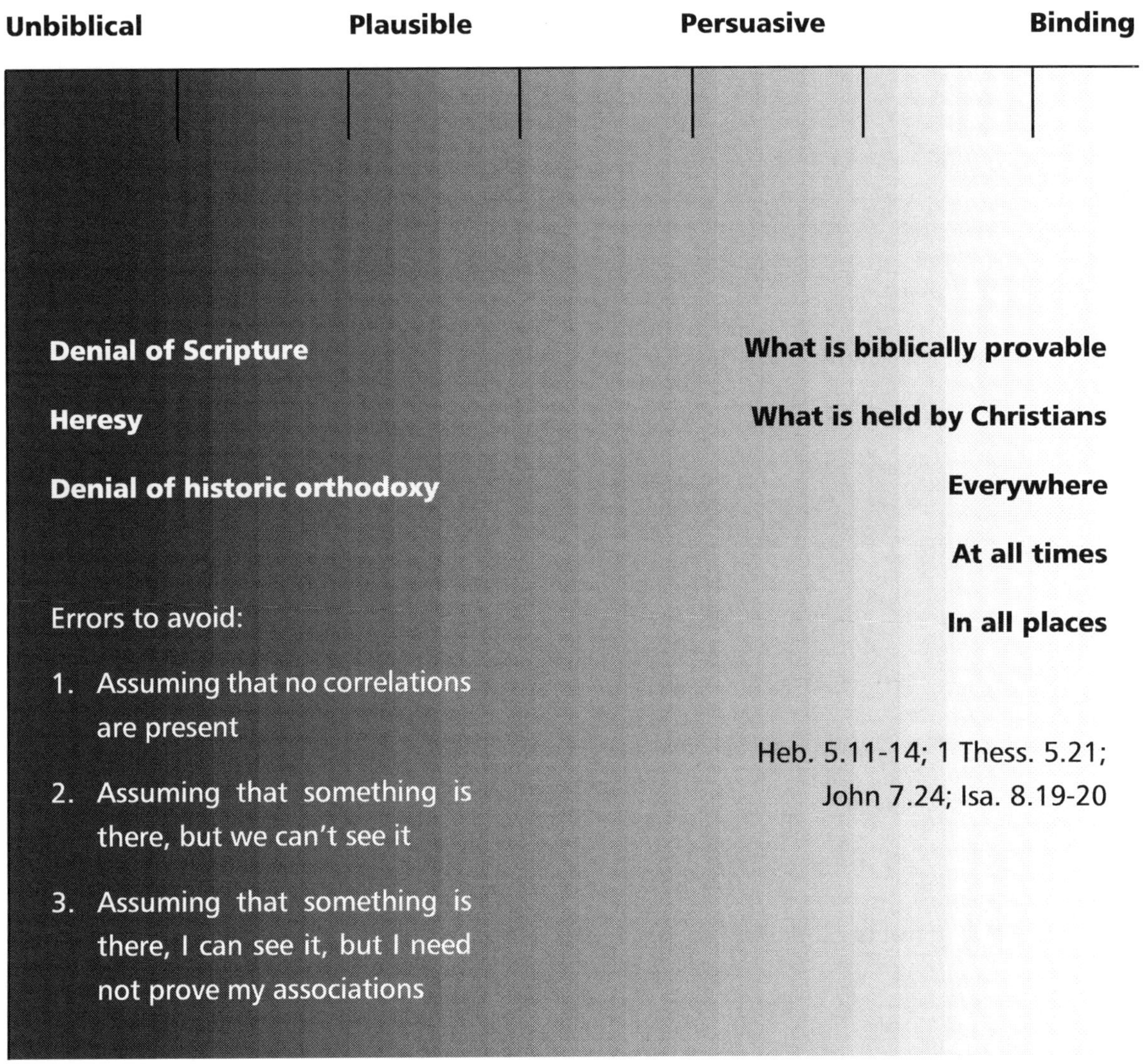

Unbiblical **Plausible** **Persuasive** **Binding**

Denial of Scripture

Heresy

Denial of historic orthodoxy

Errors to avoid:

1. Assuming that no correlations are present
2. Assuming that something is there, but we can't see it
3. Assuming that something is there, I can see it, but I need not prove my associations

What is biblically provable

What is held by Christians

Everywhere

At all times

In all places

Heb. 5.11-14; 1 Thess. 5.21; John 7.24; Isa. 8.19-20

APPENDIX 42

Checklist of Narrative Elements

Adapted from Leland Ryken. How to Read the Bible as Literature.

I. What Is the *Setting* of the Story?

A. Physical surroundings

B. Historical environment

C. Cultural situation

D. Interpersonal relationships and situation

II. Who Are the *Characters* in the Story?

A. Who are the main/supporting players in the story?

B. Who is the "protagonist?" Who is the "antagonist?"

C. How does the author describe the character's development?

D. What is the final outcome of the character's life and choices?

III. What Plot *Conflicts* Exist within the Story?

A. What are the central conflicts with God?

B. What are the central conflicts with others?

C. What are the central conflicts within the characters themselves?

D. What are the central conflicts between the character and their situation?

IV. What Are the Aspects of *Narrative Suspense* Revealed in the Story?

A. What influences make us sympathize with the characters?

B. What produces disgust and aversion between us and the characters?

C. How are we made to approve of what the characters did?

D. What events or happenings cause us to disapprove of the characters?

Checklist of Narrative Elements (continued)

V. What Insight Do the Characters Give Us as a "*Commentary on Living*"?

A. Reality: What is the view of reality portrayed in the story and the character?

B. Morality: What constitutes good and bad in the context of this story?

C. Value: What is of ultimate concern and value in the story?

VI. How Does the Story *Unify* Itself in its Various Parts?

A. How does the organization of the story contribute to its unity?

B. What is the sequence of events in this story? (Beginning, Middle, and End)

C. In what way does the story's end resolve the questions raised at the beginning?

VII. How Are the Characters *Tested*, and What *Choices* Do They Make?

A. What is the dilemma/problem/conflict the protagonist is seeking to overcome?

B. What character quality is tested in the protagonist ?

C. What alternative life choices are open to the characters in the story?

D. Which decisions do the characters make, and what is the result of their decisions?

VIII. How Do the Characters *Progress and Grow* (or Decline and Fall) in the Story?

A. Where do the characters begin in the story?

B. How do the experiences of the character affect their development?

C. Where do the individual characters eventually wind up as a result of their experiences, and the choices they made within them?

Checklist of Narrative Elements (continued)

IX. What *Foils, Dramatic Irony, and Poetic Justice* Are Used in the Story?

A. Foils: what characters are set against each other as foes in the story?

B. Dramatic irony: When is the reader informed of situations and realities that the characters themselves are unaware of?

X. What Items Are *Repeated, Highlighted, and Foregrounded* in the Story?

A. Repetition: what phrases, items, themes, issues, or actions are repeated?

B. Highlighting: what things in the characters and events are emphasized above other things?

C. Foregrounding: what things are made to stand out "center stage" in the flow of the story?

XI. What Is the *Point of View* of the Author of the Story?

A. What comments does the author give us about the characters and events in the story?

B. What feelings do you believe the story is intending to generate?

C. How are the materials and details arranged to communicate the author's viewpoint clearly?

APPENDIX 43

Documenting Your Work

A Guide to Help You Give Credit Where Credit Is Due

The Urban Ministry Institute

Avoiding Plagiarism

Plagiarism is using another person's ideas as if they belonged to you without giving them proper credit. In academic work it is just as wrong to steal a person's ideas as it is to steal a person's property. These ideas may come from the author of a book, an article you have read, or from a fellow student. The way to avoid plagiarism is to carefully use "notes" (textnotes, footnotes, endnotes, etc.) and a "Works Cited" section to help people who read your work know when an idea is one you thought of, and when you are borrowing an idea from another person.

Using Citation References

A citation reference is required in a paper whenever you use ideas or information that came from another person's work.

All citation references involve two parts:

- Notes in the body of your paper placed next to each quotation which came from an outside source.
- A "Works Cited" page at the end of your paper or project which gives information about the sources you have used

Using Notes in Your Paper

There are three basic kinds of notes: parenthetical notes, footnotes, and endnotes. At The Urban Ministry Institute, we recommend that students use parenthetical notes. These notes give the author's last name(s), the date the book was published, and the page number(s) on which you found the information. Example:

> In trying to understand the meaning of Genesis 14.1-24, it is important to recognize that in biblical stories "the place where dialogue is first introduced will be an important moment in revealing the character of the speaker . . ." (Kaiser and Silva 1994, 73). This is certainly true of the character of Melchizedek who speaks words of blessing. This identification of Melchizedek as a positive spiritual influence is reinforced by the fact that he is the King of Salem, since Salem means "safe, at peace" (Wiseman 1996, 1045).

Documenting Your Work (continued)

Creating a Works Cited Page

A "Works Cited" page should be placed at the end of your paper. This page:

- lists every source you quoted in your paper
- is in alphabetical order by author's last name
- includes the date of publication and information about the publisher

The following formatting rules should be followed:

1. **Title**

   The title "Works Cited" should be used and centered on the first line of the page following the top margin.

2. **Content**

   Each reference should list:

   - the author's full name (last name first)
   - the date of publication
   - the title and any special information (Revised edition, 2nd edition, reprint) taken from the cover or title page should be noted
   - the city where the publisher is headquartered followed by a colon and the name of the publisher

3. **Basic form**

   - Each piece of information should be separated by a period.
   - The second line of a reference (and all following lines) should be indented.
   - Book titles should be underlined (or italicized).
   - Article titles should be placed in quotes.

Example:

Fee, Gordon D. 1991. *Gospel and Spirit: Issues in New Testament Hermeneutics.* Peabody, MA: Hendrickson Publishers.

Documenting Your Work (continued)

4. Special Forms

A book with multiple authors:

Kaiser, Walter C., and Moisés Silva. 1994. *An Introduction to Biblical Hermeneutics: The Search for Meaning.* Grand Rapids: Zondervan Publishing House.

An edited book:

Greenway, Roger S., ed. 1992. *Discipling the City: A Comprehensive Approach to Urban Mission.* 2nd ed. Grand Rapids: Baker Book House.

A book that is part of a series:

Morris, Leon. 1971. *The Gospel According to John.* Grand Rapids: Wm. B. Eerdmans Publishing Co. The New International Commentary on the New Testament. Gen. ed. F. F. Bruce.

An article in a reference book:

Wiseman, D. J. "Salem." 1982. In *New Bible Dictionary.* Leicester, England - Downers Grove, IL: InterVarsity Press. Eds. I. H. Marshall and others.

(An example of a "Works Cited" page is located on the next page.)

For Further Research

Standard guides to documenting academic work in the areas of philosophy, religion, theology, and ethics include:

Atchert, Walter S., and Joseph Gibaldi. 1985. *The MLA Style Manual.* New York: Modern Language Association.

The Chicago Manual of Style. 1993. 14th ed. Chicago: The University of Chicago Press.

Turabian, Kate L. 1987. *A Manual for Writers of Term Papers, Theses, and Dissertations.* 5th edition. Bonnie Bertwistle Honigsblum, ed. Chicago: The University of Chicago Press.

Documenting Your Work (continued)

Works Cited

Fee, Gordon D. 1991. *Gospel and Spirit: Issues in New Testament Hermeneutics*. Peabody, MA: Hendrickson Publishers.

Greenway, Roger S., ed. 1992. *Discipling the City: A Comprehensive Approach to Urban Mission*. 2nd ed. Grand Rapids: Baker Book House.

Kaiser, Walter C., and Moisés Silva. 1994. *An Introduction to Biblical Hermeneutics: The Search for Meaning*. Grand Rapids: Zondervan Publishing House.

Morris, Leon. 1971. *The Gospel According to John*. Grand Rapids: Wm. B. Eerdmans Publishing Co. *The New International Commentary on the New Testament.* Gen. ed. F. F. Bruce.

Wiseman, D. J. "Salem." 1982. In *New Bible Dictionary*. Leicester, England-Downers Grove, IL: InterVarsity Press. Eds. I. H. Marshall and others.

Made in the USA
Las Vegas, NV
12 March 2024